The Modernist Nation

The Modernist Nation

Generation, Renaissance, and Twentieth-Century American Literature

MICHAEL SOTO

THE UNIVERSITY OF ALABAMA PRESS
Tuscaloosa

The University of Alabama Press
Tuscaloosa, Alabama 35487-0380
uapress.ua.edu

Typeface: Minion and Goudy Sans

Paperback ISBN: 978-0-8173-5467-1
E-ISBN: 978-0-8173-8050-2

Cataloging-in-Publication data is available from the Library of Congress.
ISBN: 978-0-8173-1392-0 (cloth)

for Alejo Xoaquín

Contents

Acknowledgments

Drafts of selected portions of *The Modernist Nation* were presented as papers to the American Studies Association, the Hemingway Society, and the Society for Multi-Ethnic Studies: Europe and the Americas; I am grateful to these conference participants for their many helpful comments. Parts of this book also appeared in earlier print versions in the *Hemingway Review* and *Literature on the Move: Comparing the Diasporic Ethnicities in Europe and the Americas* (Universitätsverlag C. Winter), edited by Dominique Marçais, Mark Niemeyer, Bernard Vincent, and Cathy Waegener. I gratefully acknowledge these editors and publishers.

Many thanks go as well to my friends, colleagues, and teachers at Harvard University for their help with a less mature version of this project, which originated as a dissertation. As the cliché goes, there are far too many names to list here. However, a few must not escape mention, particularly my advisers at Harvard, Lawrence Buell and Werner Sollors. There were also numerous friends who sustained me through a difficult time, especially Ricardo Acuña, J. Carlos Bernal, Terri Oliver, Gabi Starr, George Trone, and Chris Woods. My earliest efforts were stirred by Christine Marie Campbell; her friendship and support are greatly missed.

Acknowledgment is also given to my friends and colleagues at Trinity University—especially Ed Curtis, Jack Kerkering, Char Miller, Willis Salomon, and Claudia Stokes—for their insight and encouragement. Trinity University provided generous financial support in the form of a Summer Research Stipend. The staffs of the various libraries at Harvard University, Trinity University, and Yale University have also been kind with their time and talent.

I wish to thank the anonymous reviewers for the University of Alabama

Press for their intelligence and insight; and copyeditor Jonathan Lawrence for his scrupulous attention to detail.

I owe a great debt of gratitude to my family. My parents, Josefina and Paulo Soto, my brothers and sister-in-law, and my new in-laws in the Peña Sanchez family sustain me with unconditional love and support. To my wife, Celina Peña, I owe the happiest moments of my life: you inspire me daily.

Finally, I dedicate this book to the next generation, my son, Alejo Xoaquín Peña Soto: *M'ijo,* I hope when you're old enough to read this that you might see yourself in its pages.

The Modernist Nation

Introduction: America, Modernism, and All That Jazz

> jazz (dʒæz), *sb.* orig. *U.S. slang.* Also = jas, jascz, jass, jasz, jaz. [Origin unknown: see quots. for some of the many suggested derivations. Cf. jazzbo.] 1. A kind of ragtime dance (see quot. 1919); hence, the kind of music to which this is danced; (the usual sense) a type of music originating among American Negroes, characterized by its use of improvisation, syncopated phrasing, a regular or forceful rhythm, often in common time, and a 'swinging' quality. . . . 2. *transf.* Energy, excitement, 'pep'. . . . 3. Meaningless or empty talk, nonsense, rot, 'rubbish'; unnecessary ornamentation; anything unpleasant or disagreeable. . . . 4. *slang.* Sexual intercourse. Cf. jazzing . . .
>
> Oxford English Dictionary

The "American Century" and the Cultural Field

Imagine for a moment that Ralph Waldo Emerson had been born and raised in the Midwest, say, Cincinnati, and spent the bulk of his writing career in Berlin or Paris: Emerson's poetry and prose might have assumed another shape and treated entirely different themes; the so-called American Renaissance of the mid-nineteenth century might be known today by another name; perhaps the American Renaissance might never have taken place. As is well known, Emerson's time overseas had a profound impact on his opinion of American literature and obviously colored his view of U.S. cultural institutions; still, the Emerson we know best is as New England as cranberry harvests and clambakes. Indeed, a series of part-for-whole geographic substitutions has become a truism of American literary history, so that Emersonianism stands for New England transcendentalism, and New England transcendentalism for Americanism. No less an authority than F. O. Matthiessen observes that after his return from Europe in 1833, Emerson "could rejoice that his advantages were 'the total New England,' and the promise of American life in its first years of mature fulfillment gave [Emerson] his special tone: 'Of every storied bay and cliff and plain, we will make something infinitely nobler than Salamis or Marathon. This pale Massachusetts sky, this sandy soil and raw wind, all shall nurture us. Unlike all the world before us, our own age and land shall be classic to ourselves' " (*American* 12).[1]

Difficult as it may be to conjure an American literary history with its central nineteenth-century voice in anything but an organic relationship with the rugged soil of New England, this is precisely what we must do for virtually every major twentieth-century U.S. writer, an important detail borne out in the myth that American modernists were a "lost" generation. We almost demand of American modernists that they embark on at least a token overseas apprenticeship: for every homebound Wallace Stevens there are a dozen or so expatriate Gertrude Steins. And yet during the years that constitute literary modernism in the United States—for the sake of flexibility I will let this represent the period from the late nineteenth century to the present—an animated if sometimes blurry debate about the state of American literature took place in a host of venues: newspapers, mainstream journals, "little magazines," critical textbooks, even in works of poetry and prose fiction.[2] To an extent only now becoming clear, this discussion brought in a remarkably diverse group: men and women of all economic classes and age groups, from each region of the country, representing every conceivable racial or ethnic background, reflecting a variety of sexual orientations, and even speaking in languages other than English. With such wide-ranging and often bitterly opposed voices clamoring at once, how did American modernists make sense of their historical and cultural situation? How can figures with as little in common as poets T. S. Eliot and Amiri Baraka, novelists Jack Kerouac and Maxine Hong Kingston, and critics Harry Levin and Houston Baker speak in a common language, even if only to disagree?

In each of these cases, the latter writer famously quarreled with the former,[3] but even when the thread of influence is not so readily apparent, twentieth-century American writers, expressing themselves either creatively or critically, access a surprisingly narrow vocabulary to convey their views. The American century may have been invented by a magazine editor (Henry Luce in 1941) with military interventionist interests in mind, but the century's literary culture, at least as seen in that ever-evolving body of authors and texts we refer to as the canon, emerged as the dominant force in Anglophone writing by virtually all measures, from marketplace muscle to the more subjective realm of aesthetic value. The discourse of American modernism paved the way for this success, at least in part, by imagining the triumphant rise of U.S. literature and cultural institutions as a natural, inevitable step in the evolution of American society. While Emerson's contemporaries rarely, if ever, viewed their "own age and land" as "classic" to themselves, his twentieth-century heirs did so with a vengeance. When the Modern Library recently announced its list of the "100 Best Novels" published in English since 1900—a publicity gimmick devised by Random House—a seemingly endless stream of complaints about the list and its board ensued, primarily because the writers on the list, like the board who made the selections, were mostly white and mostly male. No one seemed to care that the list was also mostly American. It's not uncommon these days for American critics to snigger about the supposed dearth of contemporary British poetry and fiction, not unlike their British counterparts who pondered the state of American letters a century ago. And yet, curiously, the academic study of American modernism has apparently fallen behind the popular curve.

Scholarly accounts of "modernism" and its defining characteristics are notoriously vague, and often in debates about the subject the only principle that can be agreed upon is modernism's vagueness, its difficulty to define.[4] From the outset, then, I wish to make clear that this study of American literary modernism limits itself to an area of modernist studies in which there already exists a fair degree of consensus: one of the distinguishing features of modernism, as Renato Poggioli and others point out, is located in the artistic milieu and avant-garde lifestyle from which the modern arts derive, and the history of modernist literature, they suggest, reflects the history of modernist literary movements. *The Modernist Nation,* then, takes up the question of modernist movements in the United States—or, more precisely, *of* the United States, since so much of American modernism takes place "over there." Until recently, studies of modernist literature stressed the cosmopolitan context of most modern movements, and the cosmopolitan orientation of most modern writers, by emphasizing the porousness of national boundaries and the antiparochial posturing of avant-garde circles. "The [modernist] movement was by tacit definition international, and no one worked in the country of his birth," Hugh Kenner notes in his study of *American* modernism. His examples should come as no surprise: "Joyce (of Dublin) toiled in Trieste, in Zurich, in Paris; Ezra Pound (of Idaho and Pennsylvania) in London, Paris, Rapallo; T. S. Eliot (of St. Louis, Mo.) in Paris, Oxford, London; Picasso (the Catalan) by the Seine" (xii–xiii). This critical presupposition largely excludes twentieth-century U.S. literary movements from seminal discussions of modernism and the avant-garde. Within the "What Was Modernism?" genre of literary criticism—that is, within attempts to identify and analyze "modernism" systematically, exemplified by such critics as Levin ("What Was Modernism?" [1960]), Maurice Beebe ("What Modernism Was" [1974]), Robert Martin Adams ("What Was Modernism?" [1978]), and many others—the European avatars of the movement (Gide, Joyce, Mann, Proust, Woolf, Yeats) occasionally enjoy the company of those whose "Americanism" is very much in doubt (Eliot, Pound). This is not to suggest that U.S. writers, including those happy to be called "American," have been left out of studies of modernist literature. Edmund Wilson was prescient enough to include Stein and single out Poe as an early prophet of symbolism in his *Axel's Castle* (1931); however, Wilson emphasizes that it was Baudelaire who transformed Poe's ill-defined romantic tendencies into an aesthetic program known as the symbolist movement. Not unlike Atlantis, it would seem that Axel's castle lies somewhere well beneath the ocean's surface.

When in the spring of 1987 the American Studies Association put together a special number of *American Quarterly* on "Modernist Culture" in the United States, Daniel Joseph Singal, the editor of the issue, could date the intersection of American studies and modernist studies no further back than the "past decade or so." Before that time, Singal points out, "the reigning assumption held that Modernism was, for the most part, an exclusively European phenomenon that somehow couldn't happen here" (5). On or about 1976—or 1975, the year Kenner's *A Homemade World* appeared—the character of American studies changed; it caught up to (or began chasing in earnest) the century with which it shares its name. Since Kenner isolated an Americanist "doctrine of perception" to account for a modernist "reshaping of the American language" (xviii), dozens of scholarly books and hundreds of journal articles have been added to the field, as have numerous reprints, critical editions, and similar apparatuses of literary scholarship. Plunging into the discussion at this particular moment, in the American century's wake, I feel both privileged and disadvantaged because so much work has been done in recent years specifically on American modernism.

If the last decade provides any indication of things to come, then the twenty-first century may well turn out to be the "modernist American studies century" (my apologies for lacking Luce's marketing panache).[5] Since the mid-1990s alone, a steady and important stream of contributions to American studies, building on three decades of African Americanist and feminist revisionism, has grappled with American literary modernism, including the important presence of "traditions" outside the masculinist, Anglocentric mainstream. In this vein, Michael North's *The Dialect of Modernism* (1994) reconsiders Anglo-American modernism as a response to the pressures of language standardization, as well as the impact of nonstandard English dialects (especially minstrelsy) on avant-garde expression. Ann Douglas's *Terrible Honesty* (1995) extensively chronicles the role of black *and* white Manhattan in what might be described as the masculinization of American culture during the 1920s, a process in which Stein and William James stand alongside Freud as modernism's "founding fathers." George Hutchinson's *The Harlem Renaissance in Black and White* (1995) addresses the interracial dynamics, institutional and otherwise, of early-twentieth-century American cultural nationalism; indeed, "American Modernism in a Rainbow of Colors" might be a more accurate title for his impressive study. Walter Benn Michaels's *Our America* (1995) looks at the rise of "nativist modernism" in the United States during the period following the Great War. While I quibble at times with some of their specific conclusions, I must acknowledge a profound debt to these and similar examples of recent, pathbreaking scholarship. Unlike earlier examinations of literary modernism, each of these critics foregrounds the relationship between the conditions of modernity specific to the U.S. context and the specifically modernist elements of U.S. literary culture.

When I began *The Modernist Nation,* I wanted to know in the broadest possible terms how modernist movements in the United States have been symbolically imagined, and I wanted to map out the contours of the field as I saw it. How and why have literary movements been identified by American writers working within or against their stated or implicit frameworks? How and why have these movements been introduced into academic discourse? Whether one prefers to think in terms of a Kantian "regulative idea" (as do René Wellek and Austin Warren) or in terms of "discursive formations" (as does Michel Foucault), it is necessary to bear in mind the often unstated relationship between literary periods and movements and the cultural norms and expectations these categories presuppose. The various tags applied to modernist literary movements—and as Astradur Eysteinsson has shown, even the movement and period marker "modernism"—tend to function as totalizing nomenclatures, with implicit (and often explicit) guidelines for inclusion and exclusion. Movement labels serve as species markers whose influence can be seen in academia, in the publishing industry, and at times in "popular" responses to literary works; they govern how we organize and what we title our courses, our books, our reviews—our thoughts.

My first step in addressing these issues was almost embarrassingly inductive: I looked to well-known histories and encyclopedias of American literature to determine what field-organizing principles had been adopted in the past. What, in other words, have I been taught to call American modernism by those who came before me? The most obvious American literary movements, at least among those that can be called modernist, often are closely associated with a journal (Others, New York School), a university (Black Mountain School), or both (Fugitives/Agrarians), although these are few in number. An even smaller number derive their names and group identities from a clearly articulated aesthetic program (Imagism, L=A=N=G=U=A=G=E Poetry). Instead, most of the names assigned to modernist literary movements in the United States suggest a greater sociohistorical than aesthetic significance; specifically, literary generations (Younger, Lost, Beat, Silent, X, and scores of immigrant generations) and renaissances (Chicago, Little, Harlem, Southern, San Francisco, Chicano, Native American, and Queer) make up an unlikely proportion of America's modernist literary movements. The Lost Generation and the Harlem Renaissance (or the "Negro Renaissance," as it was called at the time) clearly represent the two most significant movements associated with American literary modernism, and for that reason they furnish the primary focus of my research. (My long appreciation for and enjoyment of such writers as Fauset and Fitzgerald, Hemingway and Hurston, made the choice an easy one.) The next set of questions I asked was much more focused, much more tangible, as they dealt explicitly with philological and literary historical issues: When and where did the phrases "Lost Generation" and "Harlem Renaissance" originate, and perhaps more important, why? Who counts as a member of these groups, and who need not apply? What are the groups' identity markers, and how do rites of membership inform literary texts? How were the Lost Generation and the Harlem Renaissance brought into American literary scholarship? In keeping with what I will loosely describe as a sociology of aesthetics perspective, I hoped to uncover the aesthetic, economic, and otherwise ideological interests served by referring to modernist literature in these terms.

Pierre Bourdieu's sociological critique of a "pure" aesthetic begins with a premise that is easily accepted, at least within the context of a discussion of modern art: before cultural artifacts can be considered art objects, they require an "artworld," a "social universe that confers upon [an artifact] the status of a candidate for aesthetic appreciation" ("Historical" 147). The critical vocabulary Bourdieu brings to his discussion of aesthetics is fertile in spite of (perhaps because of) its scantiness: a nebulous historical institution (the artworld) composed of two mutually founded objects, the cultured *habitus* and the artistic field, endows the art object with its unique status in society.[6] In Bourdieu's own words, "Given that the work of art exists as such, (namely as a symbolic object endowed with meaning and value) only if it is apprehended by spectators possessing the disposition and the aesthetic competence which are tacitly required, one could then say that it is the aesthete's eye which constitutes the work of art as a work of art. But, one must also remember immediately that this is possible only to the extent that the aesthete himself is the product of a long exposure to artworks" (150). Art objects are therefore social constructs, and their social constructedness ironically depends in part on the degree to which artists (writers, painters, musicians, etc.) and consumers (readers, spectators, listeners, etc.) can agree upon an art object's aesthetic autonomy. While I do not subscribe to the overall tone of Bourdieu's analysis, which tends to view cultural practices and institutions as elaborate conspiracies perpetrated by a monolithic cultural elite, his generalization lends itself to a wide range of discussion, including an account of the social pressures that shaped the literary movements known as the Lost Generation and the Harlem Renaissance.

In *The Modernist Nation* I assess the degree to which these movement labels encode the social, political, and economic changes that gave rise more generally to modernist literary culture in the United States. If the literary artistic field can be described as a generation or a renaissance, then these metaphors surely endow the literary artifacts falling within their rubrics with a socially significant aura; they teach us not just *what* to read, what counts as literature, but also *how* to read, why literature counts as literature. I therefore discuss the impact of what I call "generational rhetoric" and "renaissance rhetoric" on the thematic and formal development of twentieth-century American narrative. A number of additional questions developed out of these concerns: What do "generation" and "renaissance" metaphorize, and what do they exclude from their figurative universe? How do the temporal and social structures these terms imply circumscribe or resist an avant-garde aesthetic? To what extent have such metaphors shaped academic discourse? How did they displace alternatives for identifying modernist literary movements? How are generations and rebirth evoked thematically, and are there specific narrative structures lending themselves to a concern with generations and rebirth?

Words, Words, . . . Rhetoric?

"It is too soon to write about the Jazz Age with perspective, and without being suspected of premature arteriosclerosis," mused Fitzgerald in "Echoes of the Jazz Age," a kind of personal and professional self-analysis published in *Esquire* in late 1931. The thirty-five-year-old Fitzgerald was accustomed at this stage of his career to speak on behalf of his generation, now well into its adulthood, and he comments on the youthful expressions of the Jazz Age:

"Many people still succumb to violent retching when they happen upon any of its characteristic words—words which have since yielded in vividness the coinages of the underworld" (*Crack-Up* 13). In many respects my critical approach in *The Modernist Nation* can be described as an effort to allow the words to which Fitzgerald alludes to yield their vividness by re-creating the dynamics of their public performance. Such words reveal important features not just of the linguistic underworld from which they derive, as Fitzgerald is right to insist, but, as he further indicates, of the wider U.S. culture in which they are sometimes allowed to circulate. As I hope the epigraphs at the start of each chapter demonstrate in miniature, key words and phrases used to identify modernist literary movements in the United States—including "Lost Generation," "Harlem Renaissance," and Fitzgerald's own coinage, "Jazz Age"—vividly reflect larger preoccupations about American literary culture and, by extension, American identity. The constant return to "generation" and "renaissance," and especially "jazz," reveals that American writers have been profoundly concerned with their "modernism" in the sense supplied by Lionel Trilling, who defines modern literature as that which reflects "the disenchantment of our culture with culture itself—it seems to me that the characteristic element of modern literature, or at least of the most highly developed modern literature, is the bitter line of hostility to civilization which runs through it" (3).

Ironically, the oppositional, agonistic attitude that Trilling singles out has been largely taken for granted in studies of those movements which, until recently at least, dominated the twentieth-century American canon, the Lost Generation and the Beat Generation. However, generational and renaissance rhetoric run much deeper in U.S. literary culture; in fact, it is not too farfetched to say that generations and rebirths constitute American modernism. In many cases the recognition that American modernism functions as a form of cultural critique merely confirms widely held opinions about avant-garde iconoclasts like H.D. or Allen Ginsberg; more important, it suggests the need to reevaluate the equally ubiquitous opinion that Jessie Fauset (for example) was strictly or even primarily concerned with establishing genteel credentials for the New Negro movement. As a champion of young African American writers, Fauset contributed to a national discussion of American cultural values, and her critique extends far beyond the important questions of race and gender. The larger rhetorical context for the movements with which writers such as Fauset and Ginsberg are associated locates them, whether they would admit the description or not, as (in Trilling's words) "people who adopt the adversary program" (xiii). And yet it remains to be specified: what exactly does this "adversary program" oppose?

Although Trilling deploys the familiar international array of examples in his discussion of modern literature, the categories against which he positions the modernists, "civilization" and "culture," are chiefly conceived and manifest during the twentieth century as *national* institutions. As George Hutchinson (following Martin J. Sklar) has already pointed out, "Among the general trends associated with the shift to corporate capitalism from the 1890s to the 1920s, nationalization appears again and again in intimate relation with modernization. . . . It should not be surprising that the issue of American cultural nationalism would, in these circumstances, achieve a dynamic significance unmatched since the years of the 'American Renaissance' just preceding the Civil War" (9). The "defenders" of "culture" in the United States, particularly during the early part of the twentieth century, routinely imagine their role as a form of gatekeeping, protecting the nation's borders and its citizens from external influence, from cultural invasion. It is no surprise, then, that the American avant-garde saw itself as tearing down barriers, both literal and figurative.

Both generations and renaissances invoke the ideal of an organic relationship between "America" (its landscape, its racial and ethnic composition, its mythic past) and the character (or "nature") of "American" expression. As Hutchinson implies, we expect cultural nationalism in a movement labeled a renaissance—thus Emerson's New English identity and its role in shaping the "American Renaissance"—but the same must also be said about literary generations. A preoccupation with a generation's "lostness" or "beatness" sometimes obscures the degree to which the metaphor insists on biologically determined cultural evolution. While literary generations and literary renaissances have been identified outside the United States—indeed, as I demonstrate later, the cultural models for the Lost Generation and the Harlem Renaissance were imported from overseas—it is in the American context that they took firm hold. What's more, the Lost Generation and the Harlem Renaissance express their adversary programs with national culture and national institutions very much in view, particularly when these are seen as inadequate and inhospitable. American cultural nationalism depends on sweeping changes in America's cultural institutions during the late nineteenth and early twentieth centuries, changes that create for the first time in U.S. history a national youth identity. Often, a generation defines itself in opposition to the very same cultural institutions that make youth identity possible in the first place (as I illustrate more fully in chapter 1).

Moreover, recent analysts of globalization—including Arjun Appadurai, Frederick Buell, and Roland Robertson—highlight a central paradox built into the complex interaction between global and local forces: global economic and cultural systems disseminate and sustain seemingly intractable nationalisms and ethnic fundamentalisms. Ethnic and nationalist intellectuals know their roles because they have seen them performed by others. This paradox also finds its way into the discourse of American modernism. The very simple notion that U.S. literature must exhibit "American" traits depends upon the circulation of romantic nationalist theory originally produced by European thinkers. More paradoxically, the sense of urgency present in so many of the examples of American cultural nationalism discussed in *The Modernist Nation* owes something to the rise of comparative cultural analysis (anthropology, archetypal psychology, comparative literature and philology, folklore, myth criticism, religious history) within the Euro-American academy. If *they* could produce a viable national literature, American modernists often ask, why can't *we*? This preoccupation is not so much blind to the influence of global U.S. imperialism as it is too quick to identify parallels between "primitive" impulses in America and in the far reaches of the globe. No one these days would identify Melville or Poe as an "ethnic" writer, but in the 1920s D. H. Lawrence and William Carlos Williams discussed the achievement of their predecessors in terms of a primordial nationalism. American modernism, I argue throughout this book, routinely imagined its nationalist project in what we would describe today as following a racial or ethnic pattern.

Both generational and renaissance rhetoric, then, inform a transnational, polyethnic discourse concerned with articulating a cultural nationalist aesthetic stance and with archiving the emergence of American literature. I demonstrate throughout this study the degree to which generational and renaissance rhetoric overlap and constitute each other; I also suggest that the various social relationships these metaphors encode—youth versus age, bohemian versus philistine, present versus tradition, group identity versus national culture—are always provisional, always contingent upon the specific power dynamics embedded in the historical moment. Their pivotal roles in American literary history notwithstanding, "generation" and "renaissance" signal discursive conflict at least as often as ideological consensus.

Again Bourdieu provides a useful analytic insight, this time in the form of a warning: "As soon as one treats language as an autonomous object, accepting the radical separations which Saussure made between internal and external linguistics, between the science of language and the science of the social uses of language, one is condemned to looking within words for the power of words, that is, looking for it where it is not to be found" (*Language* 107). The modernist obsession with the ontological status of the sign—with the arbitrariness or the "thingness" of language in itself—will not suffice in a study looking for the power dynamics buried beneath simple words, which is why my interest lies in generational and renaissance *rhetoric.* "Rhetoric," which implies a measure of consistency in language's capacity "to represent" or "to mean" (and is thus often synonymous with stylistics, the distinction between the "what" and "how" of a literary text), overlooks or undervalues the real force of expressions in public circulation. Nevertheless, I think that the semantic histories located in this study convey something of the evolving institutional sanction of specific objects of discourse; I am less interested in the "meaning" of the "Lost Generation" and the "Harlem Renaissance" than in the degree to which meaning is assumed by acts of verbal performance. Still, I prefer "rhetoric" to the usual choice in this type of analysis, "discourse," because the latter term implies a kind of polar relationship between the dominant and the dominated, between center and margin—static categories that are of little use when addressing the phenomenon of emergent literatures. As Foucault wrote, "we must conceive discourse as a series of discontinuous segments whose tactical function is neither uniform nor stable. To be more precise, we must not imagine a world of discourse divided between accepted discourse and excluded discourse, or between dominant discourse and dominated discourse; but as a multiplicity of discursive elements" (*History* 100). With "rhetoric" I wish to signify the "segments" out of which a discourse is fashioned, tactically or accidentally. I will reserve "discourse" for those configurations of rhetoric that have attained some level of explicit institutional sanction: legal discourse, medical discourse, the discourse of American studies, and the like.

A more immediate word of warning: I have divided this study into two rather distinct parts for the simple reason that my critical approach shifts abruptly between parts 1 and 2. The first part, "Inventing the Modern," addresses the place of generational and renaissance rhetoric in Euro-American intellectual history and in the institutional history of American literary studies. While I refer on occasion to examples from creative writing, especially modernist fiction, I direct considerably more attention to the critical discourse of American modernism, to essays and book-length reflections on the terrain. Chapters 1 ("Generational Rhetoric and American Avant-Gardism") and 2 ("Renaissance Rhetoric and American Cultural Nationalism") examine the role of generational and renaissance rhetoric in shaping literary production and in determining the scope of critical responses to literary works. Both the Lost Generation and the Harlem Renaissance derive from roughly contemporaneous European expressions: lost generations had already been identified in France (as *la génération perdue*) and Germany (as *die verlorene Generation*) before an American version was recognized, and the so-called

Irish Renaissance (or Celtic Revival) served as the primary model for several modernist movements in the United States; a generation or a renaissance was simply what one looked for during the early twentieth century. Significantly, both generations and renaissances signify cultural evolution away from Anglo-Saxon roots, a heritage that is often blamed for an atavistic puritanism or the debilitating acquisitiveness of pioneer life.

The second part of this book, "Living the Modern," undertakes in a more direct way the analysis of modernist American literature, in particular modernist novels and memoirs. Chapters 3 ("American Modernism Is Born") and 4 ("The Modernist Generation") examine an important development in twentieth-century aesthetics, the modernist preoccupation with narrative strategies variously known as "self-reflexive," "introverted," or "involuted." My primary concern here is with the thematic expression of self-reflexivity, namely, as it is realized in novels and literary memoirs representing artistic emergence in terms of immersion into bohemian subcultures. Again, I trace the European origins of the genre, as well as the Americanization of bohemian identity. The rapid proliferation of the bohemian artist narrative in the United States reveals an increasing concern not only with the inner world created by literature but also with the outer world in which literature is created and sustained, including the social worlds imagined as the Lost Generation and the Harlem Renaissance. Bohemian artist narratives in the United States, I further demonstrate, rehearse immersion into a uniquely American idiom, jazz, to celebrate national identity and simultaneously to reject imported European standards of civilization.

The Modernist Nation provides useful points of entry into the movements associated with literary modernism in the United States, and in particular the generations and renaissances making up the field. This is not the only way to discuss American modernism, nor do I pretend that it is the best. For example, my focus excludes almost entirely those writers who were either too politically radical (on the left *and* the right) or too "regional" to be considered avant-garde. I also tend not to address legitimate concerns that have been raised by gender theorists, even when the specific text under consideration screams for such attention. And as much as I would like to address individually the wide range of late-capitalist institutions against which American modernism stands in sharp contrast, to do so adequately would require another book altogether. However, my approach, which is at once thematic and historicist, does suggest that the seemingly divergent currents of U.S. literary culture derive from similar (if not the same) sources and, further, identifies important interrelationships across ethnic and national boundaries. This study demonstrates how writers such as James Weldon Johnson,

Gertrude Stein, William Carlos Williams, Scott Fitzgerald, Ernest Hemingway, Claude McKay, Henry Miller, Zora Neale Hurston, John Clellon Holmes, Diane Di Prima, Oscar Zeta Acosta, and Joyce Johnson, and critics like Barrett Wendell, W. E. B. Du Bois, Alain Locke, Florence Valentine Keys, Van Wyck Brooks, and Malcolm Cowley imaginatively conceive of American literary emergence in terms of symbolic birth (or rebirth) into a generation. I believe that the conversation begun by Eliot and Baraka, Kerouac and Kingston, and Baker and Levin, in spite of its occasional rancor, is far too important not to carry on into our new century.

I
INVENTING THE MODERN

1

Generational Rhetoric and American Avant-Gardism

> Here was a new generation, shouting the old cries, learning the old creeds, through a revery of long days and nights; destined finally to go out into that dirty gray turmoil to follow love and pride; a new generation dedicated more than the last to the fear of poverty and the worship of success; grown up to find all Gods dead, all wars fought, all faiths in man shaken.
>
> Scott Fitzgerald, *This Side of Paradise* (1920)

Emerson and the Entente des Anciens et des Modernes

The monumental and today much-maligned *Literary History of the United States* (1948) begins with a prominent trope in American literary historiography, one with deep roots: "Each generation should produce at least one literary history of the United States, for each generation must define the past in its own terms" (Spiller et al. vii). Since then virtually every major contribution to this field—including *The Literature of the American People* (1951), the *Columbia Literary History of the United States* (1988), and the *Cambridge History of American Literature* (1994–)—invokes more or less explicitly the notion that the act of historical revision remains the prerogative of each succeeding generation, a kind of institutional birthright whose metaphoricity gets lost in the presence of other, more pressing areas of theoretical contestation ("American," "literary," "history"). The most famous example of this generational rhetoric, one regularly but casually cited by literary historians, is Ralph Waldo Emerson's so-called declaration of cultural independence, the "American Scholar" address delivered before the Phi Beta Kappa Society of Harvard in 1837, roughly the moment when the earliest American literary histories were being published. The passage in question develops a metaphor for books as peculiar as it is complex. Books are imperfect, Emerson argues, like nineteenth-century vacuum chambers: "As no air-pump can by any means make a perfect vacuum, so neither can any artist entirely exclude the conventional, the local, the perishable from his book, or write a book of pure thought, that shall be as efficient, in all respects, to a remote posterity, as to contemporaries, or rather to the second age. Each age, it is found, must write its own books; or rather, each generation for the next succeeding. The books of an older period will not fit this" (*Works* 1:55–56).

The larger context for this crescendo of figurative language, which accelerates wildly from one metaphor to another, generally escapes notice by critics eager to seize upon the cultural nationalist implications of the oration or to see the American scholar as another version of the Emersonian freethinking individualist. These metaphors (for books, artists, and periods) make up one small facet of Emerson's appropriation and ultimate dismissal of the centuries-old *querelle* between the ancients and moderns, rendered in English as the "battle of the books" since Jonathan Swift. Rather than draw the expected strict comparisons between ancient and modern, or between pagan and Christian, or even between more and less perfected, Emerson sets up an opposition between a solipsistic self-understanding ("the ancient precept, 'Know thyself' ") and an environmentally located self-consciousness ("the modern precept, 'Study nature' "). However, the distinction rings hollow, as these modes of analysis "become at last one maxim." Not only has Emerson the naturalist introduced a measure of scientism absent from previous versions of the ancients-versus-moderns debate (even if he remains ironically distanced from an aesthetic of "efficiency" and the science of vacuums), but he has also introduced a subtle historicism into an equation that normally privileges the "either" (antiquity) or the "or" (modernity). Moderns, he suggests, look to nature because all knowledge and all cultural artifacts remain grounded in, stained by, their immediate historical circumstances. Modern literature is not inherently superior to that of the past; it is simply less remote, more relevant. Although he never defines "generation" with any precision, we can be sure that it signifies a time span far briefer than any referenced during the heyday of the *querelle.*

I find myself drawn to this example from Emerson because it incorporates two important elements commonly found in generational rhetoric. First, it focuses attention on the local, on a geographically and chronologically palpable sociohistorical milieu. Emerson's artist, and presumably his cultural historian, measures progress as a succession of discrete generations, not as ages or epochs.[1] Here Emerson's literary historical chronometer is more in synch with Ezra Pound's than with Samuel Johnson's. And as a theorist of literature, Emerson resembles those counterparts in the United States and elsewhere—Herder, Scott, and Bancroft, for example—who argue that a literature of universal significance can only be distilled from "local" (which is often synonymous with "national" and "ethnic") cultural traditions. Second, and just as important, Emerson's use of generational rhetoric elevates local forms of knowledge against any pseudo-universalist bookishness in what amounts to an avant-gardist repudiation of received tradition. This is one of the key reasons Emerson serves as a rare hero for America's most famous literary generations, the Lost and the Beat. Even if the vying precepts become in the end "one maxim," Emerson alludes, after all, to a *battle* between ancient and modern books. Scholarship makes use of books and book learning, but the American scholar bursts through the library's walls like a runaway intellectual train: modernity dictates that the "sluggard intellect of this continent will look from under its iron lids and fill the postponed expectation of the world with something better than the exertions of mechanical skill. Our day of dependence, our long apprenticeship to the learning of other lands, draws to a close" (*Works* 1:52).

Generations and battles go hand in hand, although these so-called conflicts rarely contribute to any lasting damage. Because generational conflict and succession bear so much metaphorical weight throughout human history, it is no surprise that the concept of literary generations has also proven considerably powerful. This chapter explores the profound impact of generational rhetoric first on significant contributions to the sociology of knowledge, and later on U.S. literary modernism and avant-gardism more generally. The Lost Generation proves a particularly lasting mythology, one with far-reaching theoretical and practical effects, so it will be the object of first concern. Our understanding of the Lost Generation, and its varied applications over the years, play out in the organization of literary histories and anthologies; in the publication of journals and critical studies; and in the conceptualization of films, plays, and musicals (there's even a Lost Generation cookbook). Theorists of American modernism routinely take for granted this ubiquitous and powerful discursive object, often at the expense of those authors who lie outside the Lost Generation rubric. An obvious problem can be detected in the unacknowledged and typically hard-and-fast distinction between the Lost Generation and the Harlem Renaissance (a fallacy addressed throughout this study), but the myth also fails to account for other important literary figures, mostly women and "regional" writers, who do not quite fit the Lost Generation mold.[2]

I am also drawn to Emerson's example because the "one maxim" forged out of antiquity and modernity, out of the self and nature, out of books and life, might be taken as a friendly note of caution. Even in his most messianic celebrations of a life removed from the fetters of books and empiricism, Emerson pays homage to an ancient tradition of world literature. And he can be downright bookish at times. In the second number of the *Dial* he published his "Thoughts on Modern Literature" (1840), a meditation on the role of "subjectiveness" in modern literary history, what we now refer to as the rise of the romantic ego during the eighteenth and nineteenth centuries. Emerson applies his idealistic worldview to an evaluation of individual literary works and to the idea of literary tradition in general. Literature expresses what is best in humankind, reflecting centuries of learning and a multiplicity of discourses. All of these are available to the individual reader: "Another element of the modern poetry akin to this subjective tendency . . . is, the Feeling of the Infinite. Of the perception now fast becoming a conscious fact,—that there is One Mind, and that all the powers and privileges which lie in any, lie in all; that I as a man may claim and appropriate whatever of true or fair or good or strong has anywhere been exhibited; that Moses and Confucius, Montaigne and Leibnitz are not so much individuals as they are parts of man and parts of me, and my intelligence proves them my own,—literature is far the best expression" (141).

This notion that literature embodies the infinite derives from a presumed dialectic of literary history (or the history of ideas) and individual growth. Culture proceeds biologically, like an organism with a card catalog, while biology proceeds culturally, like a library composed of brain tissue. To be sure, Emerson holds no special place for modern literature other than to acknowledge its belatedness—the library of the present age is an "immense miscellany," it "prints a vast carcass of tradition." Nor does he privilege the modern reader, who must wade through this mess. But significantly, only the modern library contains "all books":

> [Modern literature] reprints the wisdom of the world. How can the age be a bad one, which gives me Plato and Paul and Plutarch, St. Augustine, Spinoza, Chapman, Beaumont and Fletcher, Donne and Sir Thomas Brown, besides its own riches? Our presses groan every year with new editions of all the select pieces of the first of mankind—meditations, history, classifications, opinions, epics, lyrics, which the age adopts by quoting them. If we should designate favorite studies in which the age delights more than in the rest of this great mass of the permanent literature of the human race, one or two instances would

> be conspicuous. First; the prodigious growth and influence of the genius of Shakespeare, in the last one hundred and fifty years, is itself a fact of the first importance. It almost alone has called out the genius of the German nation into activity, which spreading from the poetic into the scientific, religious, and philosophical domains, has made theirs now at last the paramount intellectual influence of the world, reacting with great energy on England and America. Society becomes an immense Shakespeare. (141–42)

Were he forced to take sides in the battle of the books, Emerson would surely choose the moderns—at least judging by this example. After all, the modern reader has the shoulders of the past on which to stand. But Emerson's logic necessarily sacrifices the individual (the dwarf) to the ideal of individualism (the view from the shoulders of giants). Subsumed under a broader generational identity, the Emersonian reader experiences the infinite: he or she figuratively becomes not only Shakespeare but Plato, Paul, and Plutarch as well—an experience shared by Chapman and Spinoza not so long before. Rather than lament the gulf between individual experience and the human spirit, Emerson advances a generational model of literary history because it offers an organic alternative to static notions of ages, epochs, or other more "objective" alternatives to periodization. One is not born into a generation, he suggests; one *lives* into it, one *reads* into it. Emerson's generational model also bridges individual and collective historiography, each of which lends metaphorical potency to the other—just as each of his representative men stands for something greater than a single life. Individual growth and intellectual development mirror the evolution of the world spirit. After all, ages cannot literally quote from texts, but individuals can and do. Conversely, as the library of the imagination grows, so too does the reader.

Nothing, it often seems, could be more natural than generations. Everyone, with one or two well-known exceptions, was born of a biological mother and father, and most children have at least figurative parents. Like the concepts "nation" and "race"—the latter is a close etymological cousin to "generation"—generations simply *are.* But as omnipresent and powerful as these concepts may be, a great difficulty lies in providing anything but reductive or romantic definitions for them; it is especially difficult to achieve a semblance of critical distance, to locate a place outside their magnetic force. "As a vast, solid phalanx the generations come on," Emerson wrote in his *Journals* in 1841, not too long after his "American Scholar" address. "All wear the same expression, but it is this which they do not detect in each other. It is the one life which ponders in the philosophers, which drudges in the laborers, which basks in the poets, which dilates in the love of the women." Writing of the need to surrender the self to the larger social good, to the "great destiny which comes in with this as with every age" (8:81), Emerson anticipates the rhetoric of the historical avant-garde ("solid phalanx") and rehearses the views of a number of generational theorists since the Enlightenment, many of whom adopt a similarly romantic view of generations. A generational identity—the one that ponders, drudges, basks, and dilates—inescapably defines the individual self.

Generations cannot and should not be avoided, Emerson insists; at the same time, their "expression" is lost in translation from one age to the next. It proves difficult to fix lived experience—in particular the unavoidable facts of birth, maturation, and death—as an object of critical discourse. Before continuing, then, it is appropriate to summarize the Emersonian position and, finally, to provide a definition of literary generations by invoking the twentieth-century writer who perhaps more than any other embodies the Emersonian tradition, Octavio Paz. He applies an almost identical understanding, at once persuasive and puzzling because it relies on the romantic conflation of social and biological forces, to his succinct definition of literary generations:

> The history of a literature is the history of select works and the authors of these works. But in between the works and the authors there is a third position, a bridge between the writers and their social location, between the works and their first readers: literary generations. A literary generation is a society within a society and, at times, in front of it. It is a biological and also a social fact: the generation is a group of youth of the same age, born into the same class and the same country, readers of the same books, and possessed of the same passions and aesthetic and moral interests. . . . [T]he vital roots of their members are the same; what distinguishes one generation from another isn't so much the ideas as the sensibility, the attitudes, the likes and dislikes; in a word: the *mood.* (94; my trans.)

Generations, along with the literary products that record and transmit their vocabulary, form "a bridge between the writers and their social location" and thus embody revolutionary probes into future social formations. This is a tremendous weight for any artist to bear, and indeed many have chosen to shirk the responsibility; American literary history, however, reads like a catalog of those men and women who have chosen otherwise.

Generations: Their Problems and Their Solutions

Although generations have proven a ubiquitous interpretive category in all varieties of cultural history, few theorists bother to provide a workable definition of the concept, let alone acknowledge its metaphoricity. Karl Mannheim, the Hungarian German social theorist who spent much of his career in England, exiled from the Third Reich, offers a measure of precision. In a 1927 essay, "The Problem of Generations," Mannheim outlines two basic approaches that interfere with generational analysis: positivist and romantic-historical formulations of the "problem."[3] The positivists, "anxious to find a general law to express the rhythm of historical development" (353), derive a mathematical formula for generational duration (most set the figure at thirty years, the number still preferred by demographers) and superimpose this static figure onto human history. Mannheim argues that thinkers such as Hume and Comte explain the most complex historical dynamics with a reductive anthropomorphic model, projecting the human life span onto a vast array of sociohistorical phenomena. Human biology thus determines social and cultural change.[4] The romantic-historicists, on the other hand, replace the quantitative treatment of historical phenomena with the qualitative treatment of eras "felt" by a historically situated mind. "The problem of generations is seen here as the problem of the existence of an interior time that cannot be measured but only experienced in purely qualitative terms" (356), Mannheim writes. In this case, the denotative function of language gives way to its connotative other; thus "generations" furnish Dilthey, Heidegger, and Pinder with a palpable figure for expressing headier and considerably more inclusive historical concepts, including volksgeist ("spirit of the people"), zeitgeist ("spirit of the age"), and even "culture." More important, the romantic-historical view opens up the possibility of Pinder's "noncontemporaneity of the contemporaneous," that is, the insight that multiple generations might coexist in time and space, if only metaphorically. However, Mannheim warns that this approach threatens to become "dangerously inimical to the scientific spirit" (361) so important to the sociology of knowledge.[5]

Although Mannheim's essay suffers from the conflation of sociohistorical method and the history of national thought—for Mannheim, positivism is a French prejudice, romanticism a German one—he nonetheless develops a fruitful alternative to positivist and romantic extremes. He acknowledges that biological factors (the inevitability of life and death, of physical and emotional development, of aging, of a limited life span) play important roles in generational identity formation. However, "anthropology and biology . . .

offer no explanation of the relevance these primary factors have for the shaping of social interrelationships in their historic flux" (365); that is, there must be rhyme and reason behind the superimposition of the life span onto historical change. Mannheim therefore develops a cultural rather than biological theory of "social location" to account for generational identity: a "generation" cannot be described as a "concrete group" ("a group which cannot exist without its members having concrete knowledge of each other" [363]); nor can it be described as a formally defined association with institutional apparatuses; rather, one belongs to a generation as one belongs to a social class. Thus, "'generation' represents . . . a particular kind of identity of location, embracing related 'age groups' embedded in a historical-social process" (367). Members belong to a generation by being "similarly located" in terms of chronology and sociohistorical space (which for Mannheim, as for Paz, means nation-space); in other words, they experience the same sociohistorical phenomena in similar fashion, with the same vocabulary, so to speak. But this describes only the inherent *potential* of a generation. A "generation as an actuality" exists only "in so far as [individuals of the same age] participate in the characteristic social and intellectual currents of their society and period, and in so far as they have an active or passive experience of the interactions of forces which made up the new situation" (379).

In Mannheim's somewhat idealistic and even Emersonian terms, a generation as an actuality participates in the "common destiny" (378) of the times. This is not to say that all members of a generation react to their historical location in identical fashion. Mannheim makes the further distinction of "generation units," a category representing "a much more concrete bond than the actual generation as such" because it expresses ideological differences on the symbolic level: "Youth experiencing the same concrete historical problems may be said to be part of the same actual generation; while those groups within the same actual generation which work up the material of their common experiences in different specific ways, constitute separate generation units" (379).[6] A specific example relevant to this study would be the generation of Americans who entered into adulthood just after World War II. This might be described as the actual Silent Generation, but we have come to know them as discrete units called the "Beats" and the "Squares." Mannheim's theory also helps to explain why William S. Burroughs (born 1914) might belong to the same generation as Amiri Baraka and Diane Di Prima, even though they were twenty years his junior, and even why an eighty-three-year-old former heroin addict (Burroughs's age at the time of his death) might sell Macintosh computers and Nike running shoes to 1990s teenagers.

Youth Identity and the Younger Generation

Many twentieth-century cultural critics regard "generations" as completely arbitrary markers for distinguishing between periods; in fact, the theme of chronological imprecision plays a significant role in generational rhetoric at a time when positivist accuracy held sway in the human sciences. Both Paul Rosenfeld and Alfred Stieglitz remarked that a new literary generation takes shape in America every five years. "At this rate, and since everything is relative," wrote Van Wyck Brooks, who reported Stieglitz's comments in 1921, "a spectator whose memory of the American literary scene extends over thirty years is, in a way, a sort of Methuselah" ("Literary" 58; Rosenfeld 53). Percy H. Boynton, professor of literature at the University of Chicago during the interwar period, noted in 1924 that the "younger set"—a term describing Mencken's antipuritan intellectual coterie—referred to itself as such "without indicating *de senectute* where old age begins" (232). Alain Locke reflected in 1928 that the "accumulated spiritual momentum of one knows not how many generations has suddenly precipitated a phenomenal burst" of Negro creativity, all in the three years since he edited *The New Negro* (1925), an anthology dedicated to the "Younger Generation" of Negro artists ("Negro Contributions" 242).[7] (Elsewhere in the same article Locke writes that the "Negro novel of ten or even five years back seems generations less mature" than Claude McKay's recently published *Home to Harlem* [1928].) And Malcolm Cowley, the poet and critic who is perhaps the most important chronicler of the Lost Generation, noted in 1980 that "the 'generations,' or age groups . . . had been succeeding each other every ten or a dozen years" (*Dream* 136). In the area of cultural criticism, unlike psychology and sociology, there appears to be little consensus as to the length of generational duration precisely because "generations" signify a figurative (or cultural) instead of a literal (or biological) relationship between the old and the young.

Even writers who count themselves among the members of a generation—not always the younger one—settle upon arbitrary or imprecise measures for their own and opposing camps. Just as important, writers continually bring the figurative nature of the relationship between young and old into sharp focus. Henry Seidel Canby, one of the twentieth century's most influential literary critics (he taught English at Yale, founded the *Saturday Review*, chaired the Book-of-the-Month Club selection committee, and helped edit the *Literary History of the United States*), publicized the "younger generation" of writers, which he identified in 1922 by virtue of birth after the 1880s—it includes John Dos Passos and Scott Fitzgerald (both born 1896). According to Canby, this generation invented itself in contrast to a putative "older generation" of Victorians: "Perhaps when the younger generation pretend to confuse their immediate predecessors with Ruskin and Carlyle, with Browning, Emerson, Hawthorne, Longfellow, and Matthew Arnold, they are merely strategic. . . . It is far easier to assume that [the Victorians] are still alive in pallid survival, and to attack a hypothetic older generation, which, representing nothing real, can therefore not strike back" (168–69). Without naming names, Amy Lowell in 1923 identified a younger generation who published in *Poetry* (presumably including herself) in contrast to the older generation who published in more genteel venues. The former, a "handful of young persons, growing up in the seventies and eighties, . . . found themselves out of sympathy with the chaste and saccharine music wandering through the ambient air of current periodicals" like *Century* or *Atlantic Monthly* ("Two" 1). In 1930, Virginia Moore—who would later make her mark as a poet, biographer, critic, and historian—set out to describe the younger generation in an article published by Canby's *Saturday Review* (she won a contest for essayists under thirty years of age). Although she borrows the language of the biological essentialist—members of the younger generation "resemble each other like the members of a family, all with hook noses. In spite of differences of disposition, of tastes, of capacity, the same blood colors their arteries" (673)—her lists of old and young writers cover more territory than any biological model since the days of Methuselah. The elder group, which spans over half a century of birth years, includes the likes of Thomas Hardy (born 1840) and Edna St. Vincent Millay (born 1892). It also includes *both* Arnold Bennett (born 1867) *and* Virginia Woolf (born 1882). Significantly, there is considerable chronological overlap between generations. Moore's "younger generation" consists of Elizabeth Madox Roberts (born 1886), Ernest Hemingway (born 1899), and Moore herself (born 1903).

Several fictional characters central to American modernism happen to be twenty-nine years old—just on the cusp of the all-important generational milestone—which suggests that writers do in fact take the literal, demographic aspect of generational identity very seriously. At "nearly thirty years of age," transplanted southerner Basil Ransom, the protagonist of Henry James's *The Bostonians* (1886), betrays a "premature wrinkle, on either side of the mouth" (43, 36). The product of a timeworn era, he stands in sharp contrast to the "thoroughly modern young man" (140), Mr. Pardon, who is a sprightly twenty-eight. At an early moment in Kate Chopin's *The Awakening* (1899), Edna Pontellier finds herself troubled by a "vague, tangled, chaotic, and exceedingly disturbing" self-awareness, a "ponderous weight of wisdom to descend upon the soul of a young woman of twenty-eight" (14); by the end of the novel, which marks her twenty-ninth birthday celebration among a dozen or so carefully chosen dinner guests, Edna is well on her way to a tragic recognition of her limited options in life. Edith Wharton's *The House of Mirth* (1905) traces the similarly tragic fall of Lily Barth, a barely fashionable twenty-eight-year-old when the novel opens (at least "her rivals credited" Lily with reaching that age [6]) and a broken woman on the verge of her thirties at the novel's end. Perhaps the best-known twenty-nine-year-old in American fiction is Nick Carraway, the affable narrator of Fitzgerald's *The Great Gatsby* (1925). Well into his narrative, Nick laments, "I was thirty. Before me stretched the portentous menacing road of a new decade" (143). And Douglas Coupland's *Generation X* (1991) more recently reminds us that (according to one chapter title) we are "Dead at 30 Buried at 70." However, if the dividing line between twenty-nine and thirty figures in some symbolic way in these well-known examples, then surely the symbolism unravels the moment additional characters, of all different ages, pass back and forth across the figurative generational dividing line. For every troubled twenty-nine-year-old in American fiction, we find a host of ageless Madame Reitzes, Lawrence Seldens, and Jay Gatsbys. Surely they cannot be pinned down by any hard-and-fast generational label, either young or old.

The protean status of generational identity—and particularly that of the "younger generation"—was very much on the mind of critic and historian Bernard DeVoto, who put on a cantankerously literal-minded hat when he wrote in 1936 that "nobody can decide just what a literary generation is":

> The time scale is ambiguous: the first novelist of the Younger Generation began publishing in 1900, its first poet died in 1886, and its twilight genius is only thirty-five. No date can be agreed on for its beginning: Mr. [Carl] Van Doren believes that it began with the Armistice, but surely it was in full cry as early as 1912 and most of the rebellions for which it is celebrated were current during its early adolescence, among the muckrakers, the crusaders, and the Ur-Greenwich-Villagers of the preceding ten years. The end is also undetermined. We are told that the period closed with 1929 and the Wall Street crash, with 1932 and the bottom of the trough, with 1934 and the crest of the New Deal, and with 1936 and the possible success of Mr. Lippmann's candidate. But wherever you fix a date for the beginning of dotage, you find that nine-tenths of the reasonably good writing since that deadline has been done by men you have extinguished. (3)

Not to be outdone, Van Wyck Brooks, in *New England: Indian Summer* (1940), reached all the way back to the 1870s to locate a "younger generation" consisting of the deracinated, adventure-seeking progeny of antebellum America's literary and social elite—that is, the sons of George Bancroft (Hubert, born 1832), Louis Agassiz (Alexander, born 1835), Charles Francis Adams (Henry, born 1838), Henry James Sr. (William and Henry, born 1842 and 1843), and Nathaniel Hawthorne (Julian, born 1846). Without indicating as much, Brooks has in mind a model of second-generation declension like that developed by psychoanalysts and immigration scholars. (Brooks also has in mind Henry Adams's autobiography, which assembled an almost identical cast of characters.) Still, Brooks is no simple positivist. The exemplary life of this generation, at least according to Brooks, belonged to the geologist Clarence King: "If King's life had a moral, as all his friends seemed to feel, if it was symptomatic and symbolic, of what was it the symbol? The waste of the brightest faculties unemployed by civilization, the *zeitgeist,* the time and the country. . . . The old culture had broken down, the old causes were dead and forgotten, and no new ideal had arisen to rally the minds of the younger men; and, while many turned westward, almost as many turned to Europe, in despair of the civilization they saw before them" (189). In other words, King—and with him the Younger Generation—symbolizes cultural critique; following Lionel Trilling's definition of "modernism," we might say that King represents "the disenchantment of our culture with culture itself" (3).

Difficult as it may be to believe, in the United States there simply was no younger generation before Brook's "Younger Generation of 1870." Children and parents abounded, to be sure, and children and old fogies make up some of nineteenth-century America's most memorable literary characters. And yet we remember Little Eva and Rip Van Winkle because they are cultural aberrations, not because they represent the social norm. Edward L. Widmer demonstrates that generational dynamics played a central role in antebellum literary and political rhetoric, particularly in the nation's emergent center of power, New York. As Widmer points out, the members of this group—rather, two groups with divergent interests—called themselves "Young America." However, a truly *national* youth culture did not exist in the United States until the aftermath of the Civil War, and only in subsequent years did the machinery of national culture allow for a coherent identity among the majority of American youth.

As the U.S. population pressed further and further westward in the years following the Civil War, several mutually constitutive factors contributed to the emergence and crystallization of a national, even transcontinental, youth culture.[8] During the late nineteenth and early twentieth centuries, the population of youth followed the larger pattern of movement from rural to urban settings, a result of the rapid industrialization of the U.S. economy. Population density in the United States grew from 7.9 persons per square mile in 1850 to 25.6 in 1900 and to 50.7 in 1950 (Taeuber and Taeuber 20). If we cross-tabulate these figures with the percentage of the population under twenty years of age, then there were 11.3 youth per square mile in 1900 and 17.3 by 1950. At the dawn of the twentieth century over 40 percent of the U.S. population lived in a metropolitan center, and by 1930 this figure increased to 52.7 percent (Taeuber and Taeuber 24).

Along with the growth in numbers of young people came the rapid implementation of compulsory primary education and, to a lesser extent, uniform curricular standards. The so-called common school movement, which sprang up in New England during the 1830s and 1840s, spread after the Civil War throughout the West, and later, thanks to strict congressional guidelines for Reconstruction, the South.[9] Between 1860 and 1890, the school enrollment rate for five- to nineteen-year-olds rose from 49 to 64 percent, in large part because of new compulsory attendance laws (Urban and Wagoner 164). As a result of these measures, the number of students in public high schools jumped from fewer than 25,000 in 1875 to 200,000 in 1890 to well over 500,000 in 1900 (Pulliam 90; Brubacher and Rudy 157). Nationwide shifts in educational policies had striking, positive effects, particularly in the area of basic literacy. Between 1850 and 1900 the illiteracy rate among whites fell from 10.7 percent to 6.2 percent (Kaestle et al. 25); by 1940, the national illiteracy rate for all racial and ethnic groups had dropped to just 3 percent (Kaestle 211).[10] There were, however, additional results of the sweeping changes in American education that were felt with more ambivalence. Local communities suffered the loss of defining characteristics due to the growing secularization of American education and the strictly monolingual emphasis of teaching and assessment. As Joel Spring writes, the "common school movement attempted to ensure that Protestant Anglo-American culture remained dominant, as large groups of immigrants with differing religious and cultural values entered American life" (120). By the time the GI Bill passed in 1944, and much sooner in urban centers, American colleges could depend on a predictable set of skills among graduating high school seniors.

For those families that could afford to send their children to college—once a luxury, but in an era of unprecedented professional specialization almost a necessity—the boom in land-grant universities spurred by the Merrill Acts of 1860 and 1890 provided new avenues for attaining a higher degree. Increases in college enrollment figures easily outpaced population gains during the latter part of the nineteenth century: from 1885 to 1895 alone, enrollment at private eastern colleges increased by 20 percent; at state universities, enrollment grew by 32 percent (Brubacher and Rudy 158). For those who could not afford college, military service remained an option, and during times of war it was a compulsory rite of passage. After the Civil War and up to the Spanish-American War, the number of active-duty military personnel held steady between 20,000 and 40,000. In the twentieth century, the number of active duty military personnel ranged from approximately 100,000 to 200,000 during times of peace. However, these numbers spiked appreciably during the Spanish-American War (209,714 in 1898), World War I (2,395,742 in 1918), and World War II (8,267,958 in 1945) (Weigley 598–99).

Reform movements, representing all corners of American political life, also expanded their reach across the continent, and their activities extended to cultural as well as strictly political issues. The universal suffrage movement, led by the American Woman Suffrage Association and the National Woman Suffrage Association (both headquartered in the East), achieved its earliest victories in newly incorporated Western states. The National Association for the Advancement of Colored People, founded in 1909, organized the first nationwide civil rights protest in 1915 against D. W. Griffith's racist film *The Birth of a Nation.* Politically progressive groups tended to include a greater number of young members than their more conservative counterparts such as the Rotary Club or the Daughters of the American Revolution, which required (explicitly or not) pedigree and wealth for membership; more important, the rhetoric of progressive reform movements—particularly the loose assemblage of groups and individuals known as the New Woman and New Negro movements—drew from and contributed to the critical vocabulary of the younger generation. This is a far cry from the schoolmarm stereotype associated with progressive movements (including abolitionism and suffrage efforts) of the mid-nineteenth century.

A complex yet vital force in the shaping of an American youth culture was the development of new communications technologies and, with these, the rise of mass media. By the end of World War I, youth all across the nation could listen to the latest jazz hit on a disk recording. To meet the growing demand, Tin Pan Alley happily spun out hit after youth-oriented hit, with such seemingly frivolous titles as "Ain't We Got Fun" (1921), "Yes! We Have No Bananas" (1923), and "Makin' Whoopee" (1928). Annual sales of phonographs in the United States reached $27.1 million in 1914 and skyrocketed to $158.7 million by 1919 (S. Douglas 84). In 1921 alone, Americans purchased over 100 million records (S. Douglas 84), or roughly one record for every person in the country. By the end of 1922, a network of radio broadcast towers spread from the New York area to every major city, and many more small towns, in the country. The number of radio broadcasters rose exponentially during this period. From January to November 1921, the Department of Commerce issued just 5 commercial broadcast licenses; in December, however, it issued 23. During 1922, the number of licenses issued virtually exploded from January (8) and February (24) to March (77), April (76), May (97), June (72), and July (76) (Barnouw 1:91). Sales of radio receiver sets and parts boomed as well: annual sales reached $60 million in 1922, $136 million in 1923, $358 million in 1924, $430 million in 1925, and $506 million in 1926 (Barnouw 1:125, 210). (RCA, the leading manufacturer of radio receiver sets—its signature product was the so-called Radio Music Box—had sales of $11 million during 1922, the first year of production, and $50 million the following year [Barnouw 1:79].) The national emergence of television during the 1940s and 1950s merely continued, and magnified, the earlier trend toward a commercial mass media.

The cultural contact zone known as mass-market publishing provided additional venues for the consolidation of a national youth identity. New York publishing firms—including the once-pathbreaking Boni and Liveright, Benjamin Heubsch, Alfred Knopf, Modern Library, and Viking Press—issued a challenge to the genteel publishing establishment, or what was perceived to be the genteel establishment, centered in Boston. New genres tailored specifically to younger readers, including children's magazines and comic books, joined the remarkably diverse fare pitched to the wider public. Even if a child could not afford to purchase the readily available supply of discounted titles (including dime novels and even cheaper novelettes), he or she could always borrow a title from the growing number of lending libraries located in all but the remotest corners of the continent. The first publicly financed library was established in Boston in 1854, and by 1875 there were 275 public libraries, primarily in urban centers. Andrew Carnegie's donation of $50 million between 1881 and 1920 led to the creation of an additional 1,412 public libraries in all parts of the country. By 1926 nearly six thousand public libraries serviced 57 percent of the total U.S. population (Wiegand and Davis 520–21).

The various "younger generations" previously mentioned bear a striking family resemblance to what we have come to know as the "Lost Generation"; their examples indicate that by the early 1930s the Lost Generation myth was the single most important prism through which America's moderns, even America's nineteenth-century moderns, were routinely viewed. This is consistent with a framework already finding widespread prominence during the 1910s and 1920s: the notion that the "younger generation" had been supplanted, finally, by "*The* Younger Generation." Canby reflected in 1922 that "we have talked about the younger generation as if youth were a new phenomenon that had to be named and described, like a strange animal in the

Garden of Eden. No wonder our juniors have become self-conscious and have begun to defend themselves" (149). It is at roughly this point that we are able to witness the transformation of the "younger generation" from relatively hollow substantive into what we now describe as an "object of discourse," a precritical linguistic formulation with the power to emerge as a tool of critical insight and shape social reality. It would become, in fact, the rough equivalent of the "Lost Generation," a group usually defined against the backdrop of a spiritually bankrupt mass market, the very same cultural institutions that gave it birth.

John Peale Bishop, who after World War I gave up an editorship at *Vanity Fair* for expatriate life in Paris (he was also the inspiration for Thomas Park D'Invilliers in Fitzgerald's *This Side of Paradise*), put his finger on this important transformation in a brief literary memoir, "The Missing All" (1937):

> Fitzgerald and Hemingway belong to what was in its day the Younger Generation. It was certainly not the first to be called so, but it was the first to gain capitals from the press. And, as Malcolm Cowley has pointed out, it was really the first literary generation in America. . . . They were those who were of an age to be combatant when America declared war on the Central Powers.
>
> Not all of them fought; but most of them had of their own choice supported a uniform of some sort. When they returned from arms, it was in revolt. What they protested against was called Puritanism, which is a fairer name than it deserves; for the enemy was the New England idea, not in its original purity, but in that corrupt state to which it had arrived through the hundred and more years in which the West was settled. (111–12)

The ubiquity of this idea—that the Younger Generation had finally arrived and now stood poised for a final showdown against its elders—clearly troubled critic Frank Swinnerton, who in 1927 disparagingly wrote of publicity-hungry youngsters who purveyed an empty vogue: "The young man who cares first of all for his *work* can afford to disregard adverse comment. But the young man who is bent upon cutting a figure in the world thinks less of the work than of the effect which it is to produce. It is the second young man who is desirous of obtaining press publicity, who resents criticism, who engages in leagues with others of his own age and styles his league 'the Younger Generation'" (422). The "younger generation" evolved during the turn of the century from a haphazard conjunction of words with understandably protean features to a specific, uppercase literary movement with genuine if not altogether clear aims and practices. "Younger" in this sense signifies not only the comparative degree of "young" (as in the *OED* definition for the term, "of less age, that has lived a shorter time") but also something less descriptive, more substantive (as in the latter part of the *OED* definition, "more youthful (in years, or fig. in disposition, etc.)." In Mannheimian terms, positivism gives way to romanticism. What was once a quantitative measure, however ill-defined and slippery, emerged as something that was felt so strongly that it elicited the most visceral responses.

Randolph Bourne, the outspoken radical whose acid views necessitated a journeyman's lifestyle, flitting from one magazine job to another, died before he could cement his position as the premier spokesman for the Younger Generation. Still, he felt his generational status as strongly as anyone before or since, leading Brooks to describe Bourne's as "one of the fullest, richest, and most significant lives of the younger generation" (Brooks even described Bourne as the incarnation of "Emerson's 'American scholar' at last") (Bourne, *History* ix, xiv). In *Youth and Life* (1913), Bourne put a figure on the age of the Younger Generation—like him, they were born ten or so years before the turn of the century—but no mere number does justice to the passion capable of sustaining youth indefinitely: "This is the great divergence which sets youth not only against old age, but against youth itself: the undying spirit of youth that seems to be fed by an unquenchable fire, that does not burn itself out but seems to grow steadier as life goes on, against the fragile, quickly tarnished type that passes relentlessly into middle life" (5). Youth against itself, or the noncontemporaneity of the contemporaneous: Bourne's urgent mood captures in few words the condition of lostness that would define his literary heirs.

Unearthing the Lost Generation

Her description of the landscape, studied and serene in spite of the conflict raging nearby, betrays an artist's temperament. Overall it is an eerie portrayal of the relatively conflict-free Franco-Swiss border—eerie for all that remains left out of the picture. She begins by invoking a timeless tradition of thinkers and writers, appropriate for a piece written in the elegiac mode: "The lake, which has sustained in turn the gaze of Calvin and Voltaire, of Gibbon and Madame de Stael, of Byron and Rousseau,—the lake lies shimmering in the haze that almost veils the Alps and Jura and softens the stony bastion of the Mont Saléve. It is an afternoon, like all autumn afternoons, for memories; above all, for memories of the significant dead." Her narrative, once the tone is set with still more thick description, develops slowly, wandering over the scene's unsettling incongruities: "the air, still as the in-drawn breath of the intently listening, the white ribboning road, the autumn fields, [and] the sunshine on the village roofs" give way to French border guards "stand[ing] red-trousered by their boxes, with fixed bayonets, by the corner of peaceful hayfields, where old men and very young boys are at work, or only women and girls." She gathers information about the family she once visited long ago, and about her former host, Mr. B—, from an old French widow who hangs the wash out to dry. The two women discuss the countryside, friendships held in common, and of course the war. All three of the widow's sons remain stationed at the front. There the world is seen in a different, dimmer light. There lives are irreparably damaged if not destroyed altogether.

"They say," she prods the widow, "that men fall beside you, and die; and you take no notice."

"[I]t's a generation lost," the widow responds, "*une génération perdue.* For of those that come back,—they won't be the same."

This conversation, which took place sometime before the Armistice, found an American audience in November 1920, when it was depicted in Florence Valentine Keys's *North American Review* article "A Generation Lost?" It marks the first instance that the "lost generation" entered into American public discourse, at least in the United States and in English, a full six years before Ernest Hemingway popularized the phrase with his epigraph for *The Sun Also Rises* (1926). And this was hardly the first instance that the "lost generation" of youth was identified. You might say that the "lost generation" was in the atmosphere, waiting for the right circumstances to fall from the skies of war-torn Europe. The semantic history of the "Lost Generation" provides a number of twists and turns, and I approach the task from the relatively privileged position of being at least the fourth person to provide such an analysis.[11] It might be argued that this kind of intense scrutiny of a simple phrase is mere pedantic trivia; however, at least four salient features are embedded in the history of the phrase.

First is the sheer ubiquity of the Lost Generation (with and without the capital letters). As we shall see, the Lost Generation is hardly a strictly American phenomenon, and perhaps more surprisingly, it is hardly confined to the Jazz Age. Second is the indeterminacy and instability of the Lost Generation: its capacity to mean depends upon key variables embedded in the history of the verbal act (who, where, when, and of course, how). Like its predecessor, the Younger Generation, the shape of the myth was largely up for grabs for at least two decades, and it did not evolve into a hard fact of literary scholarship until after World War II. Third is the sheer power of the Lost Generation myth in shaping contemporary views of American modernism. The concept has had a spellbinding and little-acknowledged impact on literary studies since the 1940s. Since the Cold War the Lost Generation has fallen snugly into place in the now-standard genealogy of American literary history, which traces successive generations from the puritan founders to the early national forefathers to the New England Renaissance romantics, and so on. Fourth, the Lost Generation embodies a more or less explicit cultural critique, in particular a critique of national cultural institutions (often identified by the label "civilization").

Robert Wohl has gone furthest in showing just how widespread and penetrating generational thinking was during the early twentieth century in his comprehensive historical study *The Generation of 1914* (1979). Wohl attempts "to rescue the generation of 1914 from the shadowland of myth and to restore it to the realm of history" (2) by exploring key generational thinkers in France, Germany, England, Spain, and Italy (although he also alludes to the Lost Generation of American expatriates). Without claiming to do so, Wohl highlights the first instance in which the phrase "lost generation" was used in a manner approximating our contemporary understanding of the term. According to Wohl, the left-leaning editor and publisher Franz Pfemfert introduced the phrase "lost generation" in 1912 in his expressionist weekly *Die Aktion.* Pfemfert was not unlike a German version of Randolph Bourne; as Wohl points out, Pfemfert "deplored the backwardness of German culture, the cowardice of the German bourgeoisie, the reformism of German Social Democracy, the heavy-handed and dangerous militarism of German foreign policy, the authoritarianism of German schools, the lack of political consciousness among German university students, the dishonesty of the German press—in fact anything and everything that crossed the horizon of his searching gaze" (45). As might be expected, Pfemfert was an ardent ideological and financial supporter of the Youth Movement. Ironically, he applied the "lost generation" tag not to the *Wandervögel,* whose members would later be killed in startling numbers during the war, but to official Germany, which "groped in vain after salvation and self-preservation" (trans. Wohl 45).[12] Pfemfert desired above all that Germany fulfill its true destiny by abandoning partisan politics, by sloughing off the dead tissue of tradition, and he imagined that the Youth Movement would show the way. What this entails is never quite made clear; the urgency and impressionism of Pfemfert's generational rhetoric drowns out any practical advice: "Be neither 'radical' in the sense of day-to-day politics nor 'nationalist.' Be young! Struggle for the right to be young against a narrow-minded and ossified world!" (trans. Wohl 45)[13]

Florence Valentine Keys, as I mention above, introduced the phrase to an

American audience in 1920, although in its somewhat unconventional form, "generation lost" (since she was rendering *génération perdue* with an awkwardly literal translation). Born in Toronto in 1868, Keys was educated in Germany, Switzerland, and France before receiving a degree from the University of Toronto. She briefly taught Greek at Bryn Mawr and was professor of English at Vassar when she was not traveling in Europe. Her cosmopolitan experience gave her a unique perspective on the war—her friends fought and died on both sides of the battlefront—and Keys's written legacy primarily consists of war correspondence for the *North American Review*, including her article that asks in its title whether the war generation is, in fact, lost.[14] One assumes that the answer to her question is "yes"; however, the generation is lost in more ways than one. As I have already suggested, Keys identifies a "lost generation" of soldiers, including the widow's three sons, who if they survive cannot simply pick up their lives where they left off. But Keys continues her episodic sketch by describing encounters with others in the Savoy region: a postmistress from whom Keys solicits direction, and a frail old man who, like Keys, searches for ties to the past. The old man locates his missing daughter, but the distance between the members of this reunited family provides Keys with another context for the "lost generation." As we might expect, the phrase registers the symbolic aggression of the young toward the old: "Soon from beyond the hedge and shrubbery comes the sound of voices; a young voice, pouring forth in a torrent of resentment and revolt, and an old voice, faint and trembling. . . . A moment later they pass across an elbow of the road; a young woman with stormy shoulders; the tiny old man; and between them, two toddling children. A gap; *une génération perdue*" (685). Thus the generation is lost not only demographically but also spiritually. A psychologist might say that nurture has become unhinged from nature.

Pfemfert and Keys (and presumably other contemporaneous writers who have yet to come to light) cast a very wide net to capture their "lost generations." Their views might best be described as more demographic than symbolic—their "lost generations" cannot yet be equated with the Younger Generation—but their analyses rest upon cultural rather than strictly biological foundations. (Their lost generations are aberrations rather than the norm; they do not necessarily represent entire populations of age cohorts.) There were numerous other potential candidates for "lost generation" status during the period immediately following the war, and indeed a few of these have been so dubbed by scholars writing with the benefit of hindsight. Just about any nation that suffered severe losses during the war might be considered a candidate. So too the exiles of failed revolutions (in Moscow, Berlin, Mexico, Lisbon, and elsewhere) or the ethnic groups swallowed up or cleft in two by post-Versailles national boundaries. Nevertheless, the "lost generation" that ultimately settled into place as the Lost Generation was the one given currency by Ernest Hemingway, in the famous pair of epigraphs to *The Sun Also Rises:*

> "You are all a lost generation."
>
> Gertrude Stein in conversation

> "Vanity of vanities, saith the Preacher, vanity of vanities; all is vanity. . . . One generation passeth away, and another generation cometh; but the earth abideth forever. . . . The sun also ariseth, and the sun goeth down, and hasteth to the place where he arose. . . . The wind goeth toward the south, and turneth about unto the north; it whirleth about continually, and the wind returneth again according to its circuits. . . . All the rivers run into the sea; yet the sea is not full; unto the place from whence the rivers come, thither they return again."
>
> Ecclesiastes [1:2, 4–7]

Hemingway was so taken by Stein's "lost generation" moniker that he almost chose it for the title of his novel instead of the title inspired by the Old Testament.[15] (In fact, the choice of title was an unsettled matter for quite some time. *Fiesta* was the title of the work in progress, and Hemingway also considered *River to the Sea* and *Two Lie Together* [both inspired by Ecclesiastes] as well as *The Old Leaven* [after a passage in 1 Corinthians]. *The Lost Generation* appears to have been the front-runner for a brief spell, and Hemingway even wrote a foreword explaining the choice [facsimile ed. xiii].) The novel's epigraphs, to borrow a cliché, function as windows into the text, although contradictory ones: Hemingway saw the latter as a correction to the former, and in November 1926 he wrote to his editor Maxwell Perkins that "the point of the book to me was that the earth abideth forever—having a great deal of fondness for the earth and not a whole hell of a lot for my generation. . . . I didn't mean the book to be hollow or bitter satire but a damn tragedy with the earth abiding forever as the hero" (*Letters* 208).

The epigraphs exerted considerable influence in determining the shape and scope of early reviews of the novel, far more influence than the novel's title (which, if we run with the cliché, might be considered an unlocked front door into the text). The majority of the novel's first American critics refer to the phrase attributed to Stein, and for many it serves as a kind of literary benchmark, a standard with which to gauge Hemingway's success or failure. (This is not the case in England, where the novel was published in 1927 as

Fiesta, without the epigraphs.) For example, John Dos Passos, in "A Lost Generation," a review of the novel for the *New Masses,* observes that "it's a dangerous thing to quote the Bible in the beginning of a book. It raises the readers' hopes as to the meatiness of the matters to be served up by the author" (92)—and then Dos Passos offers a mixed review of the book on the basis of both Ecclesiastes and Stein. In a *New York World* review, Herbert S. Gorman writes that *The Sun Also Rises* is "the tale of a great spiritual debacle, of a generation that has lost its guiding purpose and has been driven by time, fate or nerves (whatever one desires to call it) into the feverish atmosphere of strained passions" (Stephens 38). An anonymous *Springfield (Mass.) Republican* reviewer argues that "in choosing a title from the passage in Ecclesiasticus beginning 'Vanity of vanities, saith the preacher,' Ernest Hemingway sounds a keynote of disillusionment which echoes throughout the book. His characters belong to that generation (ever dear to the realist) whose ideals were smashed by the war" (Stephens 40). Writing for the *New Republic,* Lawrence S. Morris describes the novel's characters as "stumbling through life like a man lost in a forest: attracted to this side by what appears to be a clearing, repelled when the clearing is found to be a marsh." They represent "the bewildered anguish of an aimless generation" (Stephens 44, 45). Even critics who disagree with the tag felt compelled to disagree publicly. "Gertrude Stein told Ernest Hemingway once, 'You are all a lost generation,' and the remark seems to have impressed him unduly," writes Schuyler Ashley in a review for the *Kansas City Star,* where Hemingway found a job after high school. Ashley continues: "The gentle tug of the ordinary tides of life, business, marriage, getting-on-in-the-world, have set most of the stranded ships afloat again. Jake Barnes' generation is not 'lost,' though it has suffered heavy casualties" (Stephens 40–41). In fact, at least one early reviewer saw the "lost generation" as a figure for American society in general, a part-for-whole version of the American dream gone awry. In the *Boston Evening Transcript,* "K.J.W." writes that "one is inclined to view that these are not a lost generation, Miss Stein to the contrary. As spiritual bankrupts they are not so segregated, after all; they are very closely related to the so-called 'iron grip' generation now holding forth. Almost any country's condition can be deduced from the vices and virtues of the expatriates. In them the native attributes are in excess, merely because they live outside the fatherland they represent. Our sun also rises with theirs and goes down and hastes to the place where he arose, even as their sun" (Stephens 37).

It is easy to overestimate Hemingway's influence on the shape of his generation's critique of American culture; after all, older figures such as Mencken and Sinclair Lewis had already paved the way for lost-generation rhetoric by belittling puritan bogeys and denigrating holdovers from the pioneer days. Still, while the early critical fanfare for *The Sun Also Rises* was drowned out by raves for more established writers, the novel soon became a life handbook for young Americans at home and abroad. "It was a good novel and became a craze," Cowley writes, "young men tried to get as imperturbably drunk as the hero, young women of good families took a succession of lovers in the same heartbroken fashion as the heroine, they all talked like Hemingway heroes and the name was fixed" (*Exile's* 3).[16] We need look no further than *Only Yesterday* (1931), Frederick Lewis Allen's "informal history" of the 1920s, for confirmation that the name, if not the condition it describes, was "fixed," as Cowley put it. According to Allen, "To many men and women the new day so sonorously heralded by the optimists and propagandists of the war-time had turned into night before it ever arrived, and in the uncertain blackness they did not know which way to turn. They could revolt against stupidity and mediocrity, they could derive a meager pleasure from regarding themselves with pity as members of a lost generation, but they could not find peace" (203).

Although I am reluctant to commit the sin of ascribing authorial intention, in this case it is fairly easy to state that Hemingway felt his novel had been utterly misread. For Cowley, the Lost Generation was in essence the same thing as the Younger Generation he had already identified in 1921; for Allen, the Lost Generation expanded to include the entire set of "highbrows" led in revolt by Mencken; however, for Hemingway, the Lost Generation signified a much more specific condition, almost like a fast-acting, terminal disease. It was a phrase best applied in retrospect. In his abandoned foreword to the novel, when it was still called *The Lost Generation,* he explains in Steinian fashion that "there is only this then to say that this generation that is lost has nothing to do with any Younger Generation about whose outcome much literary speculation occurred in times past. This is not a question of what kind of mothers will flappers make or where is bobbed hair leading us. This is about something that is already finished. For whatever is going to happen to the generation of which I am a part has already happened" (facsimile ed. 627). The faintly fatalistic chord that Hemingway apparently hoped to strike with the epigraph gradually grew louder and louder and was eventually harmonized with *the* Younger Generation of writers about whom I have already written, until the Lost Generation was in fact about bob-haired flapper mothers, about would-be Brett Ashleys and Jake Barneses carrying on failed affairs and drunkenly speaking out of the sides of their mouths.

The Lost Generation mythology was not without its naysayers, nor even its satirists, a clear indication of the myth's widespread acceptance as a cultural touchstone. As early as 1922, in *The Beautiful and Damned,* Fitzgerald offered a scathing critique of the generation he helped invent just two years before in *This Side of Paradise.* In 1925, Anita Loos satirized American expatriate life in her *Gentlemen Prefer Blondes,* which sends the cerebrally challenged flapper Lorelei Lee to Europe where she hobnobs with "Dr Froyd" and "Sinclare Lewis." Even more to the point, Michael Arlen in 1929 published his short story "The 'Lost Generation,'" a narrative that begins as a straightforward, whimsical satire but ultimately takes a tragic turn so common in the work of Lost Generation writers. The story reads as an emblem of the larger movement from which it derives its name: a fragile, farcical gaiety only temporarily obscures a more deep-seated cynicism and tragedy. Arlen begins with a wink at the reader as he introduces the story's main character: "Hemingway was one of those men whom you don't associate with romance, and even less with sentimentality. That is to say, he liked to see exactly what it was that lay in front of him, and you couldn't imagine him being led by the nose into positions over which he had no control. He liked to have control over everything in sight, did Hemingway" (*Babes* 181).

Hemingway is not a tough young writer of hard-boiled prose, as one might expect; instead, he's a forty-year-old (and therefore ancient) English mining engineer with neither social nor romantic ambitions. That is, until he meets the fashionable American expatriate Beulah Ley, a sort of worldly-wise Lorelei Lee. The two fall in love during the course of an off-again, on-again romance, and she inevitably breaks his heart at a poolside party on the Riviera, but not before Arlen engages the rhetoric behind the Lost Generation myth. "Yes," Hemingway thinks to himself, "she was one of the 'lost generation,' born thirty or so years ago, the children of a decaying continent." He continues:

> Well, wasn't Europe decaying while you looked at it? And did these clever young people, the "lost generation," do anything for it? On the contrary, their spiritual word was "departure"—a restless flitting about from one thing to another. Wanderers without luggage, that was what they were. Unhappy? Of course, and why the devil not? No, they got no fun out of it in the end. Good Lord, fun! Beulah, for instance—he had always felt there was something sorrowful about Beulah's radiant beauty. The hue of death, as in autumn sunshine. Yes, the hue of death. In the twilight of the world the gods went out hunting and killing souls. And they chose the clever souls first. Yes, Beulah was a poor devil, really. And her friends too, those clever young puppies, those pale

> young men, inclined to prance as they walked. One had to be sorry for them—the poor brainy filleted bright young people—castrated and damned. Poor devils! (*Babes* 194)

Born in 1895 in Bulgaria to Armenian parents (his original name was Dikran Kouyoumdjian), Arlen moved to England as a child and later found himself a among London's bohemian literati, forming part of the circle that included D. H. Lawrence, Aldous Huxley, and Nancy Cunard. (Cunard was the model for Iris March, the heroine of Arlen's best-selling novel *The Green Hat* [1924].) Arlen's relationship with the Lost Generation ends neither at the title of his story nor at the not-so-subtle references to the novels of Hemingway ("castrated") and Fitzgerald ("damned"). In fact, this story appears to be at least in part a response to Arlen's association with the Lost Generation in the public eye. One reviewer, writing for the *New York Times* in 1928, viewed Arlen as "an English F. Scott Fitzgerald who has still to achieve his *The Great Gatsby*" (qtd. in Keyishian 95). Fitzgerald was a dedicated Arlen fan, at least before his opinion soured; and he once described the Englishman as "my successor" (*Letters* 108) even though Arlen was one year his senior. Much later, Hemingway reminisced how Fitzgerald "would tell me the plots and describe the characters" of Arlen's novels. "[Fitzgerald] gave me a sort of oral Ph.D. thesis on Michael Arlen" (*Moveable* 175). Judging by the dozens of reviewers who identified Brett Ashley as a latter-day Irish March, it appears that Hemingway learned something from the lessons.

The mythic status and stature of the Lost Generation can also be measured by how quickly and thoroughly Stein's remark "in conversation," as the epigraph mentions, evolved into the stuff of legend. It is one of a handful of phrases closely associated with American modernism ("jazz" is probably the most important) whose etymology and social meaning—whose myth of origins—became a site of public controversy. Hemingway describes the putative origins of the phrase in the foreword he abandoned along with the title *The Lost Generation.* He writes, "One day last summer Gertrude Stein stopped in a small town . . . to have a valve fixed in her Ford car. The young mechanic who fixed it was very good and quick and skilled." The legend begins simply enough in Hemingway's account, with Stein asking the garage owner:

> "Where do you get boys to work like that? . . . I thought you couldn't get boys to work anymore."
>
> "Oh yes," the garage owner said. "You can get very good boys now. I've taken all these and trained them myself. It is the ones between

twenty two and thirty that are no good. C'est un generation perdu. No one wants them. They are no good. They were spoiled. The young ones, the new ones are all right again."

"What became of the others?"

"Nothing. They know they are no good. C'est un generation 'perdu.' —A little hard on them," he added. (facsimile ed. 626)

Hemingway would salvage some of the material from this foreword in his posthumously published memoir, *A Moveable Feast* (1964), although with noticeable differences. Some are relatively minor: in 1964 it was the ignition, not a valve; the young mechanic does a poor job, not a good one; and the garage owner addresses the young mechanic directly ("The *patron* had said to him, 'You are all a *génération perdue*'" [29]) rather than address Stein abstractly. Also, in the 1964 version Stein repeats the phrase to Hemingway: "'Don't argue with me, Hemingway,' Miss Stein said. 'It does no good at all. You're all a lost generation, exactly as the garage keeper said'" (29). Hemingway and Stein had had a falling out long before the memoir was written, and he was able to add to this later version, "I thought that all generations were lost by something and always had been and always would be. . . . But the hell with her lost-generation talk and all the dirty, easy labels" (30).

During the considerable time lag between the novel's publication and the appearance of this published explanation of the epigraph, many contradictory takes on the origin of the phrase found their way into print. Stein herself fails to mention the garage episode in *The Autobiography of Alice B. Toklas* (1933),[17] and she recalls an entirely different, tongue-in-cheek version of the phrase's origin in its sequel, *Everybody's Autobiography* (1937):

> It was this hotel keeper who said what it is said I said that the war generation was a lost generation. And he said it in this way. He said that every man becomes civilized between the ages of eighteen and twenty-five. If he does not go through a civilizing experience at that time in his life he will not be a civilized man. And the men who went to the war at eighteen missed the period of civilizing, and they could never be civilized. They were a lost generation. Naturally if they are at war they do not have the influences of women of parents and of preparation.
>
> Everybody says something, certainly everybody here does. (53)

Had Stein's autobiographies been written after the publication of *A Moveable Feast,* it might be possible to read them as parodies of Hemingway's bitter, deadpan memoir. At any rate, it must be remembered how thin the line between literary memoirs and fiction really is—Hemingway even invites us to view his memoir as a work of fiction—and we have no solid evidence to believe either Hemingway or Stein in this specific matter. Most critics who delve seriously into the issue tend to side with Hemingway's version of events, if only because Hemingway's is the more popular memoir. Hemingway's hard-boiled critique of American culture thus trumps Stein's defense of a feminized "civilization," at least until the belated revision of U.S. cultural history undertaken by feminist cultural theorists. Others simply attribute the phrase to Stein without delving into the details of the matter; for example, the *OED* entry for "generation" cites her as the source. And a few have added touches that are apocryphal if not outright fabrications: the entry for "generation" in the *New Quotable Woman* attributes the phrase to a letter from Stein to Hemingway; Malcolm Bradbury remarks that the phrase originated with a petrol attendant in Spain (78); and Arthur Mizener attributes the phrase to "one of [Stein's] interminable monologues to Ernest Hemingway in her flat at 27 rue de Fleurus" (1). There are doubtless other examples I have overlooked, each with a self-confidently specific, fly-on-the-wall claim for the phrase's moment of origin. Searching for this holy grail quickly becomes a task of Arthurian proportions. But what cannot be escaped is the improbable ease with which the Lost Generation has been incorporated into literary histories big and small.

The Anatomy of the Lost Generation

If most critics of the sundry younger generations were unwilling or unable to put forward a concrete definition of their subject matter, by the end of the 1920s they were happy to do so for the Lost Generation. The Lost Generation stands apart from contemporaneous literary movements not only because its name derives from an ill-defined accident of literary history (although dada's origin bears some comparison in this respect) but also because the movement had no self-appointed tom-tom beater (such as Tristan Tzara for the dadaists and André Breton for the surrealists), no closely affiliated literary organ (such as *Poetry* for the imagists and *Blast!* for the vorticists), no readily identifiable manifesto or statement of aims (such as countless futurist pamphlets and *I'll Take My Stand* for the Agrarians). In spite of these factors, though, the Lost Generation is consistently viewed as America's first coherent literary generation, if not its first literary movement. No one has done more to outline the shape of the movement than the poet, critic, and editor Malcolm Cowley, himself a member of the Lost Generation. Cowley made a career of writing about his generation, and it is only fitting to turn to him for its species markers. *Exile's Return* (1934), written while Cowley was on sabbatical from an editorship at the *New Republic*—he wrote part of the manuscript while staying among the Fugitive group in Tennessee—identifies at least five salient points of Lost Generation social location. While Cowley tends to draw on very specific personal experiences to illustrate these points, he carefully positions himself as a generational Everyman.

First, there is a year of birth sometime around 1900, give or take a few years. (Cowley was born in 1898.) In the 1951 revised edition of *Exile's Return,* Cowley added a "Years of Birth" appendix listing 236 writers born between 1891 and 1905, from Herbert Asbury to Robert Penn Warren. A categorically hard-and-fast if aesthetically ambiguous hierarchy determines who's in and who's out: Cowley explains that his list is composed mostly of American writers from *Twentieth Century Authors* minus "Western writers, mystery writers (except Dashiell Hammett, who had an effect on narrative technique; Raymond Chandler had one too, but was born before 1890), popular romancers, one-book authors (unless the book was famous), scholars and scientists (except those like Crane Brinton and Margaret Mead who also write for the public), children's authors and writers on public affairs (except those who are also novelists or critics)" (311).

Second, there is the matter of educational background, including one's experiences at "Big-Town High School" and, more important, at "American College, 1916." "In college, the process of deracination went on remorselessly," observes Cowley, who uses his own tenure at Harvard to illustrate the conversion experience. "We were not being prepared for citizenship in a town, a state, or a nation; . . . instead we were being exhorted to enter that international republic of learning whose traditions are those of Athens, Florence, Paris, Berlin and Oxford. The immigrant into that high disembodied realm is supposed to come with empty hands and naked mind, like a recruit into the army" (28).

Third is the Great War, not necessarily experienced directly, but experienced nonetheless. Service in an ambulance unit might be seen as a corollary, since so many Lost Generation writers—Cowley mentions Louis Bromfield, Slater Brown, Harry Crosby, E. E. Cummings, Julian Green, Dashiell Hammett, Ernest Hemingway, Robert Hillyer, Sidney Howard, John Howard Lawson, John Dos Passos, William Seabrook, and himself—found themselves behind the wheel, so to speak.

Fourth is the "War in Bohemia," that is, a quasi-religious initiation into an unconventional artistic lifestyle in the big city—specifically, Greenwich Village. "Here, apparently, was a symbolic struggle," Cowley offers, "on the one side, the great megaphone of middle-class America; on the other, the

American disciples of art and artistic living. Here, in its latest incarnation, was the eternal warfare of bohemian against bourgeois, poet against propriety" (53). (More about this feature of generational rhetoric in chapters 3 and 4.)

Fifth is the condition of exile, which functions as an extension of the psychic alienation (from family and from mainstream society) already present. The spiritual wanderer usually winds up in Paris, but also in England or Russia or Latin America, or wherever the exchange rate is favorable: "The exiles of 1921 came to Europe seeking one thing and found another. They came to recover the good life and the traditions of art, to free themselves from organized stupidity, to win their deserved place in the hierarchy of the intellect. Having come in search of values, they found valuta" (81).

The Lost Generation has its mother and father figures—including Sherwood Anderson, Sylvia Beach, Mabel Dodge, Lowell, Mencken, Harriet Monroe, Stein, Stieglitz, and William Carlos Williams—all of whom are strategically exempt from inclusion in the "Older Generation," and some are occasionally added to lists of Lost Generation writers. These figurative parents were much more than inspiration in the traditional sense of literary influence; very often they played crucial roles in advancing the careers of their "offspring" as editors or as advocates before publishers, or as publishers themselves. Different lists of Lost Generation members vary as widely as the critics who adopt the rubric, but a core group can still be discerned, clustered around Stein in Paris and Stieglitz in New York. Not all of the 236 writers in Cowley's appendix conform precisely to the biographical criteria he outlines, but the few who do not still bear striking resemblance to their counterparts in terms of literary output.

"Now at last they had a slogan [the Lost Generation] that proclaimed their feeling of separation from older writers and of kinship with one another," continues Cowley. "In the slogan the noun was more important than the adjective. They might or might not be lost, the future would decide that point; but they already had the common adventures and formed the common attitude that made it possible to describe them as a generation" (4). While the five attributes listed above form a biographical nucleus around which a generation of location might be identified, Cowley's description of his cohorts betrays further ideological posturing. Implicit in the Lost Generation tag is a symbolic kinship with additional political and aesthetic dimensions. The "common attitude" reveals itself in a remarkably limited variety of ways, giving rise to a symbolic aggression (against the Older Generation and against American "civilization," the Older Generation writ large) that further distinguishes the Lost Generation as a generation unit. Historians typically describe the 1920s as a period marked by the "return to normalcy," an uncritical acceptance of laissez-faire conformity and the puritan values of Middletown's booboisie, to mix several metaphors making the rounds at the time. Against this (also mythical) background, the antipuritan fervor, the willful deracination, and the eventual spiritual disillusionment of the Lost Generation stand in sharp relief. The "play hard, work hard" stereotype of the Lost Generation mirrors the allegedly puritan ethic of the larger culture as would a camera obscura, by standing the image on its head. As Cowley observes:

> In spite of their achievements the generation deserved for a long time the adjective that Gertrude Stein had applied to it. . . . It was lost, first of all, because it was uprooted, schooled away and almost wrenched away from its attachment to any region or tradition. It was lost because its training had prepared it for another world than existed after the war (and because the war prepared it only for travel and excitement). It was lost because it tried to live in exile. It was lost because it accepted no older guides to conduct and because it had formed a false picture of society and the writer's place in it. (9)

These sentiments have been repeated too often by literary critics and historians to rehearse in great detail here. Virtually every "dictionary of" and "companion to" American literature includes an entry on the Lost Generation. These inevitably strike a chord similar to Cowley's or else cite his work directly. All of the major encyclopedias of American literature index the Lost Generation in their most recent editions (although this never occurred before 1940 or so). The most striking feature of the Lost Generation's place in subsequent literary history—its most troubling one in this era of the New American Studies, an approach characterized by institutionalized decentering practices—has to be the regular substitution of the Lost Generation for the whole of American modernism.

Archiving the Lost Generation

"The group of intellectuals most associated with the twenties," cultural historian Lynn Dumenil offers in a recent study of the decade, "was the one Gertrude Stein labeled the Lost Generation—the white writers and artists who came to maturity with World War I and whose disaffection with American culture led many to artistic exile in Paris and elsewhere in Europe" (149–50). Dumenil stands on solid ground with this assertion; indeed, the very association between the Lost Generation and the 1920s has a long history. As early as 1932, in *Infants of the Spring,* Wallace Thurman's Harlem Renaissance *roman à clef,* the book's narrator remarks that "Hemingway exemplified the spirit of the twenties in America more vividly than any other contemporary American novelist" (35). The revised edition of Russell Blankenship's triumphalist record of cultural nationalism, *American Literature as an Expression of the National Mind* (1949), adds a new section on "The Present Confusion," with a lengthy treatment of "The 1920's and the Lost Generation." With a pained ambivalence that commonly enters discussions of the decade, Blankenship writes: "In all American history we have had no decade more interesting or more deplorable than the 1920's" (726). He goes even further by defining the decade according to its most representative (in various senses of the word) movement: "The members of the Lost Generation, however, gave the most vivid portrayal of the period. Of the writers who belonged to this group Hemingway and Fitzgerald are the most notable, and they are the ones whose comments and portraits are the most typical and probably the most enduring" (730).

This version of part-for-whole cultural inquiry, in which the fate of the Lost Generation indexes wider cultural trends, came to dominate the analysis of American modernism during the middle of the twentieth century. The revised edition of the *Literary History of the United States* (1953) indexes the Lost Generation for the first time and adds a "Postscript at Mid-Century," written by Willard Thorp and Robert E. Spiller. Here the Lost Generation finds itself in a much more prominent position:

> [The Lost Generation's] technical experiments alone were enough to change the course of American literary history.
>
> The impetus of this group was sustained until about 1927, but then seemed to falter. Whether the stock-market crash of 1929 was cause or symptom of a deeper failure, the period from 1927 to 1932 seems to have been one of creative pause and moral inventory. Then with Malcolm Cowley's *Exile's Return* (1934), the "lost" generation was back on the job again, ready to take up the responsibility for the American literary life. (1394)

This passage not only conflates the Lost Generation with high modernist experimentation in the United States (and thus portrays the movement as a watershed in American literary history) but performs the additional task of explaining historical change according to the life span and professional career of the Lost Generation. As the Lost Generation goes, so goes the nation, from Roaring Twenties exuberance to Wall Street crash to Great Depression trough to New Deal recovery. Chastened by its own excess, the Lost Generation could pull itself—and America—up by the literary bootstraps.

This analytical model of substituting part for whole—or rather part (Hemingway and Fitzgerald) for part (Lost Generation) for whole (American modernism)—happens with considerable frequency, if only for convenience's sake. It was, in fact, invited by the writers of the Lost Generation themselves. Cowley often pointed out that the writers of the Lost Generation, because they were born around 1900, "fell into the habit of identifying themselves with the century" (*Exile's* 8). Hemingway's halfhearted attempts to disguise the real persons behind his literary personae—Harold Loeb, the model for Robert Cohn in *The Sun Also Rises,* is widely reported to have threatened Hemingway's life, and Left Bank cognoscenti dubbed the novel "Six Characters in Search of an Author, With a Gun Apiece"—led to the immediate conflation of Hemingway and his "heroes" (always in quotation marks) and quickly blossomed into the myth of Papa.[18] Baldly autobiographical novels and confessional memoirs were a staple of the Lost Generation, and in fact greatly contribute to its generational location.[19] Cowley regularly looks to the fiction of his cohorts as an anthropologist would examine the folk expressions of a primitive culture. As Marc Dolan points out, Marxian cultural critics writing in the late 1920s and early 1930s (such as Charles and Mary Beard, Joseph Wood Krutch, and Walter Lippmann) often turned to the Lost Generation's fictional characters for sociological evidence.

In part because the Lost Generation so eagerly lived its private life in public, airing its dirty laundry on page after page, literary critics in the years following World War II, the first to appraise systematically what we now call modernism, looked no further than to the Lost Generation to describe what American modernism *really* was. Alfred Kazin's *On Native Grounds* (1942) hinges upon the Lost Generation's artistic repudiation of the "old" realism and on its subsequent "revival" of naturalism. In 1951, John Aldridge could safely title his study of postmodern American literature, in the sense that "postmodern" refers to literature appearing in the wake of high modernism, *After the Lost Generation.* This trend is roughly contemporaneous with the emergence of the Beat Generation, which tended to depict itself as heir to the Lost Generation's place in literary history.[20] In 1961, "The Lost Generation" was one of fifteen Voice of America radio lectures on modern American literature, but its writers crop up again and again in the series transcripts.[21]

If scholarly titles can be taken as a register of larger trends, then the Lost Generation remains as fashionable as ever. In recent years the literary marketplace produced a bumper crop of examples. Beginning in 1971, the *Lost Generation Journal* published articles and memoirs devoted exclusively to the movement, although its tone is largely fan clubbish. The MLA Bibliography lists dozens of articles indexed under the subject "Lost Generation" since 1970. Most contributors to the *Columbia Literary History of the United States* (1988) feel uncomfortable with the Lost Generation cliché—it is "much too vague to subsume the diverse group of writers and artists, the serious ones and the fakes" (Elliott 743), writes Daniel Aaron—but its seven index entries ranks it just below the "Jazz Age" (eight) and "Modernism" (ten), and well above "World War I" (four). In 1994, Suzanne Rodriguez-Hunter published *Found Meals of the Lost Generation,* a collection of recipes and anecdotes (heavy on the cholesterol and spirits) from 1920s expatriate Paris.

An amusing but not insignificant curiosity of literary history is the extent to which the "Lost Generation" has been able to detach itself from its standard referent and reattach itself elsewhere (often as *la generación perdida, la génération perdue,* or *die verlorene Generation*)—one might even say that the Lost Generation has had its capital letters forcibly removed. Ever since the Lost Generation took shape as an object of scholarly discourse and emerged during the Cold War as the definitive movement of American modernism, the phrase has been used to describe an astounding range of movements, literary and otherwise, beyond the borders of the United States, and even well beyond the purview of modernist studies. Premodern "lost generations" are still quite rare, but at least one critic, Laura L. Nash, has identified a lost generation in ancient Greece. Larzer Ziff, taking his cue from Cowley, has argued extensively that American writers during the 1890s were even more lost than their 1920s successors—the 1890s were "truly lost"—because by 1900 the decade's greatest writers were either not yet recognized or already dead. Still others have looked to the rubric of lost generations to analyze British, Canadian, or French literature from World War I. Literary lost generations have more recently been located in 1910s and contemporary Mexico, in Cold War and Cultural Revolution China, in Japan during the 1960s, and in contemporary Brazil. During the 1930s, social critics such as Walter B. Pitkin and Maxine Davis described *all* American youth as a lost generation. Additional demographic lost generations have been found in the Netherlands during the 1950s and 1960s, in contemporary South Africa, and in countless first- and third-world urban ghettos. The tragedy of AIDS often evokes lost-generation analyses in the popular press. A professorial glut in academia resulted in what has been described as a lost generation of scholars during the 1980s. The list extends with dizzying indefiniteness and indeterminacy. The only rule that might be discerned by looking at the constellation of lost generations, once the phrase extends beyond the historical accident of war, is the vague one that might have been supplied by post-Freudian psychoanalysis: a hodgepodge of daughters and sons somehow alienated from their natural position in society. But the Lost Generation, along with its flapper mothers with bobbed hair, its Brett Ashleys and Jake Barneses, and its ability to mean beyond language's denotative capacities, lurks somewhere in the background.

Generations, Avant-Gardism, and American Cultural Nationalism

To engage avant-gardism by way of generational rhetoric is to engage it uncritically, on its own terms, rather than from some objective, exterior position. The avant-garde's use of generational rhetoric proves so widespread, so deep-seated, and at times so virulent that the German poet and critic Hans Magnus Enzensberger wrote with obvious exasperation: "Unhistoric, not merely hackneyed, is the blind trust [partisans of the avant-garde] are happy to put in the threadbare concept of generations, quite as if it were the life of the arts, rather than that of trichinae, that is subject to the biological law of the life cycle; or as if the content of a hymn by Hölderlin or a play by Brecht could be read off the author's 'vintage.' Whoever distinguishes between old and new, or old and young, in such comfortable fashion, agrees by his very choice of criteria with the philistines" (17). Like his counterparts in the Frankfurt school, Enzensberger bemoans the ease with which the culture industry (or the "consciousness industry," in his terms) outstrips the avant-garde's capacity for meaningful criticism, particularly when generational rhetoric occupies such a large space in its critical vocabulary. He argues that banal distinctions based on this rhetoric—age versus youth, old versus new, ancient versus modern—fit all too easily into the Manichaean schemata of rightist and leftist regimes, a political flexibility that accounts in part for the longevity of avant-gardism. Enzensberger adds that the ideological plasticity of avant-garde movements and the thin line between aesthetic cultism and political repression require the avant-garde's blindness to its own aporias: "The movement as a doctrinairely conceived collective, as invented fifty or thirty years ago for the purpose of shattering the resistance of a compact society, did not survive the historic conditions that elicited it. Conspiring in the name of the arts is only possible where they are being suppressed. An avant-garde that suffers itself to be furthered by the state has forfeited its rights" (40). A literary movement so thoroughly committed to the idea of generational emergence, it would seem by this account, inevitably serves statist, rather than more broadly cultural, aims.

Very few of America's moderns, and almost none of those I have thus far mentioned, referred to themselves as part of the avant-garde; and, thanks in large measure to Peter Bürger's and Renato Poggioli's efforts to define a so-called historical avant-garde (even if their methodologies clash rather discordantly), contemporary critics reserve the term to describe more definitively avant-gardist European movements (dadaism, futurism, surrealism, etc.). The extent to which American modernism struggled to shape social reality has been measured primarily in cultural or (broadly speaking) racial terms, and rightly so—the social function of art in the United States must be seen as a corollary to these wider goals. (Head-on engagement with politics tends to exclude American writers, for better or for worse, from identification with the modernist movement.) I would like to consider here the extent to which a rhetoric that might easily be described as generational also penetrates discourses that are rarely considered overlapping: avant-gardism and cultural nationalism.

Avant-gardes, generations, and nations are defined in explicit structural opposition to that which they would exclude. The avant-garde artist, Poggioli observes, "replaces that particular environment, determined by his family and social origins, with what the French call *milieu artiste*" (31); he or she thus belongs to one society by casting off another. The individual member of the Lost Generation, as so many novels tell us, sneers at her or his elders, slams the tattered pages of tradition against the table in disgust, surrounded by allies in a Greenwich Village studio or a Left Bank café. In like fashion, the nation, as Partha Chatterjee and Benedict Anderson remind us, constructs its Other at the same time that it imagines the community for which national subjects must sometimes fight and die. George Devereux, in his analysis of ethnic identity formation, labels such relationships "dysfunctional-dissociative" in the sense that identity predicated upon difference (that is, dissociative identity) often subordinates the intricate web of human experience to a single facet of existence, straitjacketing the individual into a set of social expectations that may not be to her or his best interests as an individual. According to this logic, Ezra Pound is *either* an imagist *or* a vorticist; T. S. Eliot is *either* American *or* British; and Nella Larsen is *either* black *or* white—but we seldom recognize them for anything beyond such differential boundaries.

Beyond structural similarities, there are areas of significant rhetorical overlap among the presumably distinct discourses of avant-gardism, generationalism, and nationalism. It is widely acknowledged that the avant-gardist is generational and that nation building often takes place in accordance with a specifically generational framework. Yet nationalism and avant-gardism rarely cross paths, so an examination of where they do intersect sheds important light on the rhetoric of literary emergence and the ideological machinations of cultural nationalism. We have already seen how generational rhetoric regularly utilizes the language of the avant-garde, imagining militant bohemian enclaves in contrast to a larger society of philistines. The converse is also true, as Enzensberger laments and Poggioli describes less passionately.[22] Just as important, avant-gardist and nationalist discourses frequently absorb the rhetoric of generational sacrifice, the surrender to what both Emerson and Mannheim (and countless others) describe as the "common destiny" of the times. Anderson points out that "in an age when it is so common for progressive, cosmopolitan intellectuals (particularly in Europe?) to insist on the near-pathological character of nationalism, its roots in fear and hatred of the Other, and its affinities with racism, it is useful to remind ourselves that nations inspire love, and often profoundly self-sacrificing love" (141). Meanwhile, Poggioli's analysis of avant-garde psychology couples subject-based pathologies ("agonism," "nihilism") with socially determined varieties of alienation ("economic," "cultural") and a profound ethos of self-sacrifice to the collective goals of the movement. A cursory glance at those writers affiliated with the Lost Generation reveals a wide range of relationships to the discourses of avant-gardism and nationalism. Some were so cosmopolitan (for example, Stein and Eliot) or so committed to regional pieties (like Tate and Warren) that they would no doubt laugh at attempts to describe them as "American" cultural nationalists, while others, including those who went furthest to define the Lost Generation (such as Cowley, Dos Passos, Hemingway, and Harold Stearns), repeatedly argued for the reinvigoration of literature according to a specifically national framework and borrowing frankly nationalist terminology.

Brooks, in his 1921 essay on "Literary Generations," develops perhaps the most systematic theory of generational aesthetics to arise from the Lost Generation itself. Much as Poggioli would later distinguish between movements and schools, Brooks focuses on the relationship between literary generations and literary schools, an analysis he manages to fit into the pattern developed in the wide arc of his career; that is, Brooks attempts to rescue American culture from its thin-blooded puritan heritage. His definition of a literary generation does not jibe with his view of American culture: "What constitutes a real generation in literature is, no doubt, the emergence and the dominance of some one writer, of two or three writers perhaps, powerful enough to impose their ideas upon the mass" (60). Having already described the younger generation of American writers as a wave "breaking on our turbulent literary beach," Brooks complicates his view of what the metaphor signifies: "To speak more strictly, of course, these 'waves' are not waves at all.

The sea that breaks on our literary beach is a sea without a ground-swell; it is a choppy sea, incessantly arriving, without rhythm and without intention. For, to drop the figure, one has only to compare the creed of our youngest writers with the creed, let us say, of Stephen Crane, to realize that no decisive change has taken place in our literature" (58, 59). No literary generations can be discerned in the United States, Brooks argues, because no youthful leader has yet risen to the fore, no one has shown her or his generation its true path.

Brooks drowns the generational metaphor, in a sense, calling attention to its limited ability to provide an accurate measure of time—where does one wave, one generation, end and another begin?—although this limit only applies on American shores. Literary generations can be discovered, to be sure, in France and England, where a "literary generation . . . accompanies a generation in thought, in feeling, in manners; it signifies a movement forward, whether 'progressive' or not, and the finger never turns back to quite the same impression again." Not so in America, where "a complete anarchy prevails." The individual American writer may have talent, Brooks suggests, but no sense of tradition. As a result, American literature—all of it, give or take a temporary flowering here or there—remains incoherent, atrophied, literally untutored. "To say, therefore, that we have a new generation every five years," he continues, "is to say not only that we have no authoritative writers but also perhaps that we lack the disposition to recognize them. We are not accustomed—it is a racial habit—to distinguishing between the greater and the less, we do not assimilate ideas with a firm grasp and hold fast to those that are important: we are too generally the victims of a short memory and an easily sated appetite" (59, 60, 61).

Brooks's uneasy relationship with democracy in America—his discussion of literary generations in essence indicts societies of equals—registers as one in a long and distinguished lineage of similar critiques of American culture, from Tocqueville to the present. However, Brooks has not completely given up on his patient, and he thus prescribes a cultural bromide, something to soothe the turbulent waters of American letters. The medicine assumes the shape of a literary school. Brooks agrees with André Gide (whom he quotes at length) that a school provides a foundation of mediocre talent upon which a "few great spirits . . . erect themselves." "Where these great spirits exist," Brooks continues, "the rank and file experience no humiliation in remaining the rank and file, in immolating themselves, as it might seem. For literally they gain their own souls by losing them; they find, that is, by immolating themselves, or rather by subordinating themselves, a direction which they cannot find alone." American literature lacks, then, a school of self-sacrificing avant-gardists, which is why American literature fails to measure up to the Brooksian cultural nationalist yardstick, why there are no literary generations in the United States—why there is no truly *American* literature. "The majority of American writers," Brooks concludes, "unaware that such a thing has ever existed, and incapable therefore even of desiring it, go their own way; and the more they 'strike out' for themselves, and the more they lose that sense of general momentum which all writers have in their youth, even where no school exists, owing to a vague feeling of association with other young writers, the more they come to resemble so many peas in a pod" (65, 66). Brooks waved the cultural nationalist flag so often during his career that he overlooked the cosmopolitan alternative offered nearly a century before by Emerson, as if the lessons Brooks learned from Ireland or Russia or France apply to him and him alone. Instead, his potential generations, who anguish "in despair of the civilization they saw before them," like Clarence King from the "Younger Generation of 1870," strike out west, into the great frontier. In exile.

Although historians have quibbled over the precise date of the closing of the American frontier since Frederick Jackson Turner, in the era of rapid transit and industrialization it becomes increasingly difficult to escape society by striking out west. Like Brooks's "Younger Generation of 1870," the writers of the Lost Generation were more likely to represent physical uprootedness by boarding a ship to Europe or Latin America than by rafting down the Mississippi or fishing the unspoiled lakes of Michigan. (These latter gestures are much more likely from the members of the irony-hungry Beat Generation.) When members of the Lost Generation did venture west it was usually to Hollywood, a move at best seen as a temporary sellout to the culture industry, while at worst it was, as Nathanael West wrote, where people went to die. Harold Stearns, whose *Civilization in the United States* (1922) was something of a bible for America's disaffected young intelligentsia, sounded a rallying cry heard far and wide. His disgruntled move overseas served as a model for countless lives and almost as many novels, including *The Sun Also Rises;* less so his humiliating return. And for the left-leaning members of the Lost Generation, pilgrimage to the young Soviet Union ranked as a necessity.

A more common flight from the trappings of American cultural and intellectual impoverishment took place on a strictly abstract level. Waldo Frank wrote, after all, that "ours is the first generation of America engaged in a *spiritual* pioneering" (9, my emphasis). After the frontier closes, a willful forgetting, the pathbreaking gesture necessary before one can make it new, remains possible in the form of generational conflict, a paradigm often associated with ethnogenesis and national foundations, particularly in the United States. Marcus Lee Hansen, a student of Turner's at Harvard, developed what has solidified into "Hansen's Law" to explain the cultural evolution of American immigrant communities according to a biological line of generational succession. The oft-cited kernel of Hansen's Law, "what the son wishes to forget the grandson wishes to remember" (495), has proven remarkably influential even if not entirely accurate. Hansen's Law echoes the assertion of Lewis Mumford in 1931 that the "commonest axiom of history is that every generation revolts against its fathers and makes friends with its grandfathers" (3) as well as the observation of Gertrude Stein that "one is always naturally antagonistic to one's parents and sympathetic to one's grandparents" (*The Autobiography* 78). But even more important, as Werner Sollors demonstrates, Hansen's Law parallels the trope of generational declension widely found in community-building puritan historiography, and later in early national attempts to figure the young republic as a New English child rebelling against a repressive Old English father (*Beyond* 208 ff.).

Although nationalisms of all varieties attempt to erase their cultural roots, replacing them with the fiction of immutable essence, these roots nevertheless inspire colossal human sacrifice. Ironically, the generational model so common in American historiography—including literary history, where the myth of the Lost Generation continues to define American modernism—functions both as an index of the cultural constructedness of nationalist discourse and as an instrument with which the national community is naturalized, rendered as an essence with biological foundations. Perhaps even more ironically, the trauma and tragedy associated with war and social upheaval inspire both generational location and great works of art.

One final irony, derived from the typological reading of the American literary historical family tree: it has proven convenient to imagine the Lost Generation as a "second flowering" (or so Cowley puts it), part of the "Little Renaissance" of American letters during the 1910s and 1920s. This seems only natural from the point of view that sees the movement as the generational successor to an earlier Brooksian flowering, the so-called New England Renaissance, which is in turn the figurative child of New England's puritan forefathers. "The New England renaissance was tardy in appearing and of brief duration," Vernon Louis Parrington wrote during the heyday of the Jazz Age, "yet in the few years of its extraordinary vigor it imparted a stimulus to American life that its historians have not greatly exaggerated. We are now far enough from it to see that it was the last flowering of a tree that was dying at the roots, but in the tumultuous [eighteen] thirties it seemed to be a new birth of the native New England mind, opening on new worlds and great adventures" (2:271). In another context and with only minor emendations, this might very well describe the Lost Generation. Parrington would declare a renaissance at the drop of a hat—by his measure, renaissances also took place in Virginia and with the slave trade—but in this case the moniker displays a tremendous staying power, at least as an object of academic discourse. As I discuss in the next chapter, it is difficult to determine exactly who coined the phrase, but the "American Renaissance" may derive, curiously enough, from Emerson himself, who had in mind a radically different, much more heterogeneous version of America's cultural heritage. As with his generations, the Emersonian renaissance exhibits a historical consciousness that is at once rooted in local traditions and global in scope: "We might call our age the age of . . . " he wrote in his *Journals* in 1861—and here Emerson crosses out "recuperation," replacing it with the more familiar "Renaissance": an "age of Renaissance." He continues, "We have recovered the Elgin marbles, Nineveh, the Pyramid frescoes, Cicero de Republica, the Tischendorf Manuscript, the Champollion inscriptions, Giotto's head of Dante, Milton's Christian Doctrine" (15:132).

2
Renaissance Rhetoric and American Cultural Nationalism

> Can we not build up a national tradition, a national literature, which shall be none the less Irish in spirit from being English in language? . . . America, which has no past to speak of, a mere "parvenue" among nations, is creating a national literature which in its most characteristic products differs almost as much from English literature as does the literature of France. Walt Whitman, Thoreau, Bret Harte, and Cable, to name no more, are very American, and yet America was once an English colony. It should be more easy for us, who have in us that wild Celtic blood, the most un-English of all things under heaven, to make such a literature.
>
> W. B. Yeats, letter to the editor of *United Ireland* (1892)

The pRE-history of the American Renaissance

For a nation that tends to see itself as youthful, and very often figuratively as a youth, the United States owes a considerable debt to the prefix "re-," which signified backward motion in early Latin. Even in modern English the prefix functions in this way, but more often these days it signals newness, a kind of conceptual motion forward, thanks largely to the semantic inventiveness of the Elizabethans (who assured the prefixal success of "re-" by attaching the letters to nouns and verbs almost indiscriminately, without regarding the root word's etymological origin).[1] And so today American historiography relies on "re-" in numerous efforts to imagine a collective past—a national family tree, so to speak—by continually invoking concepts such as "Revolution," "Reconstruction," and perhaps most important to literary history, "Renaissance." (I would be remiss if I failed to mention the contemporary proliferation of efforts to "reconceive," "reconstruct," "recover," and "revise" history of all sorts, literary and otherwise. And a happy coincidence it would be if "realism," "regionalism," and "religion" could be thrown into this mix.) But what if "re-" were to disappear? Where would Americanists be without recourse to the American Renaissance, the Chicago Renaissance, the Little Renaissance, the Harlem Renaissance, the Southern Renaissance, the San Francisco Renaissance, the Chicano Renaissance, the Native American Renaissance, or the Queer Renaissance?[2] What would we call our courses and title our books? How would we periodize?

I hope to demonstrate how and suggest why what I call "renaissance rhetoric" so often and so disarmingly informs our understanding of American literary history, and specifically American modernism. By way of illustration, this chapter provides an archaeological assessment of the Harlem Renaissance, or the "Negro Renaissance" as it was once known, but I will touch on these other examples because their mutual influence cannot be avoided. It would be misleading to suggest that just because something gets labeled a renaissance means that we can identify a coherent literary movement with well-defined principles and unswerving group loyalty; in fact, group identity labels often mask intense conflict over the public meaning of the names given literary movements and the texts allowed to fall under their net. Alain Locke and Wallace Thurman had a difficult time agreeing on where to lunch, let alone on the guiding principles of the Negro Renaissance each discussed on numerous occasions—their shibboleth is spelled the same but pronounced with different accents. Thoreau and Longfellow belong to the same renaissance more because they breathed the same New England air than for any obvious aesthetic or ideological reasons. Vachel Lindsay's poetry probably has more in common with that of Langston Hughes than with Ezra Pound's, yet Lindsay and Pound belong to the Little Renaissance; meanwhile, Hughes and *Fire!!* get anthologized and cataloged alongside Jessie Fauset and *Crisis.* The racial politics of literary history determine who belongs in one camp and who does not. I hope to suggest a way around these sometimes misguided distinctions by shedding some light on at least one common transnational source for virtually every example of American renaissance rhetoric: the so-called Irish Renaissance of the late nineteenth century grappled with many of the same issues embedded in the public discourse on U.S. modernism, and American modernists took careful note.

As with their Irish counterpart, all of America's renaissances bring with them a set of expectations for literary art and artists as well as for literary criticism and critics. American renaissance rhetoric tends to establish the following hierarchies: art over propaganda, youth over age, and "wholesome provincialism" over deracinated cosmopolitanism or xenophobic ethnocentrism.[3] All of these categories are, in a sense, up for grabs; renaissance rhetoric, however, steers them along surprisingly narrow paths. The rebirth metaphor also implies a healthy domestic literary marketplace rather than one overly dependent on foreign publishers or too steeped in crass commercialism. Just as important, these features of American renaissance rhetoric can be viewed as symptoms of an almost universal preoccupation among American modernists with defining a new and specifically New World cultural genealogy—a preoccupation that often gives way to proto-imperial, or tentatively imperialist, urges and utterances. Renaissance rhetoric signals a self-conscious emergence from colonial dependency to postcolonial self-sufficiency and even supremacy.[4] The impulse to declare a renaissance thus serves the forward-looking culture industry even as it embodies the nostalgic desires of newly ascendant middle classes fearing rapid modernization and the rise of international capitalism.

It is no accident that the renaissance and "modernism" (or "early modernism") are synonymous in attempts to periodize Western cultural history.[5] Scholars such as Jacob Burckhardt, who during the nineteenth century summed up the prevailing account of the renaissance worldview, favored this specific period marker because it captures a cultural ethos of self-discovery via an appreciation of the past (Burckhardt's "revival of antiquity"), an ethos of self-fashioning during the acclimation to post-theological frames of reference (his "discovery of the world and of man"), and with these an unprecedented conception, as Matei Calinescu points out, "of *historical time,* linear and irreversible, flowing irresistibly onwards" (13). This newborn historicism, an awareness of the pastness of the past *and* the futurity of the future, to emend T. S. Eliot, is a hallmark not only of tradition but also of modern consciousness. The various American renaissances do not necessarily proceed from an identical relationship with the past and with cultural relativism—they do not revive the ancients, and the new science had already lost some of its luster—although subsequent literary historians often cast them in a revivalist role, and the critical appropriation of renaissance rhetoric tends to invite cultural rather than strictly formal analyses of literary artifacts.[6] And even the more obviously ethnic renaissances invent more than rediscover their cultural legacy. Still, Burckhardt's "discoveries" remain a useful lens through which to view the Negro Renaissance, and indeed all of the literature of the Jazz Age, for the questions he largely takes for granted vis-à-vis

Italian civilization—"What is culture, how does it work, and for whom?" and "What is the relationship between art and society?"—necessarily preoccupied American artists and critics still uncomfortable with the shape of American letters at the dawn of the so-called American century.

The "original" Italian Renaissance—the one handed down by nineteenth-century cultural historians—also overlaps with those of the United States in an important and somewhat paradoxical area, that is, in the area of cultural nationalism, the identification of a national culture with specific varieties of cultural expression (although German romanticism outfitted American modernists with the rubric of "folk" culture to augment and revalue, but not replace entirely, earlier notions of national "civilization"). Burckhardt, an unapologetic Italophile, saw the rise of Italian statecraft and the Italian Renaissance as two sides of the same coin, writing in 1860 that "it was not the revival of antiquity alone, but its union with the genius of the Italian people, which *achieved the conquest of the Western world*" (175, my emphasis). Scholars continue to wrestle with the tension between the early modern diffusion of humanism and the concentration of political power that gave rise to the nation-state. The seductive idea of a renaissance lingers as a holdover from attempts to imagine an earlier, idealized phase of cultural history; the critical catchword arises out of modernity's search for premodern origins. At any rate, for someone like Burckhardt, the "naissance"—from *natio,* Latin for birth, race, and nation—outweighs the prefix "re-."

Ralph Waldo Emerson stands as the central figure of the earliest "American Renaissance," but if we look again at the version of a nineteenth-century "age of Renaissance" described in his *Journals,* written less than two weeks before shots were fired at Fort Sumter, we are led back to the transhistorical and transnational—one might even say transgenerational—American cultural genealogy to which Emerson often returns, even in his most independence-minded moments. As F. O. Matthiessen would stress in his *American Renaissance* (1941), Emerson qualified his view of American literature by noting that it takes place "in the optative mood," expressing desire for an America not yet arrived.[7] This age, this "Renaissance"—recall that he canceled out "recuperation" in favor of the more majestic-sounding term—gives us the "Elgin marbles, Nineveh, the Pyramid frescoes, Cicero de Republica, the Tischendorf Manuscript, the Champollion inscriptions, Giotto's head of Dante, Milton's Christian Doctrine, reading of papyri." Emerson would go on to catalog discoveries that shook faith in long-held beliefs, discoveries such as "the accurately determined age of men of the stone, bronze, & iron ages . . . insight into mythology alike everywhere in its element . . . recovery of antique statues [and] reconstruction of the ground plan & elevation of temples which war, earthquake & iconoclasts of all creeds had not been able to utterly disintegrate" (15:132). In this case, "renaissance" functions as a logical extension of the *musée imaginaire,* that fantasized cultural field in which all gazes remain pure. This passage certainly reflects democratic ideals in a way that obviates (for example) the allegorical tension between selfish art and human love in Tennyson's "Palace of Art"; probably Vachel Lindsay's "Orchard of Art" comes closer in spirit.[8] But in spite of his generosity, Emerson rarely places American artifacts into his museum of the imagination. None of his "representative men" are American (and only one wrote primarily in English), and his literary heroes are almost always European. The earliest examples of American renaissance rhetoric in literary criticism share a similar anxiety that American culture had yet to come of age, an anxiety marked by neocolonial irony, awkwardness, or both.

If we overlook this example from Emerson, then Unitarian theologian Samuel Osgood gave birth to American renaissance rhetoric in 1876 in his review of Octavius Brooks Frothingham's *Transcendentalism in New England* (1876). Osgood begins his review by arguing that New English culture and thought "have the best claim to universality" among America's various regions, an assertion that already had a familiar ring to it by the U.S. centennial, although less familiar was the typological reading given to what was christened the "New England Renaissance." Osgood argues that "Edwards and Franklin, in the last century, began the literature and philosophy which have since flowered and fruited in Channing and Bushnell, Prescott and Hawthorne, Bancroft and Motley, Whittier and Longfellow, Bryant and Emerson, and their peers" (742). The "third generation" of individuals behind the later flowering,[9] "the new school of transcendentalists," are "not unworthy successors of the old Puritans" like Edwards; but more than this, they also succeed Bunyan and Milton:

> Is it not true that the New England people have always looked upon themselves as part of the great English race and especially as heirs of the literature of England? The old Puritan fathers never for a moment thought of giving up their English birthright. . . . The later New England scholars were in a certain sense still more English; and even in their passion for progress, they laid claim to their old inheritance. Thus in what may be called the Renaissance in literature among the New England Puritans [i.e., the transcendentalists] in the nineteenth century, there is clearly a tendency to restoration as well as a spirit of progress, and the new culture went forward more bravely from being backed up by the old masters of thought. (745)

Osgood wishes to emphasize the colonial inheritance of Emerson and company —he draws attention to the almost regressive Old English influence of Spenser, Shakespeare, Bacon, and Hooker, something today's critics shy away from —and so forces American colonial and postcolonial history into the pattern set by England during the seventeenth century, from "renaissance" to "restoration." One wonders who, according to this scheme of things, the American Cromwell might be (Brown? Cooper? Irving?); a hint of irony also surfaces here, especially given Emerson's usual role as the prophet of American individualism, and indeed Osgood fleshes out the irony by drawing comparisons between the transcendentalists and the "great awakening" of German idealist thought since Winckelmann and Kant.[10]

Roughly contemporaneous instances of American renaissance rhetoric also force their discussions of nineteenth-century American literature in awkward, and more obviously neocolonial, directions. In poet and literary historian Charles F. Richardson's *American Literature, 1607–1885* (1886–88), one of the first examples of American literary history to offer an extended argument on behalf of American exceptionalism, we find a thinly veiled response to Matthew Arnold's version (in *Discourses in America* [1885]) of American cultural dependence and boorishness. Richardson concedes America's "criminal class," its "great body of ignorant voters," its "fashion of irreverence," its "fondness for display," and its "subservient and title-hunting tendency"; a "republic based upon the most liberal plan of suffrage" inevitably suffers these conditions. However, "when we take the larger view" and include an estimate of American "state-craft, social economy, scientific product, education, and books," one cannot help but conclude that "American literature is the literature of a cultured and genuine Democracy, a sort of Saxon-Greek renaissance in the New World; a liberty that is as far removed from anarchy as it is from despotism" (1:61–62).[11] Populist literary historian Fred Lewis Pattee's *A History of American Literature* (1896) takes the neocolonial example of Osgood to an almost absurdist extreme, first by defining the fifteenth century as "the age of the Renaissance,—the awakening of literature, science, and art, from the long slumber of the Dark Ages" (7) and later by dramatizing the course of nineteenth-century American literature in identical terms: "Following the first creative period [1812–37] there came an interval of barrenness during which the future of American literature looked dark and uncertain" (195). Once again, and in even jauntier fashion this time, a confusing mix of seventeenth- and eighteenth-century English political history stands in for nineteenth-century American literary history: "But the interregnum was not a long one. The years between 1831 and 1839 witnessed the publication of the first books of Whittier, Sparks, Bancroft, Holmes, Hawthorne,

Emerson, Prescott, Hildreth, Motley, Longfellow, and Margaret Fuller. The advent of these authors marks the opening of the 'Augustan Age' of American literature" (196).

This early branch American renaissance rhetoric gained its most influential spokesperson in Barrett Wendell, who launched the so-called Harvard literary revival when he helped found two important magazines during his tenures as an undergraduate and as instructor of creative writing (the *Lampoon* in 1876 and the *Monthly* in 1885). Wendell returned to his alma mater after a failed law career and taught the university's first course in American literature in 1897. The course, "Research in the Literary History of America," paved the way for his most important critical study, *A Literary History of America* (1900), and for another course, "Literary History of America," which he offered from 1898 until his retirement in 1917. As a popular teacher of English, American, and world literature—he also offered courses on Shakespeare and on comparative literature from Homer to Dante—Wendell directly influenced many of the early twentieth century's most innovative voices in poetry (Amy Lowell, Edwin Arlington Robinson, George Santayana), prose fiction (Robert Herrick), and criticism (George Pierce Baker, Van Wyck Brooks, Horace Kallen, Vernon Louis Parrington).[12] Still, he is primarily remembered as a caretaker of what Santayana disparagingly called the "Genteel Tradition." Throughout *A Literary History of America* one finds countless examples of the kind of preciousness that might be labeled "genteel," although it is a gentility of a tradition-inventing sort, always striving to calibrate American literature with the finest Western civilization has to offer. "Literature, like its most excellent phase, poetry," Wendell begins the study, "has never been satisfactorily defined. In essence it is too subtle, too elusive, too vital, to be confined within the limits of phrase" (1). However, after providing a few unequivocal examples of "literature"—the Psalms, the *Iliad,* St. Paul's epistles, the *Aeneid,* the *Divine Comedy, Don Quixote,* and *Hamlet*—Wendell distills an important common feature: because all literary expression takes place in a specific language, "literature is of all fine arts the most ineradicably national" (3).

This naturally presents Wendell with something of a problem; after all, if England and America speak the same language, how can there be such a thing as an American literature? He finds a provisional answer by locating American literature historically, as a barometer of America's political and social development away from its English origins. The result makes up in symmetry what it lacks in elegance: Books I to III cover in four chapters each the seventeenth, eighteenth, and nineteenth centuries; each book consists of a chapter devoted to English history, a chapter devoted to English literature, then American history, and finally American literature. Book IV discusses "Literature in the Middle States from 1798 to 1857," and Book V, the last in the volume, covers "The Renaissance of New England." Wendell's New England Renaissance, like Osgood's and Pattee's, conforms to a typological patterning that would make St. Augustine proud, with a seventeenth-century type and an antitype in the nineteenth century, but this time both the prophecy and its fulfillment remain firmly planted in U.S. soil. "From the time, shortly after 1720, when Franklin left Boston, where Increase and Cotton Mather were still preaching, we have paid little attention to that part of the country," Wendell writes. "For during the seventy-two years which have intervened between Cotton Mather's death and the nineteenth century, Boston was of less literary importance than it was before or than it has been since" (233).

Here is a Golden Age followed by an Age of Darkness, but in the wake of commercial and industrial development, the nineteenth century sheds light on New England once more. "And now, as one considers its century and more of history," Wendell continues, "one discerns more and more clearly why the period in which it reached its height may best be understood when we call it a period of Renaissance. Almost from the time of the Revolution, isolated New England, like the rest of America, was awakening to a sense of national consciousness" (258). Wendell's "figuring" of New English culture spans a number of discourses, including oratory, history, religion (Unitarianism), and philosophy (transcendentalism), and in each of these he identifies now-familiar elements of American exceptionalist ideology. The puritan strain ("the creed of New England had been the Calvinism of the emigrant Puritans" [275]), coupled with a new awareness of the nation's place in the history of ideas ("with the Renaissance there came at last to New England an eager knowledge of all the other phases of human thought and expression which enrich the records of modern civilisation" [373]), give rise to the Renaissance of New England, with Emerson, "whom we may call its prophet," manning the helm. We also encounter Whittier, "who so admirably phrased its aspirations for reform"; Longfellow, "its academic poet"; Lowell, "its humanist"; Holmes, "its rationalist"; and "but one other literary figure of equal eminence with these,—Nathaniel Hawthorne, above and beyond the others an artist" (425).

Given the hastily crafted derivativeness of these previous examples, it should come as no surprise that the primary model for subsequent American renaissance rhetoric was not the Italian Renaissance, nor even the English one, nor was it the profoundly influential work of cultural historians (such as Burckhardt, Jules Michelet, and Walter Pater), although these phenomena lent to the success of American renaissance rhetoric by bestowing the period marker with a rich fund of symbolic capital. We can find a more accurate early analogue for American renaissance rhetoric in the work of the seminal theorist of modern nationalism Ernest Renan, whose essay on "The Poetry of the Celtic Races" (1851) launched a midcentury revival of interest in Celtic mythology and folklore, if not a large-scale reacquaintance with the family of Celtic languages.[13] And we cannot ignore Victorian England's voice of humanism, Matthew Arnold, whose lectures *On the Study of Celtic Literature* (1867) attracted attention from Tory conservatives and Fenian radicals alike and even brought Celtic studies to Oxford. Still, Renan's and Arnold's influence on the American literary front was felt secondarily, at best, by way of the late-nineteenth-century Celtic revival that came to be known in the United States as the "Irish Renaissance."

In many cases the influence of the Irish Renaissance can be traced along a direct line from Dublin and London to Boston, New York, and Philadelphia. Ezra Pound, for instance, on two separate occasions served as personal secretary to W. B. Yeats, a role he prepared for at the University of Pennsylvania. While there he studied with Cornelius Weygandt, professor of English and one of the leading boosters of the Irish Renaissance during the first two decades of the twentieth century. Pound remembered being "drunk with 'Celticism'" at the time (*Essays* 367).[14] Similarly, Van Wyck Brooks, in his *Autobiography* (1965), recalls how John Butler Yeats influenced the *Seven Arts* group's political and aesthetic leanings, and even how the Irishman provided an Americanist reading list (including Emerson, Thoreau, and Whitman) for a nation still unsure of its literary worth. Brooks notes that "we felt we were on the verge of a not dissimilar movement of our own, the first phase of another revival that expressed an American coming-of-age, an escape from our own colonial dependence on England" (176). But even before W. B. Yeats's stunningly successful U.S. tour of 1903, and long before his father's immigration to New York in 1908, American critics looked across the Atlantic for clues in answer to the question on everyone's mind: "Have we a national literature?" While this question had been asked and at least provisionally answered in the United States since the early national era, many U.S. critics found a compelling answer to the related question, "What should American literature look like?," in late-nineteenth-century Ireland.

A handful of scholars have recently drawn comparisons between the Irish and Harlem Renaissances,[15] and there is a long-standing tradition of casual references to a relationship between the two. However, there existed a more broadly American interest in the Irish literary revival, spearheaded by the Anglo-Irish duo Yeats (who co-founded, with T. W. Rolleston, the Irish Literary Society of London in 1891) and Douglas Hyde (who founded the Gaelic League in 1893). Although the Irish movement was in reality a complex and conflicted amalgam of competing interests and ideologies, as F. S. L. Lyons has shown, in the United States it was largely viewed as a unified response to Anglo cultural hegemony.[16] "The two men of letters who stand to-day for the Celtic revival in Ireland," Stephen Gwynn wrote in a widely reprinted 1902 essay on the topic, "are Dr Douglas Hyde and Mr W. B. Yeats" (444–45), each of whom ensures that the Celtic "race survives, not only in the flesh, but also in the record of its history, and still more in its moulded thoughts, its embodied dreams" (428). Four years later, Moira L. Ray found it necessary to write an essay for the *Sewanee Review* distinguishing between Hyde's "purely Gaelic" and Yeats's "Anglo-Celtic" movements because the "simple distinction, drawn clearly in Ireland, is yet unfamiliar to the majority of American and English readers" (20).[17]

An ongoing legacy of American interest in Celtic culture can be found in the emergence of antiquarian Philo-Celtic societies from the 1870s, some of which remain active to this day, and in the institutional presence of Celtic studies throughout North American colleges. Fred Norris Robinson, professor of English at Harvard, inaugurated Celtic studies in the United States in 1896—one year before Wendell started teaching his course in American literature—and his efforts were quickly duplicated at Catholic University and later at the University of Wisconsin, Columbia University, and elsewhere in Canada and the United States.[18] But the Irish Renaissance captured the interest of more than the handful of scholars and antiquarians interested in Indo-European philology and medieval poetry. The Irish American and Catholic press introduced the Irish Renaissance to a targeted immigrant audience even before there was much of a rebirth to speak of, and the growing interest in Irish letters spilled over from regional venues, including the *Boston Pilot* and the *Providence Sunday Journal*, which published a number of Yeats's essays in the late 1880s and early 1890s, to mass-market periodicals such as the *Catholic World*, published in New Jersey but with an international readership and influence.[19] Soon Irish Americans would become familiar with the mantra with which Yeats concluded many of his American essays: "There is no great literature without nationality, no great nationality without literature." This chiastic prophecy exhibits the closed-circuit cultural calculus (nationality → literature → nationality) widely seen in cultural nationalist utterances, and it was obviously retooled by the intelligentsia of the Negro Renaissance. By the turn of the century the Irish movement, known since the 1890s as a "renaissance," along with its strategy of aggressively nationalist rhetoric, circulated widely in the mainstream media, including Lyman Abbott's *Outlook* and secular reviews such as Eliakim Littell's *Living Age* and *Current Literature* (which reprinted Irish, English, and American articles on the so-called Irish problem). The Irish Renaissance proved an especially popular topic for journals with an investment in American literary nationalism, such as *Bookman*, the *Dial*, the *Nation*, the *Sewanee Review*, and somewhat later the *American Mercury*.[20] The *North American Review* in early 1899 commissioned Yeats "to do an article . . . on The Intellectual Movement in Ireland," as he described the transaction in a letter to Lady Augusta Gregory in April of that year (*Uncollected* 2:184). Yeats received thirty pounds for his efforts, a large sum given that he had yet to achieve widespread fame in the United States, and the article, titled "The Literary Movement in Ireland," appeared in the influential journal's December issue. Nowhere in this particular article does Yeats refer to the movement as the "Irish Renaissance," but he does indicate how Hyde's special province, the Celtic language revival, "which has hitherto interested but a few cultivated people," might evolve into a more widespread flowering of Irish culture, even though most literary expression in Ireland took place in English. "We are preparing, as we hope, for a day when Ireland will speak in Gaelic," Yeats offers, perhaps somewhat overzealously, but until then it is worth noting that a "new kind of romance, a new element in thought, is being moulded out of Irish life and traditions" (*Uncollected* 2:184, 187).

Yeats's expressed desire for a Gaelic-speaking homeland, whether heartfelt or merely strategic, highlights one of the many problems arising out of the American appropriation of the Irish Renaissance as a model for achieving cultural independence. As Lyons demonstrates, Yeats and Hyde stretched the boundaries of "Irishness" by shifting the terms of the Irish question from religion, rurality, and class affiliation to language and literary heritage, making Irish identity available to anyone with a willingness to read and learn (including the Anglo-Irish middle class to which both Yeats and Hyde belonged). The Irish Renaissance was born in this conflicted milieu, and the extent to which the Irish movement succeeded or failed depended on key elements largely exclusive to Ireland's history and social structure, including Irish cultural longevity (Ireland has a past that has been traced to well before the Christian era), English colonial dominance (England's hegemony over Ireland was both centuries old, dating to the twelfth century, and encompassed all aspects of Irish daily life), and Irish cultural homogeneity (the island's linguistic and religious histories, at least, offer clear-cut alternatives, Anglo versus Irish). These factors alone suggest that any version of American renaissance rhetoric modeled after the Irish situation will appear forced, heavy-handed, and, *mutatis mutandis*, much of it is—something that has not escaped notice, even by those responsible for America's renaissances. And while a few examples of American renaissance rhetoric—such as Wendell's—remain mostly free of Yeats's and Hyde's influence, in almost all cases the Irish Renaissance left its residue, providing the backdrop of an anemic English civilization against which a primitivist folk nationalism stands in sharp contrast.

Civilization and Its Malcontents

In Freud's analysis of the pathologies arising out of civilization's inability to ensure human happiness, or at the very least to forestall suffering, he takes on a project of barely fathomable proportions, defining civilization as "the whole sum of the achievements and the regulations which distinguish our lives from those of our animal ancestors" (40). For the writer of colonial Ireland and postcolonial America, "civilization" carried with it an English cultural valence. Lawrence Levine has demonstrated at considerable length that the "highbrow/lowbrow" rift in nineteenth-century American culture made no pretense of concealing its "European/American" subtext (later supplemented with "native/immigrant" and "white/black" distinctions). During much of the nineteenth century, English literature provided the tacit yardstick of civilization and culture with which to measure Irish and American barbarism and anarchy. The late nineteenth and early twentieth centuries upset these critical poles, reversing the received hierarchy by negatively valuing English "civilization" in its myriad forms. American renaissance rhetoric, to the extent that it derives from Yeats, presented a ready-made vocabulary for what John P. Diggins describes as the "lyrical left," the loosely affiliated group of Americans engaged in defining a heterogeneous American modernism in contrast to the order-affirming tradition of gentility and propriety represented by Wendell in academics, Woodrow Wilson in politics, Henry Ford in business, and Emily Post in manners. Just as "American" has been a site of as much discursive conflict as consensus, so too is "renaissance" a category with ever shifting significance. During the period between roughly 1890 and 1930, the renaissance was stolen, as it were, from England and Italy, and by a kind of metonymic association (although the relationship is putatively one of descent) from the New England Puritans and the pioneers of the American West (that is, Mencken's puritans and Brooks's pioneers, not Perry Miller's and Frederick Jackson Turner's).[21]

Yeats's own relationship with fin de siècle English culture and literary decadence, Linda Dowling points out, must be understood as a vexed episode in literary history. When the politics suited him, Yeats would hold up English culture as old and ashen in contrast to its young and fertile counterpart in Ireland, a gesture surely not lost on his U.S. audience.[22] In an essay on "The Irish National Literary Society," published in November 1892 in the *Boston Pilot,* Yeats remarked that "in England I sometimes hear men complain that the old themes of verse and prose are used up. Here in Ireland the marble block is waiting for us almost untouched, and the statues will come as soon as we have learned to use the chisel" (*New Island* 158–59). Although Yeats admired much about England—in particular its system of higher education, including Oxford's new chair in Celtic studies—he was not above appropriating the colonial American trope of a wayward child (Ireland) rebelling against its overbearing parent (England), and ironically the ancient Celtic tradition accounts for the youth, the promise, of Irish literary expression. For example, in his *Boston Pilot* essay of April 1892 on "The Rhymers' Club," Yeats credits this coterie of aesthete poets with maintaining the youthful vigor of Irish literature, contrasting English isolationism with a French and Irish joie de vivre: "In England the writers do not form groups, but each man works by himself and for himself, for England is the land of literary Ishmaels. It is only among the sociable Celtic nations that men draw nearer to each other when they want to think and dream and work." This, then, explains why "England is old and her poets must scrape up the crumbs of an almost finished banquet, but Ireland still has full tables" (*New Island* 143, 148). And elsewhere in the *Pilot,* in an August 1889 review of Irish playwright William Wills, Yeats declares: "England is an old nation, the dramatic fervor has perhaps ebbed out of her. However that may be, most of the best dramas on the English stage from the times of Congreve and Sheridan and Goldsmith to our own day have been the work of Irishmen" (*New Island* 69).

Yeats's most important meditation on the role of racial vigor in literary expression is his pan-national essay on "The Celtic Element in Literature" (1897). After providing a brief review of Renan's and Arnold's work on the subject—via which Yeats ascribes the "charm" and "magic," the "passion" and "turbulence" of English literature to a Celtic source—Yeats historicizes the Irish Renaissance and the "romance" it generously offers as a "reaction against the rationalism of the eighteenth century . . . mingled with a reaction against the materialism of the nineteenth century" (*Essays* 187). When Yeats favored a greater degree of polemicism, as in his work for the *North American Review,* he would seamlessly attach these negative values to English writers, whose "literature takes delight in praising England and her empire, the master-work and dream of the middle class," and ascribe a hazy but obviously welcome passion to Irish writers, who have "learned from the discoveries of modern learning that the common people, wherever civilization has not driven its plough too deep, keep a watch over the roots of all religion and all romance" (*Uncollected* 2:187, 188).

Given Yeats's influence in the United States,[23] it follows that American modernism so often imagines an inverse relationship between an American cultural flowering and an English cultural decrepitude. Countless writers and critics in search of a hearty, authentic American literature found what they were looking for in the shape of an "American Renaissance"—so many, in fact, that in a series of articles for *Poetry* magazine in early 1915, Pound saw fit to write that "whether from habit, or from profound intuition, or from sheer national conceit, one is always looking in America for signs of a 'renaissance.' . . . [W]e look to the dawn, we count up our symptoms; year in and year out we say we have this and that, we have so much, and so much. Our best asset is a thing of the spirit" ("Renaissance" 283). (Three years earlier, in a letter to Harriet Monroe, Pound had gone so far as to predict that "our American Resorgimento" would "make the Italian Renaissance look like a tempest in a teapot!" [qtd. in Crunden 226].) Pound's only partly tongue-in-cheek analysis of this American Renaissance can be characterized as descriptive rather than prescriptive; although he argues that "a renaissance is a thing made—a thing made by conscious propaganda" ("Renaissance" 285), here as elsewhere Pound's interests are weighed in favor of an abstract revivalism, not necessarily an American one. Not that Pound is entirely tuned out to cultural nationalist sensibilities; like Mencken or Harold Stearns, he wished to shame America into cultural evolution. He begins the series of articles by noting, "No one wants the native American poet to be *au courant* with the literary affairs of Paris and London in order that he may make imitations of Paris and London models, but precisely in order that he shall not waste his lifetime making unconscious, or semi-conscious, imitations of French or English models thirty or forty or an hundred years old" ("Renaissance" 227). As one of the few American modernists who could be both self-consciously avant-gardist and explicitly postcolonial, Pound urges his reader to master foreign models in an almost imperialist sense: "The first step in a renaissance, or awakening, is the importation of models for painting, sculpture, or writing. We have had many 'movements,' movements stimulated by 'comparison' " ("Renaissance" 228). In other words, Pound urges American artists to appropriate the raw material of Europe, to transform it into something new, to add value, as it were.

Two years later, in her *Tendencies in Modern American Poetry* (1917), Amy Lowell observes that the "New Movement" under study "has as yet received no convenient designation. We, who are of it, naturally have not the proper perspective to see it in all its historic significance." Still, she adds that "we can safely claim it to be a 'renaissance,' a re-birth of beauty in our modern world, and the originality and honesty to affirm that beauty in whatever manner is native to the poet" (237). This last caveat, "in whatever manner is native to the poet," seems deceptively incidental to Lowell's application of renaissance rhetoric; however, her rebirth metaphor depends upon a rigid distinction between "the new race which America is producing" on the one hand and its "Anglo-Saxon inheritance" on the other. Lowell's "naissance" thus signifies the sum total of its etymological possibilities: birth, race, nation. The "new race"—this could easily be written by Charles Chesnutt or Jean Toomer instead of Lowell—arises from "the influence of other, alien, peoples, and [a] fusing [of their] exotic modes of thought" (4) with the Anglo-Saxon, whose cultural legacy lingers in an atavistic puritanism, "a virulent poison which saps vitality and brings on the convulsions of despair" (8). (Pound had earlier written that "America, from the White House to the gutter, is still dominated by a 'puritanical' hatred of what is beyond understanding" ["Renaissance" 285].) Even Lowell's Brahmin great-uncle is not spared: "Good poetry, if not strikingly great poetry, marked the epoch of Whittier, Bryant, Emerson, Lowell, Longfellow, and Holmes. They were English provincial poets, in the sense that America was still a literary province of the Mother Country" (5).

It would be difficult if not impossible to conceive of Lowell as a cultural nationalist judging by her poetry alone (one need only compare it to the early Yeats), and while she is remembered for popularizing the imagist movement, in *Tendencies* her discussion of imagism takes second stage to her vociferous literary nationalism. Sometimes her vision of the American community derives from Israel Zangwill: "The welding together of the whole country which the war has brought about . . . has produced a more poignant sense of nationality than has recently been the case in this country of enormous spaces and heterogeneous populations. Hyphens are submerged in the solid overprinting of the word 'America.' We are no more colonies of this or that other land, but ourselves, different from all other peoples whatsoever" (v); "this is indeed a melting pot, and its fumes affect the surrounding company as well as the ingredients in the crucible" (4). At other times she more closely resembles Kallen or Bourne, something indicated in her painstaking analyses of the ethnic backgrounds of individual poets. "Some day, America will be a nation; some day, we shall have a national character. Now, our population is a crazy quilt of racial samples" (201), she writes. Thus, "Mr. [Edwin Arlington] Robinson . . . comes of good Anglo-Saxon stock" (10); "Mr. [Robert] Frost is only of New England stock on his father's side. His mother was born in Edinburgh, of lowland Scottish descent" (81); Edgar Lee Masters "comes of a sturdy [Nova Scotian] stock and a pioneering [Virginian] one" (143); "Mr. [Carl] Sandburg is of Swedish stock" (201); "probably Mrs. [Hilda] Doolittle comes from that fine, undeviating people, known for more than two hundred years as the Pennsylvania Dutch" (249); and John Gould Fletcher's "father was of Scotch-Irish stock" (281). My point is not that Lowell sometimes describes poets as one might cattle but rather that she traces the history of modern American poetry in terms of genetic movement away from Anglo-Saxonism; indeed, she develops a three-stage "revolutionary" model for this very purpose: "In the first stage, beauty is a thing remembered and haunting"—this is where Robinson and Frost fit in. "In the third stage, [beauty] is rediscovered and intoxicating"—here we find H.D. and Fletcher. "But in the second, [beauty] is crowded out by the stress of travail, by the pangs of a birth which has not yet occurred" (141)—thus, Masters and Sandburg midwife the American Renaissance into existence. Lowell's nationalist poetics, her American Renaissance, resembles nothing more closely than M. L. Hansen's "Law" of immigrant generational declension. Retooled ever so slightly, her stages might read, "what the son wishes to forget the grandson wishes to remember."

Louis Untermeyer declared in his preface to *Modern American Poetry* (1919) that "'America's poetic renaissance' is no longer a phrase. It is a fact. . . . A new spirit, energetic, alert, penetrative, seems to have stirred these states" (vii). Numerous other early-twentieth-century examples of American renaissance rhetoric—many of which confine themselves to poetry, a few of which are more expansive in their reach—appear to confirm Untermeyer in this belief. Again, note the stress on art, on youth, and on wholesome provincialism. In 1916 an anonymous writer for *Century* magazine declared that "there is no more hopeful sign of the advancement of a new age of artistic appreciation in this country than the recent genuine renaissance of native and vigorous poetry, blazing new trails for itself in realism, fantasy, form, and method" ("America's Golden Age" 793). In a 1921 lecture at the Town Hall of New York, Sinclair Lewis heralded an "American 'renaissance' in letters," if only "the American public read more of its native literature and thus encouraged home production and gave the American author a chance to compete with his British brother." He further sounds the lukewarm charge by adding, "We've been thoroughly trained in the thought that the American writer is inferior to the British, but some day the American novelist will go over to England and lecture. Art is like burgundy. It is considerably improved by a sea voyage." To this the *New York Globe* responded: "American authors are free to invade England, and some of them have done so. . . . More patience, closer study of the classics, less regard for the dangerous profits of the motion-picture and the popular magazine, are parts of a prescription which might lead us in time to a veritable literary renaissance" (qtd. in "Our Literary 'Rebirth'" 23).

In 1925, Mina Loy published a manifesto on "Modern Poetry" in *Charm,* a fashion magazine for working women, in which she follows the lead of Lowell in her analysis of how "the muse of modern literature arose," her tongue having been "loosened in the melting-pot" of the American language. Loy, only a semi-permanent U.S. resident at this stage of her career, argues that the modernity of American English, its ability to evolve rapidly "while professors of Harvard and Oxford labor . . . to preserve 'God's English,'" makes it "inevitable that the renaissance of poetry should proceed out of America, where latterly a thousand languages have been born, and each one, for purposes of communication at least, English—English enriched and variegated with the grammatical structure and voice-inflection of many races" (158, 159). Allen Tate's 1929 essay on "American Poetry since 1920" takes up where Loy leaves off: "The poets who made the second decade of this century famous as the American Renaissance exhibited, in spite of their local differences, a singleness of outlook that seemed to prove that we had, after all, a national spirit and that our period of servitude to foreign models had ended" (503). Tate represents a belated Emersonian; like his New English predecessor, he insists that provincial attitudes counteract the influence of foreign (by which he mostly means English) models—a factor that he would emphasize some years later as an intellectual leader of the "Southern Renaissance."[24]

American renaissance rhetoric during this time even found its way to Europe, with several practitioners overseas taking their turn on behalf of New World writers. "Nobody in England ventures to speak of a poetic renaissance," wrote French poet and critic Valéry Larbaud in *La Revue de France* in 1921, adding, simply, "In the United States people do." Larbaud identifies Whitman as the root of American modernism, but oddly enough, he also places Whitman in the New England tradition:

> It was Whitman, and Whitman alone, who rendered possible this freedom in poetic form and in choice of subjects. It was he who taught the artists of his country, some fifty years ago, that a poet's power displays itself, not so much in the difficulties overcome as in the opportunities discovered. It was he who told them, with that strange prophetic tone, at once epic and familiar,—the tone of the old Puritan preachers, now transmuted into literary beauty,—that the subject of a poet's song ought to be "the commonplace," and also the "I," moral and physical,

> the daily spectacles of street and field, the great harbors, the factories, the work of modern man, and last of all, "these states." (589)

According to Larbaud, the puritan strain can be detected in Whitman's work more for its orality than for its ideology. The English spiritualist and crime writer Carl Eric Bechhofer, a regular contributor to the *London Times Literary Supplement,* in 1923 proved less subtle in his book-length study of *The Literary Renaissance in America.* Bechhofer heavy-handedly deploys renaissance rhetoric as a means to contrast the younger generation of critics, novelists, and playwrights with those who appeal to the "Puritan elder generation," such as Edith Wharton and Booth Tarkington (126). Indeed, he describes the American Renaissance as "a revolt against the intellectual standards that have for so long dominated American culture. One may accept the current phraseology and label the official philosophy 'Puritanism,' 'Philistinism,' or 'the optimism of the pioneer,' but the name does not much matter" (1). The younger generation's renaissance, then, takes positive shape in the "racial contrasts and incongruities" (104) of Cather's and Drieser's Midwest, for example, or negative shape in the view espoused by most contributors to Stearns's *Civilization in the United States* (1922): "American civilization is a young growth, crippled by Anglo-Saxon swaddling-clothes" (37). Similarly, Firmin Roz, a French historian writing in the *Revue des Deux Mondes* in 1925, characterizes the "New Spirit of the American Novel" as a kind of renaissance (a "metamorphosis, the inversion of values, that accounts for this awakening to consciousness" [879; my trans.]) centered in the Midwest and spearheaded by Lewis, Dreiser, and Cather. This movement, Roz argues, derives from America's youthful optimism and idealism, which signify its cultural independence from Europe.

Even when it does not make strict reference to renaissance rhetoric, American modernism famously disavows its English heritage, very often cast in the narrower terms of New England's puritan legacy, in favor of something younger and more vital, and hopefully something more American. Almost every Jazz Age writer developed her or his own version of America's literary genealogy, although this legacy is figured not so much as the New England myth of national origins traced by, for example, Wesley Frank Craven or Sacvan Bercovitch; it is more like an early, cartoon version of a 1950s "square," more George Babbitt than Judge Pyncheon. Judging by the vitriol of the lyrical left, one might think that Cotton Mather and Jonathan Edwards wrote the Eighteenth Amendment, or implemented the blue laws, or banned the importation of *Ulysses.* John Dos Passos, for example, introduced himself upon graduating from Harvard to the wider literary world with his

New Republic manifesto, "Against American Literature" (1916). American literature, because it owes so much to foreign sources—he has in mind Wharton and the latter Robert Herrick—"has become a hybrid which, like the mule, is barren and must be produced afresh each time by the crossing of other strains," hardly the kind of birth we associate with a renaissance. He further describes American literature as a "rootless product, a cutting from England's sturdy well branched oak tree" (36). Dos Passos laments the WASPish "abstract theism" such hybridity engenders: "We have none of those local saints—tamed pagan gods, most of them—that have tied the Church in Europe so tightly to the people, to the soil; to the external powers of corn and wine and resurgent earth" (37). In Russia, for example, "there is the primitive savagery, the color, the romance of an age of faith suddenly burst in upon by European science"; Americans, however, reside in the "prim colonial living room of thought, where the shades are drawn for fear the sun will fade the carpet Puritan ancestors laid there" (38).

Dos Passos offers a cynical, negative diagnosis, but one easily transformed into a positive attribute by American modernists. The absence of a deep-rooted cultural legacy readily gives way to a nationalism that need look only to the not-so-distant past, or to contemporary "primitive" cultures, for filler. For instance, William Carlos Williams's gnomic collection *Spring and All* (1923) contains some of the most avant-gardist pronouncements uttered in the English language, including diatribes against "You moderns!" (" . . . it is the death of poetry that you are accomplishing"), against an unnamed T. S. Eliot ("If I could say what is in my mind in Sanscrit or even Latin I would do so. But I cannot. . . . Kill! Kill! let there be fresh meat."), and on numerous occasions against the word "like" (*Poems* 1:177, 179, passim). Williams's unrelenting attention to "no ideas but in things" coexists, peacefully or not, with his primordialist celebration of an "Arab / Indian / dark woman" who are (is?) "rich / in savagery"—as though "Arab," "Indian," "dark," and "woman" transmit an experience unmediated and unencumbered by history or ideology. (Might we conceive of him writing something like "Pilgrim / divine / rich / in boobery"?) Williams argues that the "primitives are not back in some remote age—they are not BEHIND experience," and thus he favors "work which bridges the gap between the rigidities of vulgar experience and the imagination. . . . It is new, immediate—It is so because it is actual, always real" (*Poems* 1:220). Williams examines some of the demons impeding such work in his book-length manifesto of American cultural nationalism, *In the American Grain* (1925). The collection of historical essays attempts to purge the inhibiting puritan legacy by aligning it with the vulgarity of Victorian commercialism: "the result of that brave setting out of the Pilgrims has been an atavism that thwarts and destroys"; "to-day it is a generation of gross know-nothingism, of blackened churches where hymns groan like chants from stupefied jungles, a generation universally eager to barter permanent values (the hope of an aristocracy) in return for opportunist material advantages, a generation hating those whom it obeys" (68). In its place, Williams offers a constructivist genealogy of the American spirit—incorporating traits from the Spanish, the French, the Caribs, the Abnaki, the Negro, and elsewhere—as opposed to a genealogy traceable along bloodlines. There will be no Puritans in Williams's ideal America: "All that will be new in America will be anti-Puritan. It will be of another root" (120), he declares to Larbaud at a Paris salon, for while "we are not Indians . . . we are men of their world. The blood means nothing; the spirit, the ghost of the land moves in the blood, moves the blood" (39).[25]

The Invention of the Negro Renaissance

Wallace Thurman's *Infants of the Spring* (1932), a *roman à clef* set at Niggeratti Manor, a boardinghouse peopled by eccentric African American artists and an even greater number of would-be artists, features characters who are thinly veiled stand-ins for some of the Harlem Renaissance's leading figures (many of whom also appear in Thurman's first novel, *The Blacker the Berry* [1929]). At a literary salon organized at the behest of Alain Locke (in the novel he is Dr. A. L. Parkes, "a professor of literature in a northern Negro college . . . who, also . . . played mother hen to a brood of chicks, having appointed himself guardian angel to the current set of younger Negro artists" [180]) we encounter Zora Neale Hurston (as Sweetie May Carr, a "short story writer, more noted for her ribald wit and personal effervescence than for any actual literary work" [229]); Dorothy West and Helene Johnson (as Doris Westmore and Hazel Jamison, who "surprisingly enough for Negro prodigies . . . actually gave promise of possessing literary talent" [231]); Langston Hughes (as Tony Crews, whose "work was interesting and unusual. It was also spotty" [231]); Countee Cullen and his lover, Harold Jackman (as DeWitt Clinton, "the Negro poet laureate . . . accompanied, as usual, by his *fideles achates,* David Holloway" [232]); Aaron Douglas (as Carl Denny); Eric Walrond (as Cedric Williams); and Rudolph Fisher (as Dr. Manfred Trout).

At an early stage of the novel's development, its third-person narrator ponders the future significance of a Negro Renaissance not quite ushered in by this talented group of artists. "There had been throughout the nation an announcement of a Negro renaissance," observes the narrator, whose focus hovers around the book's main character, a novelist named Raymond. "The American Negro, it seemed, was entering a new phase in his development. He was about to become an important factor in the artistic life of the United States. As the middle westerner and the southerner had found indigenous expression, so was the Negro developing his own literary spokesmen" (61–62). The novel takes place during the 1927–28 academic year—external political developments or events of historical importance do not place the novel chronologically; rather, the publication dates of specific books do—and even at this late date, less than two years before the Great Crash would bring the Jazz Age to a close according to the standard portrayal of events, both Raymond and his close approximation in real life, Thurman, expressed considerable doubt in the mere existence of a Negro Renaissance. In a 1927 *Independent* essay, Thurman laments that "it is too bad that negro literature and literary material have had to be exploited by the fad finders and sentimentalists. Too bad that the ballyhoo brigade which fostered the so-called negro art 'renaissance' has chosen to cheer and encourage indiscriminately anything which claims a negroid ancestry or kinship" ("Nephews" 269). Meanwhile, in the novel, Raymond also worries that the Negro Renaissance is but a pretense for heaping unwarranted praise on second-rate works of art, that "very little was being done to substantiate the current fad, to make it the foundation of something truly epochal" (62).

Thurman's fears, by the time the novel made its appearance during the worst years of the Great Depression, were by no means his alone. During the 1920s and 1930s, writers and critics regularly questioned the results of the cultural project loosely designated as the Negro Renaissance. Never mind such obvious examples as George Schuyler's *Nation* article on "The Negro-Art Hokum" (1926) or Richard Wright's "Blueprint for Negro Writing" (1937) manifesto; some of the movement's leading boosters also lost faith. Even Locke would view the program he set in motion as a misguided failure, writing in 1937 that the "one great flaw of the first decade of the Negro Renaissance was its exhibitionist flair. It should have addressed itself more to the people themselves and less to the gallery of faddist Negrophiles" ("Spiritual" 85). As early as April 1927, Benjamin Brawley questioned whether or not the "so-called renaissance" might in fact be a misnomer; after all, "these men would probably have written even if there had been no 'renaissance' at all." In his view, an exoticist groping for strong effects and a willingness to place sordid, bohemian themes into free forms—especially jazz- and blues-inspired modes of expression—produce a literature devoid of standards and with little appreciation for literary tradition. The "day of jazz" so recently ushered in by Vachel Lindsay, Brawley concludes, "is over; charlatanry has defeated itself" ("Renaissance" 184). In August 1933, Du Bois wondered aloud for his *Crisis* readers, "Why was it that the Renaissance of literature which began among Negroes ten years ago has never taken real and lasting root?" His answer cemented the pattern already taking shape: "It was because it was a transplanted and exotic thing. It was a literature written for the benefit of white people and at the behest of white readers, and starting out privately from the white point of view." Du Bois expresses the militant nationalism that would characterize numerous subsequent accounts of African American literature during the Jazz Age, particularly those written during the Black Arts Movement of the 1960s and 1970s, even though this view compromises the validity of his own literary production. The renaissance "never had a real Negro constituency and it did not grow out of the inmost heart and frank experience of Negroes," Du Bois reflects; "on such an artificial basis no real literature can grow" ("Negro College" 176).

By the time Langston Hughes gave the movement its current name in *The Big Sea* (1940), he could look back and diagnose with confidence the naïveté, the pandering, and the tenuous economic footing of African American writers that still occupy the movement's critics and historians. "That spring [1931] for me (and, I guess, all of us) was the end of the Harlem Renaissance," he writes, substituting his own subjectivity for African American modernism as a whole. "We were no longer in vogue, anyway, we Negroes" (334). The Negro Renaissance became the Harlem Renaissance at precisely the moment in Hughes's narrative that the itinerant worker transforms into a professional writer, that the protégé of Godmother (Charlotte Mason) emerges as his own man, and that the Roaring Twenties become the sober thirties (both for Hughes and for the nation). All of Hughes's concerns animate contemporary Harlem Renaissance criticism, either as a legitimate response to a failed moment in cultural history (views shared by Nathan Irvin Huggins and David Levering Lewis), as a misplaced yardstick for judging the subversive modernism lurking beneath the surface of African American letters (Houston Baker), or simply as a myopic account of an African American literary success story (Ann Douglas and George Hutchinson).

But back to Thurman for a moment. Upon its publication by Macaulay, *Infants of the Spring* was viewed almost universally as a critical disaster. Rudolph Fisher's review for the *New York Herald Tribune*, "Harlem Manor," sums up the prevailing response: "The theme is the early demise of the so-called New Negro, whose literary and artistic renaissance enjoyed a fair bit of publicity five years ago, but in the course of the novel there is so much expositional and argumentative prattle on race prejudice and communism that one can not be sure at the end what the book started out to say" (16).

Perhaps not too surprisingly, the novel continues to draw readers for the very reason it drew fire from Thurman's contemporaries, namely, its excessive attention to sociology and politics, or perhaps more accurately, its propagandistic repudiation of propaganda. David Levering Lewis has written more recently that "this was hardly the stuff of a good novel, but it was a valuable first intellectual statement of the malaise of the Renaissance" (280). *Infants* was not quite the first, but it represents one of the earliest attempts to offer a posthumous explanation for the early demise of the Negro Renaissance. The suicide of the novel's most extreme decadent, Paul Arbian (modeled after Richard Bruce Nugent, or "R.B.N."), like Thurman's own tragic end, sounded the death knell for the movement.

Much as we saw with the Lost Generation, Harlem writers and critics cast individual lives (Hughes's) and deaths (Fisher's, Thurman's, the fictional Paul Arbian's) in larger roles, symbolizing entire classes of individuals. The health of the Negro Renaissance has also been gauged by the postwar economic vital signs of the nation as a whole, although during the 1920s few critics were willing to admit that the Negro Renaissance ever went into full swing. In literary history the Harlem Renaissance now registers only as a fait accompli, a discrete movement that came and went. However, Thurman's novel, like most examples of Negro Renaissance rhetoric, takes place at least partly in the optative mood; it points toward a promised land of recognition and respect, always just beyond the horizon. Just as Emerson imagined American literature, or as Yeats did the Irish Renaissance—in the future tense, or at the very least as an event only just begun—the Negro Renaissance was identified well before it ever took place. Between the turn of the century, when the phrase was born, and the early 1930s, when it was considered only in the past tense, Negro Renaissance rhetoric followed a course not unlike contemporaneous American renaissances. It functions as a discursive object with which to re-create the past and to imagine the future of African American literature. This "futurism" had a short history—Negro Renaissance rhetoric, at least as it emerged from the movement itself, came to an abrupt end around the time of Thurman's novel—but for that brief span, and with greater clarity than any of its American Renaissance counterparts, it envisioned an African American literary emergence predicated on the familiar ideals of art, youth, and provincialism.

In an Optative Mood

In November 1901, poet and editor William Stanley Braithwaite begat the idea of a "Negro Renaissance" in a review published in the *Colored American Magazine.*[26] In an otherwise unremarkable discussion of Mary Weston Fordham's *Magnolia Leaves* (1897), a collection of poems described in Braithwaite's typically impressionistic fashion ("genuine feeling and a true lyrical quality"; "musical but often carelessly considered"), he introduced what would become the overwhelmingly popular term for describing modernist African American culture: "To my mind our race should recognize that we are at the commencement of a 'Negroid' renaissance (to use the epithet, Mr. [William Hannibal] Thomas has coined for our use) that will have in time as much importance in literary history as the much spoken of and much praised Celtic and Canadian renaissance. Mr. Dunbar certainly command [*sic*] as wide a reading audience as Mr. [Bliss] Carman, leader of the Canadian school, or that fascinating elusive, Mr. W. B. Yeats of the Celtic revival" (73).[27] Significantly, Braithwaite finds it necessary to set off Thomas's anthropological term ("Negroid") in quotation marks, while the notion that a renaissance on a par with that of Ireland (and, bizarrely, Canada) is about to occur can be taken as simple fact. Braithwaite's review is thus a watershed in the history of American cultural criticism, for similar aspirations for African American literary expression—that is, for literary artistry, as opposed to the relatively common, romantic racialist view that "negroes . . . are born orators, painters, sculptors, musicians, actors, for the present dwarfed by the wicked magician OPPRESSION" (the example is that of Unitarian reformer Moncure D. Conway in 1866 [39])—only began to flourish during the turn of the century, when for the first time a sufficient number of African Americans themselves began to weigh in on the critical dialogue. Even so, the Emersonian life of the mind, the "life you grudge us, O knightly America," as Du Bois put it in *The Souls of Black Folk* (1903), remained as yet a Pisgah view of the Promised Land, a perspective from "between Philistine and Amalekite" (74). During the first two decades of the twentieth century, Negro Renaissance rhetoric offered a compelling way to voice this sense of literary belatedness, the sentiment needed to prepare for a literary coming-of-age.

In the first issue of the *Voice of the Negro* (January 1904), for example, editor J. Max Barber compared the journal's potential accomplishments, "which shall stand as the vanguard of a higher culture and a new literature," with those of the Italian Renaissance, which brought about "the enfranchisement of the human mind from the most cruel tyranny" (38). (This represents one of the extremely rare examples of Negro Renaissance rhetoric invoking a comparison with the Italian Renaissance. Locke's "Our Little Renaissance" [1927] and McKay's *A Long Way from Home* [1937] are two others.) In one of Du Bois's whirlwind tours of African American literary history, "The Negro in Literature and Art" (1913), he lays out the conceptual groundwork for the

Negro Renaissance he helped preside over by arguing that "the time has not yet come for the great development of American Negro literature. The economic stress is too great and the racial persecution too bitter to allow the leisure and the poise for which literature calls." But he quickly adds that "never in the world has a richer mass of material been accumulated by a people than that which the Negroes possess today and are becoming conscious of" (236–37). Similar sociohistorical interpretations of African American cultural history dominate the period's criticism, planting the seeds for the art-versus-propaganda rift that would develop into a vast chasm during the Great Depression. Brawley, in one of the earliest of his many articles and books bearing a title like "The Negro in Literature," repeated this sentiment that Negro life was simply too taxing to sustain a viable literature; he even extends Du Bois's answer to the question, How does it feel to be a problem? "The grand epic of the [Negro] race is yet to be produced," Brawley wrote in the *Dial* in 1916, sounding a familiar cultural nationalist note for that journal's largely white audience. But he continues with greater focus on the racial context for this message so full of desire, so much like the "national longing for form" described by Timothy Brennan: "Some day our little children will not slave in mines and mills, but will have some chance at the glory of God's creation; and some day the Negro will cease to be a problem and will be a human being. Then, in truth, we shall have the Promised Land" ("Fiction" 450). These ambitions, which today seem so remote because so taken for granted, could in retrospect lead only to frustration, only to failure; however, for the duration of the Jazz Age, a Negro Renaissance seemed an inevitable step along the path of American cultural and social evolution.

"A renaissance of American Negro literature is due," Du Bois declared in early 1920; "the material about us in the strange, heart-rending race tangle is rich beyond dream and only we can tell the tale and sing the song from the heart" ("Negro Writers" 299). From this moment forward, and particularly after the publication of *The New Negro* in 1925, Negro Renaissance rhetoric became fixed within the discourse on African American cultural appraisal. No longer were critics confined to writing about "The Negro *in* Literature," although this type of "imagology" (to borrow a term from Werner Sollors [*Neither* 26]) continues unabated to this day; instead, critics could finally speak of an African American literary tradition proper. Indeed, the transition from the study of the Negro in literature to the study of Negro literature emerged as a minor theme of African American criticism during the Jazz Age.

James Weldon Johnson reflected the views of many when he wrote that the "Negro in the United States is consuming all of his intellectual energy in this grueling race-struggle" in his famous preface to *The Book of Ameri-*

can Negro Poetry (1922). "But, even so," he would add, "the American Negro has accomplished something in pure literature" (xx, xxi). "Only gradually through the dull purgatory of the Age of Discussion," Braithwaite offers in his contribution to *The New Negro,* "has Negro life eventually issued forth to an Age of Expression" (29). And elsewhere in that foundational collection, Locke signaled a socioeconomic turning of the corner allowing for such an epochal shift: "Already enough progress has been made in this direction so that it is no longer true that the Negro mind is too engulfed in its own social dilemmas for control of the necessary perspective of art, or too depressed to attain the full horizons of self and social criticism. Indeed, by the evidence and the promise of a cultured few, we are at last spiritually free, and offer through art an emancipating vision to America" (53). By 1926, Du Bois was finally able to proclaim, "after a vast hiatus in Negro development, there is today a renaissance of Negro genius" ("Art Renaissance" 26) because a large group of African American writers—he points to Jessie Fauset and Walter White—were finally gaining a foothold in the mainstream literary marketplace. The following year Locke explained why this was so by comparing "Our Little Renaissance" with the "Grand Renaissance" in Italy centuries earlier: "It was only yesterday that we had to preach objectivity to the race artist to cure the pathetic fallacies of bathos and didactic approach. We are just beginning perhaps to shake off the artifices of that relatively early stage; so to speak the Umbrian stiffness is still upon us and the Florentine ease and urbanity looms just ahead" (118).

During the mid-1920s, a groundswell of newly published articles and books on the topic indexed the shift in purpose and perspective suggested by Du Bois and Locke. Their titles reflect the hope and ambition of the New Negro cause: Locke's *The New Negro,* of course, as well as his studies of "American Literary Tradition and the Negro" (1926), "The Negro's Contribution to American Art and Literature" (1928), and "Negro Contributions to America" (1929); Du Bois's "Negro Writers" (1920), *The Gift of Black Folk* (1924), and (from the *Survey Graphic*) "The Black Man Brings His Gifts" (1925); V. F. Calverton's article on "The Advance of the Negro" (1926); Charles S. Johnson's "The Negro Enters Literature" (1927) and "The Rise of the Negro Magazine" (1928); not to mention the many articles bearing the title "Negro Renaissance." Between 1920 and 1932 alone, variations of this latter title were adopted in literary journals by a long list of writers and critics: Benjamin Brawley, A. Calza, R. M. Fox, Martha Gruening, Alain Locke, Lloyd Morris, Franck L. Schoell, Carl Van Doren, and Walter White. (This does not even account for the anonymous editorials bearing the title, nor the many newspaper articles, including one by Du Bois, reporting on the event.) But it is not enough simply to note a proliferation of references to a Negro Renaissance or to point out that some disagreement arose out of the identification of a movement by that name. Why a Negro Renaissance, and why now? What, following René Wellek and Austin Warren, does the period reveal in the way of "literary norms, standards, and conventions" (265), not to mention extraliterary concerns? What, finally, does the Negro Renaissance *mean*?

Youth, Art, Wholesome Provincialism

Contemporary discussions of the Harlem Renaissance typically overlook the degree to which the movement's key players expressed their goals in terms of a generational passing of the torch. The absence is not total; it would be difficult not to mention that *The New Negro* was dedicated "To the Younger Generation," or that *Fire!!* was "Devoted to the Younger Negro Artists," or that its editor, Thurman, was only twenty-four when the journal appeared. And no one can overlook the intergenerational dynamics of the literary contests sponsored by *Opportunity* or *Crisis,* or the legendary Civic Club dinner of March 1924. Still, given the post–World War II emphasis on Harlem as the cultural center of the movement, most studies begin with a geosocial account of the Great Migration from the rural South to northern urban centers, a point of emphasis obscuring not only intergenerational cooperation and conflict but also the national (and even international) reach of the Negro Renaissance and its leading figures. The earliest scholarly analysis of the movement, French historian Franck L. Schoell's *Revue de Paris* article "La 'renaissance nègre' aux États-Unis" (1929), set the pattern of sociohistorical analysis later adopted by, among others, Huggins, Lewis, and to a lesser extent Douglas.[28] The utopian goals of the movement's leadership—the view that a Talented Tenth could pave the way for the remaining Untalented Nine-tenths—necessitate this mode of analysis, at least on the part of cultural historians interested in tracing larger social patterns. But this perspective also obscures the uprooted lifestyles of the movement's individual writers, most of whom lived outside Harlem, and many of whom spent considerable time overseas. That the Negro Renaissance so often made use of generational models, that it celebrated youth almost as a matter of official policy, suggests that literal geography was less important than the "spiritual pioneering" (Waldo Frank's aptly loaded phrase) of generational identification.

The NAACP, a key sponsor of the Harlem Renaissance via its publication of *Crisis,* looked to the German *Wandervögel* for inspiration on multiple occasions. In February 1924, the *Crisis* published Eugene Corbie's discussion of

"The German Youth Movement" and Du Bois and Locke's analysis of "The Younger Literary Movement" side by side. Several months earlier, in an article on "The League of Youth," Cullen remarked in the same journal that "youth the world over is undergoing a spiritual and an intellectual awakening" (167). In his groping for an appropriate model for the transformation taking place in Harlem and elsewhere, Cullen saw fit to draw direct parallels between the German Youth Movement and a contemporaneous "American Negro Youth" movement. However, after the widely reported Civic Club dinner, such comparisons were no longer necessary, and even extraneous to the cultural nationalist project of the Negro Renaissance. In May 1924, *Opportunity* took stock of the dinner as "The Debut of the Younger School of Negro Writers," in which the journal's editor and organizer of the gala, Charles S. Johnson, described a "coming out party" for Cullen, Eric Walrond, Hughes, Fauset, Gwendolyn Bennett, Jackman, Regina Anderson, "and a few others" (143). These debutantes stood before a distinguished group of well-wishing "elders," including Charles S. Johnson, Locke, Horace Liveright, Du Bois, James Weldon Johnson, Walter White, Montgomery Gregory, and Albert C. Barnes. Also on hand was Carl Van Doren, whose remarks on "The Younger Generation of Negro Writers" later appeared in *Opportunity.* An editorial in the *New York Herald Tribune* entitled "A Negro Renaissance" announced that "these young people—and youth was another striking thing about this gathering—were not trying to imitate the white man nor repeating the professional white story-teller's dreary stencils of the 'darkey.' They were expressing their own feelings, frankly and unabashed, even if it took them back to the jungle" (187). True to form, Charles S. Johnson reprinted the editorial in its entirety in *Opportunity,* and he quoted from it liberally in subsequent advertisements for the journal and its contests (although he conveniently overlooked the *Herald Tribune's* "jungle" reference).

Crisis and *Opportunity* convened virtually identical gatherings following each literary contest they sponsored, and numerous other literary journals not typically identified with the Harlem Renaissance followed suit. (The well-known rivalry between *Crisis* editor Du Bois and *Opportunity* editor Johnson for literary bragging rights was one facet of a wider talent search going on within and beyond the sphere of influence of the African American press.) It is ironic but not unexpected that many of the then-celebrity judges (such as Pearl S. Buck or Zona Gale) today find themselves displaced from the modernist American canon by the regular winners of the contests (including Hughes and Hurston). For this they owe a great debt to Locke, described by Charles S. Johnson as the "virtual dean of the movement" ("Debut" 143) gathered at the Civic Club. The degree of Locke's influence in

Harlem Renaissance circles remains a matter of some scholarly debate; however, Locke clearly developed close relationships with many of the movement's rising young stars, and perhaps more important, he is largely responsible for the conflation of the Harlem Renaissance and the whole of African American modernism in contemporary critical discourse.

The most noteworthy case in point is Locke's reinvention of the *Survey Graphic* Harlem number (March 1925) as *The New Negro*, which Albert and Charles Boni published later that year. A handful of critics have already dwelled on the impact of these changes,[29] but a few editorial choices warrant further examination. Most obviously, *The New Negro* is considerably more comprehensive in scope, both in terms of sheer size (452 pages compared to the *Survey Graphic's* 103, which includes dozens of advertisements) and in terms of editorial content (with an emphasis on national Negro culture rather than the Harlem enclave). This shift in scope also occasioned a kind of editorial gentrification: targeted toward an African American middle class and Negro college audience, *The New Negro* shelved the more politically charged discussions of urban decay found in the *Survey Graphic* and replaced these with relatively anemic articles on middle-class institutions located throughout the United States. Winold Reiss's more controversial illustrations were also jettisoned, although many of his remaining illustrations were reproduced as color plates and supplemented with the work of his protégé, Aaron Douglas. Oddly enough, the politically neutral photographs accompanying James Weldon Johnson's Harlem essay were also removed from the anthology.

Another significant and thus far overlooked change introduced in *The New Negro* is Negro Renaissance rhetoric on a grand scale and with strategic effect. In the *Survey Graphic*, only Albert C. Barnes's essay on "Negro Art and America" introduces the phrase to describe the revivalist mode of, for example, Paul Laurence Dunbar and Booker T. Washington: "The renascence of Negro art is one of the events of our age which no seeker for beauty can afford to overlook. It is as characteristically Negro as are the primitive African sculptures" (668). (This is also the thrust of Arthur A. Schomburg's "The Negro Digs Up His Past," which immediately follows Barnes's essay in the *Survey Graphic*.) Locke's Negro Renaissance rhetoric, on the other hand, virtually redirects the social reformist flow of the *Survey Graphic* into more strictly aesthetic channels previously opened by Yeats and Pound. Locke's "Negro Youth Speaks" introduces several paragraphs absent from its *Survey Graphic* counterpart ("Youth Speaks"), all of them brimming with Negro Renaissance confidence. The essay begins with an all-new, prophetic declaration:

> The Younger Generation comes, bringing his gifts. They are the first fruits of the Negro Renaissance. Youth speaks, and the voice of the New Negro is heard. What stirs inarticulately in the masses is already vocal upon the lips of the talented few, and the future listens, however the present may shut its ears. Here we have Negro youth, with arresting visions and vibrant prophesies; forecasting in the mirror of art what we must see and recognize in the streets of reality tomorrow, foretelling in new notes and accents the maturing speech of full racial utterance. (47)

In the work of this Younger Generation—Locke highlights especially Fisher, Hughes, Hurston, Walrond, Toomer, and Willis Richardson, all of whom appear in the anthology—Locke identifies a "lusty vigorous realism" that breaks free of the "trammels of Puritanism" inhibiting an older generation of Negro writers. "Just as with the Irish Renaissance," he continues, "we are having and will have turbulent discussion and dissatisfaction with the stories, plays and poems of the younger Negro group." But these writers "take their material objectively with detached artistic vision; they have no thought of their racy folk types as typical of anything but themselves or of their being taken or mistaken as racially representative" (50). Critical objectivity, the "new realist" aesthetic also favored by Braithwaite and James Weldon Johnson, figures prominently in Locke's project, much to the subsequent consternation of Du Bois: "Not all the new art is in the field of pure art values," Locke writes, "but reason and realism have cured us of sentimentality" associated with representations of the "Old Negro" soaked in humor or pathos. (It is no surprise, then, that Locke conveniently neglects to mention the impressionistic primitivism of Nugent's "Sahdji," another short story in the anthology.) "That is why," Locke writes in his introduction to *The New Negro,* in a passage that is also missing from its *Survey Graphic* counterpart ("Enter the New Negro"), "our comparison is taken with those nascent centers of folk-expression and self-determination which are playing a creative part in the world to-day. Without pretense to their political significance, Harlem has the same rôle to play for the New Negro as Dublin has had for the New Ireland or Prague for the New Czechoslovakia" (7).[30]

Thus the "re-" in Locke's Negro Renaissance is virtually interchangeable with the "new" in New Negro. Generational identification, a loosely theorized version of the new, easily lends its metaphorical weight to subsequent "discoveries" of the national spirit; that is, the Younger Generation comes of age by discovering itself in its collective past. Two years after putting together *The New Negro,* Locke argued in his *Four Negro Poets* (1927) collection that "with this generation of Negro poets [McKay, Toomer, Cullen, and

Hughes], a folk temperament flowers and a race experience bears fruit. Race is often a closer spiritual bond than nationality and group experience deeper than an individual's: here we have beauty that is born of long-suffering, truth that is derived from mass emotion and founded on collective vision. The spiritual search and discovery which is every artist's is in this case more than personal; it is the epic reach and surge of a people seeking their group character through art" (5).[31] Here Locke explicitly follows in the theoretical wake James Weldon Johnson, who argued in *The Book of American Negro Poetry* that the "power of the Negro to suck up the national spirit from the soil and create something artistic and original" would somehow lead to racial uplift because the "final measure and greatness of all peoples is the amount and standard of the literature and art they have produced. The world does not know that a people is great until that people produces great literature and art" (xix, vii). This phrasing, to anyone familiar with Yeats's American essays, is hardly unprecedented, stretching back at least to the romantic nationalism of Herder. And while Johnson elsewhere urges Negro poets to do "something like what Synge did for the Irish; he needs to find a form that will express the racial spirit by symbols from within rather than by symbols from without, such as the mere mutilation of English spelling and pronunciation" (xl–xli), much of the "provincialism" found in Negro Renaissance rhetoric sways between Yeats's modern culturalism on the one hand and Hyde's primordial racialism on the other. This vacillation within the parameters of Negro Renaissance rhetoric occurs so rapidly that it is often difficult to decide where one ends and the other begins, but perhaps such genealogical instability befits a movement so dependent on intra- and interracial cooperation and debate.

It is worth remembering that the most famous disagreement over the social meaning of the Negro Renaissance took place between George S. Schuyler, a dark-skinned editor, columnist, science fiction satirist, onetime Socialist, and later John Birch conservative from New England via upstate New York, on the one hand, and Langston Hughes, a light-skinned and always politically radical poet, fiction writer, and memoirist from the Midwest via just about everywhere else, on the other hand, in the pages of the *Nation,* one of America's leading left-wing journals. Schuyler modeled "The Negro-Art Hokum," which appeared on 16 June 1926, after the acerbic wit of his chief literary inspiration, Mencken. Schuyler begins by dismissing the idea that "Negro art 'made in America'" even exists; it is as much a figment of the imagination as "the widely advertised profundity of Cal Coolidge" or "the reported sophistication of New Yorkers." Schuyler concedes that such art exists "among the numerous black nations of Africa; but to suggest the possibility of any such development among the ten million colored people in this republic is self-evident foolishness." So, too, the Negro Renaissance. "Eager apostles from Greenwich Village, Harlem, and environs proclaimed a great renaissance of Negro art just around the corner waiting to be ushered on the scene by those whose hobby is taking races, nations, peoples, and movements under their wing. New art forms expressing the 'peculiar' psychology of the Negro were about to flood the market. In short, the art of Homo Africanus was about to electrify the waiting world. Skeptics patiently waited. They still wait" (662). Schuyler is not out to prove that no art ever emerged from African Americans; rather, his point of emphasis, to which he returns again and again, is that this is an American art, not a Negro art. Spirituals, jazz, and the Charleston, he argues, "are no more expressive or characteristic of the Negro race than the music and dancing of the Appalachian highlanders or the Dalmatian peasantry are expressive or characteristic of the Caucasian race." In other words, these forms of African American expression reflect certain regional and class influences more than they do racial psychology. Similarly, "the literature, painting, and sculpture of Aframericans—such as there is— . . . is identical in kind with the literature, painting, and sculpture of white Americans: that is, it shows more or less evidence of European influence." While this line of argument is itself somewhat reductive, it nevertheless depends on the objective analysis of cultural artifacts, not on romantic racialist presuppositions or impressionistic reactions. But Schuyler's irreverence largely drowns out his message: "the Aframerican is merely a lampblacked Anglo-Saxon," he writes, as if to invite scorn. "If the European immigrant after two or three generations of exposure to our schools, politics, advertising, moral crusades, and restaurants becomes indistinguishable from the mass of Americans of the older stock (despite the influence of the foreign-language press), how much truer must it be of the sons of Ham who have been subjected to what the uplifters call Americanism for the last three hundred years" (662).

Only Schuyler would describe three hundred years of slavery and Jim Crow as "Americanism," but his analysis of African American culture differs very little from the "opposing view" (as the *Nation* dubbed it in an editorial note) offered by Langston Hughes. "The Negro Artist and the Racial Mountain," which appeared on 23 June 1926, takes a similar view of the influence of region and class on the artistic temperament and, by extension, on art. His "Negro poet," who once said, "I want to be a poet—not a Negro poet" (he was thinking of Cullen), belongs to "what I suppose one would call the Negro middle class: people who are by no means rich yet never uncomfortable nor hungry—smug, contented, respectable folk, members of the Baptist church" (692). With this upward mobility, Hughes suggests, comes a hardly resistible desire to be a white poet, "meaning, behind that, 'I would like to be white.'" This poet is socialized to believe that all things clean, moral, and beautiful are white things; such is the racial mountain that must be overcome. Hughes adds: "One sees immediately how difficult it would be for an artist born in such a home to interest himself in interpreting the beauty of his own people. He is never taught to see that beauty." But not all is lost, he argues; indeed, "perhaps [the] common people will give to the world its truly great Negro artist, the one who is not afraid to be himself. Whereas the better-class Negro would tell the artist what to do, the people at least let him alone when he does appear. And they are not ashamed of him—if they know he exists at all" (693). And so Hughes celebrates "the low-down folks, the so-called common element" from "Seventh Street in Washington or State Street in Chicago," those who "have their hip of gin on Saturday nights" and "play awhile," "sing awhile," not worrying about social status or self-promotion. Most of all, Hughes celebrates jazz, "one of the inherent expressions of Negro life in America; the eternal tom-tom beating in the Negro soul—the tom-tom of revolt against weariness in a white world, a world of subway trains, and work, work, work; the tom-tom of joy and laughter, and pain swallowed in a smile" (694).

Hughes shares with Schuyler a belief in cultural and economic determinism as well as the widely held view that America excels at producing not the artist but the Tired Business Man. Both even find something of value in jazz. Where they disagree is in their respective views of what constitutes a wholesome provincialism. While neither uses Royce's phrase, both offer an account of the role of folk culture in artistic development, and specifically in its part-to-whole relationship with African American expression. Hughes is quite clear on the subject. For him, folk culture represents authenticity: Toomer's *Cane* and the singing of Paul Robeson are "truly racial"; jazz is an "inherent expression" of the "Negro soul"; and judging by Hughes's essay, no genuine African American household goes without its tom-tom. In contrast, Hughes's poet, the one who wants to be white, stands at the opposite end of the spectrum, deracinated, lost. For Schuyler, the racialized traits of African American culture celebrated by Hughes are more aptly described as regional elements of American culture. In his response to Hughes's essay, printed on 14 July 1926, Schuyler writes: "If there is anything 'racial' about the spirituals and the blues, then there should be immediate ability to catch the intricate rhythm on the part of Negroes from Jamaica, Zanzibar, and Sierra Leone. Such is not the case, and we must conclude that they are the products of a certain American environment: the South. They are American folk-songs, built around Anglo-Saxon religious concepts" ("Negroes and Artists" 50). These forms of expression, Schuyler insists, are comparable in scope with other varieties of local color expression.

I do not wish to side with either Hughes or Schuyler in this debate; rather, I wish to point out how the terms established by American Renaissance rhetoric lead almost inevitably to reductive critical positions, positions in which the most evident alternatives are romantic racialism and neoclassic universalism.[32] Hughes is surely correct in suggesting that jazz, for example, provided a liberating influence for those uninterested in hackneyed, "puritan" standards. But this impulse can hardly be defined as strictly African American. And Schuyler rightly insists that African American culture betrays the influence of European (especially "Anglo-Saxon") models. But years of subsequent scholarship have also revealed structural continuities between African and African American forms. In the end, Negro Renaissance rhetoric provides no clear answers to the questions, What is wholesome? What is provincial? Where do *Nigger Heaven* and *Home to Harlem* fit in relation to *There Is Confusion* and *Flight,* or Dunbar's dialect poetry in relation to a Cullen sonnet (or, for that matter, a Dunbar sonnet)? What impact do Berlin and Paris and Mexico City have on the African American literary imagination as opposed to, say, Harlem or rural Georgia? The one answer that fits all of these questions is, "In an unprecedented way. In a new way," and also "In a manner that generates healthy debate about the past and future of American culture."

Locke argued in 1928 that, because "it is based on a conscious revival of partly lapsed tradition and experience . . . it is not ineptly termed 'the Negro Renaissance.' Its general social and cultural effects will not be apparent for half a generation yet, but in its literary and artistic course it has all the earmarks of other recent folk revivals like that of the Celtic tradition in the Irish Renaissance or of the Bohemian history and folk arts in the Czecho-Slovakian developments still more contemporaneously" ("Negro's Contribution" 242–43). Locke's view is not incompatible with Walter White's assertion, in *Palms,* a little magazine published out of Guadalajara, Mexico, that from the African American experience "springs a passion, a colorfulness, a strength which gives [Negro poets] most decided advantages over their white brothers writing verse" (6–7). As we saw with Hughes and Schuyler, these opinions differ only in terms of the scope of their views: Locke offers a comparativist panorama, White a look into the psychology of individual writers. Because both stem equally from the rhetoric of the Negro Renaissance, the truest meaning of the phrase must lie somewhere in between, somewhere not too far from Carl Van Doren's account, in his essay on "The Negro Renaissance" (1926): "Something has been poured into the stream of native culture which cannot soon cease to tinge it. Something has been uttered to enlarge the imaginative sympathy between the races which is an absolute essential of any decent solution of the color problem in America. . . . And [the Negro race] swiftly flowered into utterance, much as New England, in the early part of the nineteenth century, flowered into Transcendentalism" (636–37).

We have come, then, full circle, back not so much to the New England Renaissance as to the larger idea that cultural emergence is an ongoing feature of American life. The proliferation of renaissance rhetoric during the late nineteenth and early twentieth centuries indexes several comings-of-age for American writers and critics. Locke and White, as well as Hughes and Schuyler, voiced concerns that contribute to the loud chorus of cultural nationalism central to the discourse of American modernism. But this widespread message was not limited to nonfiction prose; indeed, the idea of rebirth finds its way into the very fabric of modernist literature, including poetry and fiction. In the following chapters I will take seriously the assertion that American writers imagine their craft as a kind of childbirth, a figure of speech long connected to artistic creation. In the U.S. context, this figure takes sometimes new, sometimes familiar shapes. Let us begin in the birthplace of American modernism, part Greenwich Village, part Harlem: bohemia.

II

LIVING THE MODERN

3

American Modernism Is Born

The Rise of the Bohemian Artist Narrative

> So no wonder that in certain cities of America, in New York of course, and New Orleans, in Chicago and San Francisco and Los Angeles, in such American cities as Paris and Mexico, D.F., this particular part of a generation was attracted to what the Negro had to offer. In such places as Greenwich Village, a ménage-a-trois was completed—the bohemian and the juvenile delinquent came face-to-face with the Negro, and the hipster was a fact of American life.
>
> Norman Mailer, "The White Negro" (1957)

From *Beau Monde* to New World: Bohemianism and Cultural Critique

The symptoms are unmistakable: long, unkempt hair squirms out of a battered hat; a tufted beard; a shabby coat, dark and loose-fitting, but also with a touch of drama, including elaborate fleur-de-lis buttons and an exquisite, shiny pin; within the coat's pockets, nothing but the ripped-off stub to yesterday's matinee, a few loose pamphlets, a rumpled manuscript, and lint; a thin pair of trousers descend toward patches of dust-covered leather pretending to be shoes. He speaks in clever turns of phrase and paradoxes, so clever in fact that most remain unintelligible to the public at large. The garret he calls home, which contains little more than an odd assortment of books and unpawnable furniture, leaks water through the roof and allows drafts through the windows, but the landlord hasn't been paid in months so complaints are out of the question. He abhors society, and society returns the favor. The diagnosis: *Homo bohemianus.* Examples of such creatures in U.S.

cultural history are many and include anyone from Whistler and Whitman to Baraka and Burroughs. By adjusting the pronouns and changing only a few other details this description could just as readily apply to Janis Joplin and Joan Didion. In this chapter, though, I will focus on James Weldon Johnson, Henry Miller, Zora Neale Hurston, Oscar Zeta Acosta, Gertrude Stein, Scott Fitzgerald, Ernest Hemingway, and William Carlos Williams, although I will visit a number of other bohemians along the way. Their deployment of bohemian themes and motifs, I argue, extends well beyond mere fashion sense; indeed, they deploy the French cultural cliché to advance an Americanist cultural agenda.

German critic Helmut Kreuzer, the world's foremost authority on bohemianism, provides a succinct definition of the French term in a rare English translation of his work: "'Bohemia(nism)' denotes an intellectual subculture, in particular one within the bourgeois economic order; it is composed of marginal groups whose activities or ambitions are primarily literary, artistic, or musical, and whose behaviour and attitudes are markedly non- or even anti-bourgeois. Bohemia constitutes an antagonistic complementary phenomenon to the well-adjusted middle-classes of those industrialized or industrializing societies which provide sufficient individualistic latitude and allow symbolic aggression (*épater le bourgeois*)" (533). Bohemianism alters its appearance over time, Kreuzer adds, because it must constantly adjust to the prevailing attitudes of bourgeois society; it is, in fact, parasitic on the very categories it so vehemently opposes. Its patron saint is Ovid, for metamorphosis is bohemianism's natural condition: "Bohemian style (like the occasionally parallel individualistic-aristocratic 'style' of the literary dandyism of romantic provenance)," offers Kreuzer, "is not independent of the conventions of society, but is—as an anti-convention—negatively dependent on them (down to the extravagant details of clothing and hair styles). Bohemianism transforms itself with the changing conventions in order to maintain contrast, and is thus a form of symbolic aggression" (537). Bohemianism thus follows the oppositional pattern of avant-garde movements identified by Raymond Williams: the category "'bourgeois,' in all its rich range of meanings, turns out to be a key to the many movements which claimed to be its opposite" (53). However, the American context allows us to specify further what shape an anti-bourgeois, bohemian rhetoric assumes in translation.

Explicit discussions of bohemianism in U.S. literary history are rare, so it is worth considering one such instance in the *Literary History of the United States* (1948), which includes a chapter by Harry Levin on "The Discovery of Bohemia," nestled appropriately between chapters on two Henrys (James and Adams). "Out of the *beau monde* of Europe and the 'good society' of

New York and Boston and Newport," Levin begins, "Henry James had fashioned his novels and tales on the International Theme. This had been his way of responding to the predicament of a society which did not yet know that it had to be redeemed. A further phase of the disenchantment of the late nineteenth century was a turning aside from the materialism of the modern industrial world, the conflict of science and religion, in the quest for a happier land of carefree life and impressionistic art of a mythical Bohemia" (Spiller et al. 1065). Levin proceeds with a wide-ranging discussion of once-important nineteenth-century U.S. writers, including Ambrose Bierce, Lafcadio Hearn, Edgar Saltus, and James Gibbons Huneker. Their significance to American literary history is debatable, but it must be acknowledged that they extended the range of literary expression in the United States by detaching writing from its stubbornly pragmatic roots. "Where literature had been traditionally connected with oratory and theology," Levin writes, "it could now be envisaged through its relation to purely artistic disciplines; hence the old-fashioned didactic presuppositions gave way to aestheticism" (Spiller et al. 1077–78).

According to the now-standard version of nineteenth-century U.S. cultural history, Americans sought to widen their artistic horizons with the wealth created by Gilded Age economic expansion, and the U.S. public, including American writers, traveled to Europe in unprecedented numbers. (Meanwhile, the number of European immigrants to the United States more than doubled between 1850 and 1900.) Alfred Kazin sums up the larger socioeconomic context for this literary sea change:

> Just as in the nineteen-twenties an esthetic revolution in American writing was to be effected by a few postwar expatriates, so cultural history was made in the [eighteen] nineties by the vast numbers (after 1892 the Customs Service could report more than 90,000 American citizens returning each year from Europe) who fled the country only because they could afford to live on [newfound wealth]. Like the Wyatts and Howards and Sidneys who helped to shape the Elizabethan Renaissance by their studies in Italy, the many young writers who now turned to Europe were the progenitors of an American Renaissance, the medium through which the new currents in European art and thought began to flow. (52)

I do not wish to quarrel here with Levin or Kazin—indeed, they draw attention to the easily overlooked fact that bohemian aestheticism facilitated the transnational flow of literary ideas and modes of expression during the latter half of the nineteenth century—but I do wish to complicate their version of events by pointing out a discrepancy between premodernist and modernist American literary bohemianism. Why is the transatlantic cultural flow so one-sided before 1900 and bidirectional since then? What cultural products became newly available for export, so to speak? If young writers at the turn of the century were the "progenitors of an American Renaissance," as Kazin argues, to what exactly are they giving birth?

This chapter explores these questions both historically and thematically. First, I look briefly at the history of "bohemian" as a social category in U.S. letters because the mythical tag indexes American cultural anxiety at the onset of the modernist era; the status of bohemians in American culture reveals the pains associated with modernism's birth in the United States. Then I examine several well-known (and a few lesser-known) bohemian artist narratives, as I dub them, to illustrate the theme's centrality to U.S. literary modernism and to suggest that these narratives signify literary emergence even at improbably late stages of American history, long after the United States rose to prominence as a military and economic world power. These texts chronicle how an artist is born into a philistine society that refuses to accommodate artists and is then symbolically reborn into a bohemian one that will. Bohemian artist narratives continually return to birth and rebirth motifs, including the symbolic erasure of genealogical lines of descent; the equation of reading and sex; the birth of books; and the strategic conflation of fiction and reality, of biological and cultural evolution, which (as I demonstrate in the next chapter) achieves material status in the *roman à clef.* These motifs are hardly unprecedented in literary history, and in fact they all date back several centuries at least. However, during the twentieth century, and in the bohemian artist narrative, these motifs cluster together to form an unmistakably modernist constellation. Each motif self-referentially points back to the text by naturalizing the tumultuous process of artistic creation, putting modernist narrative involution in the service of a potent critique of modernity. Rather than assume an "art for art's sake" aloofness, bohemian artist narratives celebrate lifestyles and social systems that cut across the grain of long-standing American ideologies, including the myths of unbroken descent from puritan and pioneer origins. Bohemianism muddies the waters from which American culture springs, so to speak. It becomes possible to discuss turn-of-the-century *American* literature with Kazin's confidence only because it is also possible to identify American *bohemians.* But a sweeping claim like this requires some explanation.

The against-the-grain structural logic of bohemian identity very closely resembles that of ethnic identity, and indeed sociologist R. A. Schermerhorn's definition of an ethnic group parallels Kreuzer's discussion of bohemianism in telling ways. Schermerhorn defines an "ethnic group" as "a collectivity within a larger society having real or putative common ancestry, memories of a shared historical past, and a cultural focus on one or more symbolic elements defined as the epitome of their peoplehood" (12).[1] I would like to suggest that the nineteenth-century American appropriation of bohemianism as a yardstick of aesthetic success or failure—Kazin's "American Renaissance"—should be seen as a specifically ethnic literary emergence. *All* American literature is ethnic literature to the extent that it self-consciously departs from English literary traditions, and the U.S. adoption of bohemian rhetoric represents an important step in this movement away from Anglo cultural hegemony. Literary history plainly documents that colonial and early national American writing developed quite consciously as an offshoot of global British culture. This condition created obvious problems for American cultural nationalists. Nineteenth-century discussions of U.S. art and literature increasingly responded to the question, "What should American art and literature look like?" In most cases, three emergent models predominate: American writers, nineteenth-century critics insist, should follow the Irish example, or the Russian example, or the French example. "Bohemianism" provides a convenient shorthand for the latter.

If bohemian artist narratives owe much to the French romanticization of the artist's lifestyle, then the rise of the genre in the United States indicates a step away from English influence. Versions of this last statement have been offered as both a lament and a celebration; bohemianism represents a form of redemption or a fall from grace. Since the mid-nineteenth century, U.S. writers and critics regularly gauged the New World artistic climate by measuring American culture against an Old World bohemian yardstick; depending on one's point of view, bohemianism has been seen as a national artistic call to arms or as the unhealthy influence of a foreign fad. The science is imprecise, but we can measure the shifting levels of American postcolonial apprehension by tracing the semantic naturalization of the French term into American English; that is, the range of linguistic associations attached to the word "bohemian" reveals how the concepts of artistic iconoclasm and cultural independence mingle and even overlap with their "antagonistic complimentaries," respectable imitation and artistic conformism.

At least since Hawthorne, American writers positioned bohemian idealism (however doomed to failure) against not just bourgeois materialism but, more specifically, against a crass, stifling puritanism, the arch-signifier in the American literary imagination of an English colonial legacy. We might read this posturing, following psychoanalyst George Devereux, as a form of "dissociative identity"; that is, as a form of identity predicated almost entirely on difference ("A is an X because he is not a Y"; "B is a Y by being a non-X" [411]). But I would like to insist on the specifics of an American context, and I further suggest that we locate U.S. bohemianism as a symptom of postcolonial anxiety (in the various senses supplied by critics as diverse as Harold Bloom and Frantz Fanon) with measurable effects both for good and for ill. As Lawrence Buell has shown, many of "the practices and innovations of the iconic figures of U.S. literary history arose out of 'a culture in which the ruled were constantly tempted to fight their rulers within the psychological limits set by the latter,' to quote Ashis Nandy's characterization of the intellectual climate of colonial India" (415). Bohemianism signals local resistance to global capitalism, including the Anglophone literary marketplace centered in London. I would agree with Buell that we cannot simply apply, *mutatis mutandis*, recent postcolonial theory to a turn-of-the-century United States; nevertheless, we must recognize that American bohemianism betrays a culture not quite sure of itself, even at the crest of its imperial project. To paraphrase Devereux: "bohemianism is American by being non-English"—a strikingly threadbare cultural nationalist flag to wave.

The bohemian artist narrative landed upon U.S. shores when *Knickerbocker Magazine* published Henri Murger's *Scènes de la Vie Bohème* in a serial translation entitled "The Gypsies of Art."[2] The series, translated by Charles Astor Bristed, a dilettante New York critic writing under the pen name Carl Benson, carried the first half of the episodic novel in semi-regular monthly installments between January 1853 and May 1854. (The first full-length English translation was published in London in 1887.) According to Bristed's prefatory note, *Scènes* "depicts very faithfully and effectively the precarious life of those literary and artistic vagabonds who, with nothing to support them but their wits . . . meanwhile exist from hand to mouth till their fortune takes a decisive turn one way or the other: either they work out for themselves a position and livelihood, or they break down altogether, and sink into utter misery and a premature grave" (12). This cautionary note, together with additional textual apparatuses accompanying the *Knick's* translation, function as a morality tale with a clear message: bohemianism does not pay, and what's more, it's un-American. More precisely: bohemianism runs counter to the expected values and behavior patterns of the Anglo-American middle class. Editorial footnotes offer pithy cultural translations along with strictly linguistic decoding; in one note, for example, Bristed shares his dim view of the French predilection for publicly flaunting love affairs: this practice is a "never-failing resource for a Frenchman, as it affords abundant food for his vanity, and scope for his imagination" (597). Just in case the reader is unsure of his disposition toward bohemian tales, Bristed adds in a translator's afterword, "In America, thank God! such a story would be unnatural." While his tone is sometimes tongue-in-cheek, Bristed earnestly argues that many of the scenes depicted in the novel are "very true in the *realist* sense" but are also unfaithful to the patrician ideals art is supposed to uphold; *Scènes* is "a legitimate expression of the realist school, but none the less revolting" (489).[3]

In the years between the U.S. publication of Murger's novel and the Civil War, the first bohemian club of note gathered at Pfaff's Cellar in New York, located one block from Washington Square. Remembered today for Whitman's membership, this group's activities are chronicled in a wide range of reminiscences, including Bayard Taylor's *Diversions of the Echo Club* (1876) and William Dean Howells's *Literary Friends and Acquaintance* (1900). At the center of this polyglot group of European and American poets and wits was Ada Clare (née Jane McElheney), the so-called Queen of Bohemia. (The King of Bohemia was journalist Henry Clapp.) According to historian Albert Parry, the "few Americans who had heard of Murger's *Scènes de la vie Bohème* were wont to associate Ada's type with the frivolous Musettes and Mimis of Paris. . . . While the first men of American Bohemia were met by the public with reserved awe, she was treated with unreserved suspicion. The heroines of Theodore Dreiser and Floyd Dell had not yet come to life" (16). We might expect that the U.S. public would view Clare through the distorting lens of Murger's rakish French heroines; after all, this earliest group of American bohemians thematized cultural dependence to sound a rallying cry against an unhealthy American philistinism, predicated as it was upon Victorian ideals.

In his *Harper's Monthly* short story "The Bohemian" (1855), Fitz-James O'Brien, an Irish American member of the Pfaff's circle, voiced his ambivalence toward bohemian pretensions by pointing out bohemianism's secondhand status in the New World. "When I say I am a Bohemian, I do not wish you to understand that I am a Zingaro. I don't steal chickens, tell fortunes, or live in a camp," sniffs the story's title character, Philip Brann. "I am a social Bohemian, and fly at higher game. . . . Have you read Henry Murger's *Scènes de la Vie de Bohéme*? . . . Well, then, you can comprehend my life." The bohemian then proceeds with a comprehensive list of the uncommercial, un-American activities that occupy his time and energy: "I am clever, learned, witty, and tolerably good-looking. I can write brilliant magazine articles. . . . I can paint pictures, and what is more, sell the pictures I paint. I can compose songs, make comedies, and captivate women" (235). O'Brien's "American" bohemian, a transplant from England, proclaims his individualism by saying that he is just like a character, indeed a caricature, from a novel about the Paris underworld—a most ironic declaration of cultural independence. In contrast, the unnamed narrator, an unsuccessful lawyer by profession, spends his idle time waiting for clients to appear and laboring over a formulaic historical tale for *Harper's.* "Bohemian" thus signals a departure from the utilitarian, anti-artistic (or at best consumerist) values of a waking industrial giant.

Murger insisted in his preface to *Scènes* that "Bohemia only exists and is only possible in Paris" (xxxvi). As with this example from O'Brien, most nineteenth-century bohemian artist narratives in the United States wish to prove Murger wrong by importing bohemia—with its attendant myths and stereotypes—from France. The hoopla surrounding the U.S. publication of George Du Maurier's *Trilby* provides a memorable example of the American public's growing fascination, perhaps even ease, with bohemianism by the end of the century. Du Maurier's episodic narrative about a Parisian laundress and artists' model (the title character), three bohemian British painters, and an unsavory Jewish mesmerist (Svengali) was serialized in *Harper's* beginning in January 1894. Almost overnight, "*Trilby*-mania" swept through the United States and across the Atlantic, giving Harper and Brothers the first international best-seller following the passage of the Copyright Act of 1891 and spawning a wide range of peculiar behavior in the wider U.S. culture.[4] In addition to rekindling the nineteenth century's anti-Semitism and fascination with hypnotism, *Trilby* also engendered a national foot fetish. Trilby becomes a model because her feet, although unbecomingly large, are nevertheless perfectly proportioned. (The British artist Little Billie, named after a lyric by Thackeray, sketches her foot on his apartment wall in a parody of the "birth of art" motif in painting.) Historian L. Edward Purcell records some of the more memorable occurrences inspired by the novel:

> A broadway caterer offered his customers ice cream molded in the form of Trilby's foot. A Chicago shoe manufacturer advertised a high-heeled ladies' model, "the Trilby," for $3.00. In Philadelphia, a bootmaker promised a set of the best quality Trilby style shoes ("of kid, satin or silk lined") to the woman who could most closely match the dimensions of Trilby's foot. As his ad said, "bear in mind ladies, it need not be the smallest feet that win, but the most perfect form of a foot." For a while it was fashionable for ladies to not only be shod in Trilby style but also to sport a silver scarf pin in the image of Trilby's "nude foot." Presumably such Trilby souvenirs could most appropriately be worn while dining on "Trilby Sausage" from a Philadelphia grocer and watching a

> bare-back circus rider performing in Trilby costume under the whip of a Svengali-clad ringmaster. (74)

The novel's curious relationship with American artistic values also registers in numerous parodies for the page and stage (not to mention later film versions of the novel); one of these, *Thrilby,* presented at New York's Garrick Theatre in June 1895, was billed as an "operatic burlesque" featuring a villainous "Spaghetti" who mesmerized chairs and tables (Purcell 70).[5] As if to underscore the American public's inadequate preparation for the bohemian dimensions of *Trilby,* at least two glossaries—offering explanatory notes for such phrases as "Quartier Latin" and "cuisine bourgeoise en bohème"—were published within a year of Du Maurier's novel.[6]

Trilby-mania stands as the signal moment in the lengthy bohemianization of America, but it was not until the twentieth century that Bohemia was fully Americanized, a process that is still ongoing. The very word "bohemian," much like "avant-garde," retains an unmistakable foreignness when used to describe U.S. culture. American letters gave the English language countless homespun alternatives to "philistine" by the early twentieth century—H. L. Mencken is personally responsible for a handful—but it was not until the 1950s and 1960s that American approximations of "bohemian" (such as "beatnik" and "hippie") entered into wide circulation. As late as the 1930s writers referred to Greenwich Village as the Latin Quarter of New York, and North Beach was called the Latin Quarter of San Francisco into the 1960s. Even today, nineteenth-century U.S. bohemians are discussed as American versions of their European counterparts: Huneker is the American Pater, Saltus the American Wilde. One is tempted to call Poe the American Valéry. And yet these estranging features of bohemianism in the United States—the social category's un-American flavor—lend themselves to revisionist cultural critique. In virtually all bohemian artist narratives, linguistic and psychological "foreignness" serve as the figurative doubles of literal immigration and exile.

Bohemian rhetoric invites immigration metaphors, so I will retain the figure for a moment longer. Bohemian artist narratives, fiction and nonfiction alike, often describe literal expatriation and other modes of social alienation as exile, even though legal banishment (or extreme physical threat) rarely describes the political context of bohemian expression. Much as Renato Poggioli observes of avant-garde movements, totalitarian states simply do not tolerate bohemian enclaves; these exist only in democratic societies that are willing to turn a blind eye to bohemianism's symbolic aggression against prevailing values. However, political facts rarely deter writers from imagining local bohemian subcultures as the Republic (or Kingdom) of Bohemia, and bohemian artist narratives lavish the attention of an anthropologist visiting exotic locales—a cold-water flat or an artists' café, the Latin Quarter or Greenwich Village—with thick descriptions of geographic and societal idiosyncrasies. Bohemia may be nowhere, but its boundaries are clearly marked by sight and sound and smell, and its inhabitants at any given moment inevitably look alike (at least to the untrained eye).

A fascination with differential boundaries, with the cues distinguishing "here" from "there"—as well as "us" from "them"—significantly informs texts ranging from James Weldon Johnson's *The Autobiography of an Ex-Colored Man* (1912), with its memorable scenes of ragtime folly in the "Club"; to Claude McKay's *Home to Harlem* (1928), with its blues-rich house parties and buffet flats; to John Clellon Holmes's *Go* (1952), with its "Go Hole," a dank and seedy Times Square bar where musicians play a "rebel and nameless" (161) modern jazz; to Diane Di Prima's *Memoirs of a Beatnik* (1969), with its "Pad," home to a group of promiscuous artists and wanderers. If we look beyond U.S. borders, we could just as easily substitute the semifictional, expatriate Paris of Ernest Hemingway and Henry Miller, of Mina Loy and Gertrude Stein. Literal and figurative geographies on both sides of the Atlantic have inspired many a travel guide and walking tour; more important, they insist that art and artists flourish not on Main Street but in the underground.

Johnson's novel, for example, investigates spatial oppositions on a number of levels: Europe versus America; North versus South; passenger train smokers versus second-class cars; Harlem versus downtown Manhattan. Perhaps the most important opposition Johnson explores in *The Autobiography* is the all-encompassing one of insider versus outsider. For most of the novel, the unnamed narrator utilizes his Du Boisian gift of "second sight" to expose cultural practices on both sides of the color line, a sharp divide that "gives to every colored man, in proportion to his intellectuality, a sort of dual personality." One side of a person's divided existence, he continues, "is disclosed only in the freemasonry of his race" (14). (When the novel was first published anonymously, as a bona fide autobiography, Johnson's publishers took up the metaphor in their preface: "In these pages it is as though a veil had been drawn aside: the reader is given a view of the inner life of the Negro in America, is initiated into the 'freemasonry,' as it were, of the race" [xxxiv].) But Johnson's novel is not just about initiation into the private lives of racialized subjects; it delves into a wide spectrum of activities that can also be described in terms of "freemasonry": musical apprenticeship; literacy; Spanish (and French and German) language immersion; cigar factory culture; African American salon society; and Paris café culture, to name only a few of the more obvious examples. The narrator carefully illustrates the physical layouts of several gin joints and gambling houses during his extensive travels through Europe and the United States, paying particular attention to the interior design of the "Club," New York's "center of colored Bohemians and sports" (76), which allows him to unpack the myriad layers of social meaning in the symbolically rich strata not visible from the outside. The narrator eventually concedes, "More that I learned would be better suited to a book on social phenomena than to a narrative of my life" (79).

Significantly, Johnson ushers the reader into this bohemian enclave by updating the European immigrant narrative tradition: the ex-colored man personifies New York City as an imposing enchantress, inviting comparisons to similar arrivals upon U.S. shores, which often include an immigrant's description of the Statue of Liberty upon first landing: "New York City is the most fatally fascinating thing in America. She sits like a great witch at the gate of the country, showing her alluring white face and hiding her crooked hands and feet under the folds of her wide garments—constantly enticing thousands from far within, and tempting those who come from across the seas to go no farther. And all these become the victims of her caprice" (65).[7] Traditionally a site for symbolic interaction between native and foreign, the Statue of Liberty undergoes a revisionist interpretation here; Johnson conflates European immigrants with naive visitors from the South and West to underscore the city's estranging distance from everyday American life. Because the ex-colored man wishes to expose the "dwarfing, warping, distorting influence" (14) of American racial attitudes, the attributes normally associated with Lady Liberty since Emma Lazarus—her inviting arms, her benevolent gaze—are turned on their head. Bohemia is a foreign land indeed; however, race-blind, bohemian inhibition proves no match in the end for Jim Crow.

It is literally in a foreign land that the real promise of bohemianism enters Johnson's novel most clearly. In Berlin, the ex-colored man and his millionaire employer fall in one night with "a party of men composed of artists, musicians, writers, and, for aught I know, a count or two" (103). The occasion is typically bohemian, with drinking and smoking and talk about art. When the discussion arrives at the subject of music, the "universal language" of bohemian artist narratives, the narrator suddenly experiences a career epiphany:

> My millionaire planned, in the midst of the discussion on music, to have me play the "new American music" and astonish everybody pres-

> ent. The result was that I was more astonished than anyone else. I went to the piano and played the most intricate ragtime piece I knew. Before there was time for anybody to express an opinion on what I had done, a big bespectacled, bush-headed man rushed over, and, shoving me out of the chair, exclaimed: "Get up! Get up!" He seated himself at the piano, and, taking the theme of my ragtime, played it through first in straight chords; then varied and developed it through every known musical form. I sat amazed. I had been turning classic music into ragtime, a comparatively easy task; and this man had taken ragtime and made it classic. The thought came across me like a flash—It can be done, why can't I do it? From that moment my mind was made up. I clearly saw the way of carrying out the ambition I had formed when a boy. (103–4)

When Carl Van Vechten read this passage, he inscribed in the margin of the text, "Rhapsody in Blue foreseen" (Sollors, *Beyond* 172). Unlike Gershwin, though, the ex-colored man experiences firsthand the trauma of racial violence and forsakes his cultural "birthright" for a life of unexamined philistine ease in a downtown firm. Ironically, the narrator's facility with the Spanish language allows his entrance into the New York financial world; this linguistic marker of cultural difference proves an asset rather than a liability, and it is nothing in comparison to a racial heritage that leaves no visible traces on his person. The novel's title fixes this last, impassable boundary with its emphatic *Ex-*, a firmly placed hyphen that insists finally that *The Autobiography* should never be mistaken for an immigrant narrative.

The "new Americanist" project abandoned by the ex-colored man—the cultivation of expressive forms that are at once bohemian *and* distinctively American—has preoccupied dozens (if not hundreds) of Americans writing in Johnson's wake. During the twentieth century, bohemian cultural critique was so thoroughly Americanized, in fact, that its transnational origins and affinities often fade from view. Ragtime music provides an early example of the "distinctive American products," as Johnson put it in *The Book of American Negro Poetry* (1922), that he would champion throughout his career; he also offers such goods as the cakewalk and spirituals for export across the Atlantic. Today an international countercultural argot—which is only possible in the wake of multinational commodity distribution systems—shows traces of earlier searches for an authentic "American" language, the verification that America had produced a New World race of men and women out of its colonial heritage. To be thus reborn is to reject one past and manufacture another; as Lauren Berlant writes in another context, "collective identity is equivalent to collective amnesia: patriotism"—or, she might add, bohemianism—"is constituted by the desire to overcome political and historical memory" (199). This willful forgetting, so often figured as rebirth, constitutes another key motif in bohemian artist narratives, framing a mirror image of M. L. Hansen's "Law" of immigrant generational declension: while the son wishes to forget the father, he chooses to remember the grandfather. That is, bohemian artist narratives thematize the rejection of the near past and the recuperation of a distant (even ancient) cultural heritage.

Shallow Pockets, Deep Genealogies

In his *Garrets and Pretenders* (1933), Albert Parry suggests why the adjective so easily transfers from person to person, nation to nation, age to age: "Bohemianism is not a class feature; its adherents are not a class because there is less of a hereditary character in their group than in any other group of society. Theirs is a temporary, flexible group. Very seldom are Bohemians the sons and daughters of Bohemians and begetters of Bohemians in their turn. Artists' cafés and attics are the meeting ground for many classes, the middle-class scions predominating" (xxiii). It remains possible to place bohemians in their historical context, and even to trace distinct lineages across time, as Parry and Emily Hahn have done for the American scene and still more have done for the European version, but often this proves a difficult task; after all, we tend to regard only the Whitmans of literary history and leave out of view the Clapps and Clares and countless latter-day beer-hall wits and coffeehouse poets. We separate the respectable wheat from its bohemian chaff. The difficulty resides, I believe, in the very structure of the bohemian artist narrative.

When his *Scènes* took the shape of a book in 1851, Murger, in a lengthy preface to the volume, clearly specified who was—and just as important, who was not—a "bohemian." Such people are not "the Bohemians whom melodramatists have rendered synonymous with robbers and assassins. Neither are they recruited from among the dancing-bear leaders, sword swallowers, gilt watch-guard venders, street lottery keepers and a thousand other vague and mysterious professionals whose main business it is to have no business at all" (xxxi). Thanks to Murger's novel and its many popular offshoots—from Puccini's opera to the recent film *Moulin Rouge*—"bohemian" does not refer to a race hailing from beyond the thick-wooded mountains separating Germany from the present-day Czech Republic; rather, the category applies to a class of rootless adventurers and artistic vagabonds. Rootless, but not without a past, an invented heritage. It is only natural that Murger, the son of a concierge and a dressmaker, would look beyond his immediate social circle to fashion a literary heritage:

> The class of Bohemians referred to in this book are not a race of to-day, they have existed in all climes and ages, and can claim an illustrious descent. In ancient Greece, to go no farther back in this genealogy, there existed a celebrated Bohemian, who lived from hand to mouth round about the fertile country of Iona, eating the bread of charity, and halting in the evening to tune beside some hospitable hearth the harmonious lyre that had sung the loves of Helen and the fall of Troy. Descending down the steps of time modern Bohemia finds ancestors at every artistic and literary epoch. In the Middle Ages it perpetuates the Homeric tradition with minstrels and ballad makers, the children of the gay science, all the melodious vagabonds of Touraine, all the errant songsters who, with the beggar's wallet and the trouvère's harp slung at their backs, traversed, singing as they went, the plains of the beautiful land where the eglantine of Clémence Isaure flourished. (xxxi)

After claiming Homer and similar vagabonds in this fashion, Murger adds more homebound figures, including Michelangelo and Rousseau, to his list of bohemians. Almost as important as describing the itinerant exploits of "modern" bohemians is the simple identification of bohemian counterparts and influences in cultural history—the location of "ancestors at every artistic and literary epoch." Repudiating one's fathers becomes a redundant enterprise in the wake of such genealogical self-fashioning. Thus, acknowledging the influence of a distant past ironically doubles as a register of contemporary avant-gardism.

Henry Miller wrote to Emil Schnellock in August 1931: "I start tomorrow on the Paris book: first person, uncensored, formless—fuck everything" (Gottesman 9). First published in Paris in 1934, *Tropic of Cancer* caused a considerable stir on both sides of the Atlantic, and its first U.S. edition, which appeared in 1961, was greeted with widely publicized and extensively documented controversy. Miller's obsessive attention to sexual reproduction and otherwise prurient details placed the novel on numerous censors' lists and, presumably, on the cutting edge of literary expression. For the past two centuries at least, such "honest" depictions of sex have been signposts of a text's modernity and even modernism; sex was, after all, one of the few significant categories remaining to be explored fully and objectively, so any candid portrayal of it constitutes an experiment. When the novel's first U.S. publisher,

Grove Press, came under fire in roughly sixty court proceedings, including famous obscenity trials in Boston, Chicago, and Los Angeles,[8] it enlisted the help of several well-known literary critics and college professors, including Harry Levin, Harry T. Moore, and Mark Schorer, each of whom testified for the unsuccessful defense in Boston. (A higher court later reversed the decision ruling *Cancer* obscene.) The defense strategy reveals an interesting paradox about the function of sex in Miller's novel: on the one hand, *Cancer* represents an avant-gardist "work of art written out of a spirit of anti-art," remaining truer to life for all its gritty, anti-academic realism, as Schorer told the court on 26 September 1961 (Wickes 162); on the other hand, as Levin argued two days later, there already existed "a well-authenticated literary category for the description of Parisian low life which goes back as far as the Middle Ages and to one of the great French poets, François Villon, who wrote very elegant poems about such themes as prostitutes." If *Cancer* is obscene, so too is a large chunk of Western literature. Levin goes on to note that "Bohemia—Paris as the Bohemian center for raffish artists—has been a theme ever since the novel, on which the more famous opera is based, came out in the middle of the nineteenth century" (Wickes 168–69).

Even before the trial, critics routinely viewed Miller and his work as the post-Freudian terminus of a distinguished line of (inevitably male) sensual realists. Beat poet Kenneth Rexroth argued in 1947 that "there aren't many people like Miller in all literature. The only ones I can think of are Petronius, Casanova, and Restif. They all tried to be absolutely honest. Their books give an overwhelming feeling of being true, the real thing, completely uncooked" (Gottesman 98). For George Orwell, the closest family resemblance to Miller's vividly experiential writing can be found in the poetry of Whitman, whose acceptance of any and all experience no longer proves tenable in a world defined by the horrors of modernity, "an epoch of fear, tyranny, and regimentation. To say 'I accept' in an age like our own is to say that you accept concentration camps, rubber truncheons, Hitler, Stalin, bombs, aeroplanes, tinned food, machine guns, putches, purges, slogans, Bedaux belts, gas masks, submarines, spies, provocateurs, press censorship, secret prisons, aspirins, Hollywood films, and political murders" (Wickes 40). *Cancer*'s narrator, Henry, is even more wide-ranging than the critics in fabricating an artistic genealogy; he scours the globe and the centuries for like-minded bohemians, his literary grandfathers:

> Today I am aware of my lineage. I have no need to consult my horoscope or my genealogical chart. What is written in the stars, or in my blood, I know nothing of. I know that I spring from the mythological

> founders of the race. The man who raises the holy bottle to his lips, the criminal who kneels in the marketplace, the innocent one who discovers that *all* corpses stink, the madman who dances with lightning in his hands, the friar who lifts his skirts to pee over the world, the fanatic who ransacks libraries in order to find the Word—all these are fused in me, all these make my confusion, my ecstasy. (259)

Henry acknowledges the cultural constructedness of his past, belonging as he does to a "race" invented by "mythological founders," forged perhaps in the smithy of their souls. More precisely, he traffics in the irony of identifying a "race" of literary vagabonds, although Miller's Whitmanesque effusions, here and elsewhere in *Cancer*, have a dead serious ring to them. Edmund Wilson described *Cancer* as "the epitaph for the whole generation of American writers and artists that migrated to Paris after the war" (Wickes 26), an epitaph, in other words, for the Lost Generation.

At one point in its history, Miller planned to call his novel *The Last Book*, and indeed its narrator augurs the significance of the aborted title: "Now we shall have a vessel in which to pour the vital fluid, a bomb which, when we throw it, will set off the world. We shall put into it enough to give the writers of tomorrow their plots, their dramas, their poems, their myths, their sciences. The world will be able to feed on it for a thousand years to come. It is colossal in its pretentiousness." Henry's ecstatic prophecy, like most utterances of this sort, betrays a sense of belatedness and a deep fear of cultural atrophy: "For a hundred years or more the world, *our* world, has been dying. And not one man, in these last hundred years or so, has been crazy enough to put a bomb up the asshole of creation and set it off. The world is rotting away, dying piecemeal. But it needs the *coup de grâce*, it needs to be blown to smithereens" (27). While literal sex in *Cancer* may be dehumanized and at times literally mechanical, figurative sex, like this pornographic Molotov cocktail, invokes the legacy and lessons of the past to instruct and reorder the future. The original and ongoing critical success of the novel derives at least in part from the lasting desire of avant-garde circles—we could add T. S. Eliot, Ezra Pound, and William Carlos Williams to the list of Miller admirers—to transform the world into a more experience- and expression-friendly place, to administer a cultural enema, so to speak.

It would be difficult to imagine an American writer further afield from Miller than Zora Neale Hurston, and it can almost surely be said that she never saw herself as embodying the same tradition that gave us *Cancer;* after all, she wrote at a time and from a position in which troubled U.S. race relations were an ever-present and unavoidable concern. As Hurston puts it in her memoir, *Dust Tracks on a Road* (1942), "Negroes were supposed to write about the Race Problem" (151). Nevertheless, *Dust Tracks*—subtitled "an autobiography" since its first edition—behaves in much the same way as Miller's autobiographical novel. First, the narratives fulfill the so-called autobiographical pact by tracing the development of an individual personality in the depiction of significant life events. Second, *Cancer* and *Dust Tracks* meander from sketch to sketch in picaresque fashion, although significantly neither achieves narrative closure with the expected marriage or with the uncovering of the protagonist's distinguished lineage. Third, both narratives focus attention on the debilitating effects of conformity to a time-honored American value, namely, the nativist belief, widespread since the late nineteenth century, that a celebrated ancestry (and perhaps early arrival in the New World) lends social status to individuals and to entire social classes.

Kazin observes of the American fin de siècle: "The sedulous imitation of Europe represented a significant reversion to colonialism not much different from the sudden passion of the upper middle classes for genealogical charts, family coats of arms, and the historical romances that now became the rage. The country was prosperous, smug, relaxed" (53). Just as Miller's novel on occasion laments the "puritanical buggers back home" (309) in America, so too does *Dust Tracks* take aim at "the better-thinking Negro" (or the "think-they-are-better Negroes"), those "who claim that they are descendants of royal African blood," for they "have taken a leaf out of the book of the white ancestor-hounds in America, whose folks went to England with William the Conqueror, got restless and caught the *Mayflower* for Boston, then feeling a romantic lack, rushed down the coast and descended from Pocahontas. From the number of her children, one is forced to the conclusion that Pocahontas wasn't so poky, after all" (147). In contrast, Hurston can "boast that I am the only Negro in the United States whose grandfather on the mother's side was not an Indian chief. Neither did I descend from George Washington, Thomas Jefferson, or any Governor of a Southern state. I see no need to manufacture me a legend to beat the facts" (171). As Werner Sollors argues, an American obsession with founding fathers derives in part from the belief that "ancestors may be adopted by consent" (*Beyond* 229); that is, Washington and Jefferson and the governor of a southern state represent an ancestral ideal to which putative descendants may aspire.[9] However, Hurston's tongue-in-cheek version of ancestor worship, in which she lampoons the lengths to which people go to establish descent lines (unfair though she may be to Pocahontas), constitutes an attack on blue-blood (and blue-vein) pretensions and implicitly critiques the larger value systems these pretensions serve. This estimate may not be bohemian in any obvious sense, but it is clearly anti-bourgeois. Françoise Lionnet describes Hurston's negative reconstruction of her lineage as "an effort to be *the* voice of [an] occluded past, to fill the void of collective memory" (118). If Hurston does not descend from Washington or Jefferson or Pocahontas, who then makes up her family tree? If, as Lionnet suggests, *Dust Tracks* is an "orphan text" simultaneously appealing to and debunking cultural traditions, who are Hurston's foster parents?

An early incident in *Dust Tracks* sets in motion the answer to these questions, an answer developed throughout the memoir. At school in Eatonville one day, the young Zora Neale impresses Mrs. Johnstone and Miss Hurd, two benevolent white women from Minnesota, and in the process Zora Neale acquires her first patrons. Soon the two women lavish upon her one hundred "goldy-new pennies," secondhand clothes, and most important, parcels of books: "In that box were Gulliver's Travels, Grimm's Fairy Tales, Dick Whittington, Greek and Roman Myths, and best of all, Norse Tales." Zora Neale feels more at home in the wondrous landscapes of Norse mythology than in the barren plains of the Bible or the "thin books about this and that sweet and gentle little girl who gave up her heart to Christ and good works" (38, 39). Even in a text claiming autobiographical authenticity, Hurston regularly blurs the line separating fact and fiction, literary memory and lived experience: "Why did the Norse tales strike so deeply into my soul? I do not know, but they did. I seemed to remember seeing Thor swing his mighty short-handled hammer as he sped across the sky in rumbling thunder, lightning flashing from the tread of his steeds and the wheels of his chariot" (39). The memoir naturalizes the dualistic tension between the dizzying promise of books and the sobering reality of life by rendering the dualism as the growing pains associated with artistic emergence: "In a way this early reading gave me great anguish through all my childhood and adolescence. My soul was with the gods and my body in the village. People just would not act like gods. Stew-beef, fried fat-back and morning grits were no ambrosia from Valhalla. Raking back yards and carrying out chamber-pots, were not the tasks of Thor. I wanted to be away from drabness and to stretch my limbs in some mighty struggle" (40–41). As central to the design of *Dust Tracks* as other motifs regularly cited by critics (such as migration, trains, and of course dust), this constant recognition of literary influence bears tremendous weight in Hurston's representation of the lifelong development of Zora Neale, would-be artist. Many times during the course of the memoir, an encounter with a new book takes on the significance of a ritual event in her life.

The impressive reading list assembled along the winding roads of *Dust Tracks* also includes Milton, Gray, and the more adventuresome parts of the Old Testament, and Zora Neale's initiation into the world of literature is accompanied by visions of her own future as a storyteller, visions that produce "a feeling of difference from my fellow men" (42). With each new example from Zora Neale's early reading, it becomes more apparent that her closest bonds are not with her family, nor are they with "My People! My People!" (as she explains in a chapter bearing that title); as in Miller's novel, Hurston constructs her identity not on strict biological kinship but on an imagined relationship with those whom she encounters on the page, with "fellow pilgrims on [her] strange road" (43). Intimacy with fictional worlds effects an equal and opposite reaction to social worlds, as though the laws of physics govern personal development. Henry Louis Gates Jr. argues in his review of the second edition of *Dust Tracks* (published as an afterword to the Harper reprint) that "many events in [the] text are figured in terms of Hurston's growing awareness and mastery of books and language, language and linguistic rituals as spoken and written both by masters of the Western tradition and by ordinary members of the black community" (264). *Dust Tracks* creates ample room for both "highbrow" literary and "lowbrow" folk expression, all the while relegating middlebrow culture—the legacy of Washington and Pocahontas—to the narrative's margins.

Hurston thus constructs an individuated self by contrasting conformity to middle-class ideals (religious faith, marriage and family life, material success) with decidedly non-utilitarian modes of discursive self-fashioning. She conceives of her literary awakening in terms of gaining access to geographically and temporally fluid voices as opposed to capitulating to the restrictions of place- and time-bound alternatives. Rather than signal the death of the author, intertextual moments in *Dust Tracks* denote artistic freedom, the freedom to read and write as an artist—indeed, they enable the "auto-" in Hurston's autobiography and index her emergence from the dirt roads of the South to national acclaim as a professional writer. (The *Saturday Review* fittingly bestowed upon *Dust Tracks* its $1,000 Anisfeld-Wolf Prize in 1942 for "contributions to the field of Race Relations.") Because *Dust Tracks* acknowledges literary influence to unhinge the narrative from time and place, almost all of the memoir's intertextual references reach back centuries. Hurston could have fashioned a similar critique of contemporary philistinism with more direct reference to the bohemian ways of her colleagues and, indeed, to her own lifestyle during her Harlem years.[10] Large portions of her original manuscript—cut before the book went to press and published for the first time in the recent edition assembled by her biographer, Robert Hemenway—detail her involvement in this symbolically potent milieu; however, even this material remains more a catalog of friends and patrons than an exposé of the bohemian underworld, as though Hurston wished not to compromise her position as story consultant at Paramount Studios (where she wrote much of the memoir) or jeopardize her future with the relatively conservative publishing establishment then taking the writer under its wing.[11] In more recent years, such careful cultivation of an inscrutable public image is not only detrimental to professional writing careers but even runs counter to an emergent trend in bohemian artist narratives. Lineages of bohemian writers and artists are no longer assumed to represent ancient idealism as opposed to latter-day capitulation to worldly interests. Bohemia has been so thoroughly Americanized that bohemianism per se instead represents the trappings of conformity to a new version of American ideological consensus. This proves especially true for American ethnic writers, who are understandably suspicious of the bohemian romanticization of U.S. minority cultures. By the 1960s or so it was common for American writers, particularly those associated with the Beat Generation, to assume naively that U.S. minority cultures held the key to the imaginary, carefree Republic of Bohemia. Not surprisingly, writers from these groups took issue with the kind of romantic racialism epitomized by Norman Mailer's "The White Negro" (1957).

In Oscar Zeta Acosta's *The Autobiography of a Brown Buffalo* (1972), for example, the semifictional persona who narrates Acosta's life story, Buffalo Zeta Brown, undertakes a spiritual odyssey in keeping with the now-classic narrative arc of bohemian vagabondage. *Brown Buffalo* culls its narrative from several Beat Generation mainstays—dank, seedy bars peopled with social misfits; free-love hippie communes; separatist bunkers loaded with acid rock LPs and paramilitary firearms; Mexican red-light-district cantinas—only to find each locale devoid of lasting meaning. For Buffalo, mere bohemianism stands for a desiccated cultural cliché, an absurd, empty pose:

> I speak as a historian, a recorder of events with a sour stomach. I have no love for memories of the past. Ginsberg and those coffee houses with hungry-looking guitar players never did mean shit to me. *They* never took their drinking seriously. And the fact of the matter is they got what was coming to them. It's their tough luck if they ran out on the road with bums like Kerouac, then came back a few years later with their hair longer and fucking marijuana up their asses, shouting Love and Peace and Pot. And still broke as ever. (18)

Critics have yet to reach a consensus regarding the genre of *Brown Buffalo,* opting for either satire or autobiography in most cases, as if the two were incompatible.[12] Each camp rests on solid ground, I believe, because the narrative repeatedly projects the psychological onto the social, so that the repair of the fractured self suggests the possibility of communal rebirth; in the words of Ramón Saldívar, *Brown Buffalo* articulates a "shared desire, itself related to the historical moment of the late 1960s and early 1970s, to fashion out of the instability and fragmentation of social life a utopian vision of collective action" (74). Significantly, though, *Brown Buffalo* refuses to accept this tempestuous historical moment on its own terms. The bohemian counterculture's drugs and booze feed a bilious, bloody ulcer, which also symbolizes Buffalo's relationship with U.S. and Mexican officialdom. As a burnt-out war-on-poverty lawyer, Buffalo is rejected by his chosen profession: "[Private attorneys] just love to get ahold of Legal Aid lawyers with our blue suits from Macy's and black ties. Can you imagine me having to argue with one of those guys? They never even taught me how to cross-examine hostile witnesses in the sleazy night school I attended. And do you think the silver-haired judges come to our assistance? Shit, they too are members of the local Bar. They despise us as much as anyone else" (22). So much for Buffalo's entry into mainstream U.S. society. And following a weeklong bender in Cuidad Juarez, across the Rio Grande from his boyhood home in El Paso, Texas, Buffalo is arrested after a minor scuffle at his cold-water hotel room and lectured by a Mexican judge: "If you're a lawyer, you should act like one. Cut your hair or leave this city. We get enough of your kind around here. You spend your money on the *putas* [prostitutes] and then don't even have enough to pay for your fines when you're caught with your pants down," the judge scolds, and adding insult to injury, she asks, "Why don't you go home and learn your father's language?" (193–94).

With failure heaped upon failure, Buffalo is at home neither in the United States nor in Mexico; his ultimate autobiographical insight, his healing vision, smacks of autobiographical conversion by fiat: "What I see now, on this rainy day in January 1968, what is clear to me after this sojourn is that I am neither a Mexican nor an American. I am neither a Catholic nor a Protestant. I am a Chicano by ancestry and a Brown Buffalo by choice" (199). Unfinished business is the only appropriate ending to a narrative that refuses to fulfill the autobiographical pact; for that we must await the sequel in Acosta's *The Revolt of the Cockroach People* (1973), in which the angst-ridden self-doubter emerges as a bona fide Chicano activist. In *Brown Buffalo,* meanwhile, Acosta recognizes that the Beat Generation's bohemian rejection of the American mainstream depends upon the promise Mexico holds as a new frontier (Kerouac calls it "one vast Bohemian camp" [*On the Road* 302]), a neocolonial imperative lacking the subtlety needed to account for a Brown Buffalo who finds an unsavory puritanism on both sides of the border.[13] The Americanization of bohemia depends upon the celebration of cultural difference, and in particular ethnic and racial difference, since there lies the great drama of U.S. cultural history, a ready-made "us versus them." Acosta realizes that this is the case and suggests that bohemianism performs its countercultural surgery with a rusty hacksaw.

The same holds true for Maxine Hong Kingston in her *Tripmaster Monkey: His Fake Book* (1989), in which Kingston thematizes the rejection of her Beat Generation predecessors to find inspiration instead in a nineteenth-century bohemian, Walt Whitman, after whom the novel's protagonist is named. Wittman Ah Sing, a would-be beatnik interpreter of the Chinese American experience, wanders along Market Street in San Francisco, filling his thoughts with a Kerouac poem. For Wittman, who is loosely modeled after ardent Kingston critic Frank Chin, this Beat icon offers an emasculating stereotype of Chinese manhood that must be erased: "If King Kerouac, King of the Beats, were walking here tonight, he'd see Wittman and think, 'Twinkling little Chinese.' Refute 'little.' Gainsay 'twinkling.' A man does not twinkle. A man with balls is not little. As a matter of fact, Kerouac didn't get 'Chinese' right either." Wittman's insights quickly evolve into an ethnic diatribe against the mainstream, "American" Kerouac: "Big football player white all-American jock Kerouac. Jock Kerouac. I call into question your naming of me. I trust your sight no more. You tell people by their jobs. And by their race. And the wrong race at that. If Ah Sing were to run into Kerouac—grab him by the lapels of his lumberjack shirt. Pull him up on his toes. Listen here, you twinkling little Canuck. What do you know, Kerouac? What do you know? You don't know shit. I'm the American here" (69–70). A fifth-generation Chinese American, Wittman claims his namesake's legacy—the "naming of me"—as his own. For Kingston as for Acosta, bohemia has by the end of the twentieth century become so thoroughly Americanized that it no longer lives up to the democratic promise of America.

Conjugate Relations: Having Books and Reading Sex

I am fascinated by the ease with which Roland Barthes introduces "transgressive" writing in terms of what he labels *jouissance,* a word translated variously as "bliss," "joy," or "coming" when translations are attempted at all.[14] In his influential *The Pleasure of the Text* (1973), Barthes replaces institutionally sanctioned modes of decoding an author's intention ("as institution, the author is dead: his civil status, his biographical person have disappeared" [27]) with an explicitly eroticized relationship between a liberated reader and a textual "body"; indeed, it is only the successful text, the text desiring the reader as much as it is desired by the reader, that can be said to be embodied at all. "You address yourself to me so that I may read you," Barthes writes in a metadiscursive passage that ventriloquizes both the reader's and the text's voice, "but I am nothing to you except this address; in your eyes, I am the substitute for nothing, for no figure (hardly that of the mother); for you I am neither a body nor even an object (and I couldn't care less: I am not the one whose soul demands recognition), but merely a field, a vessel for expansion. It can be said that after all you have written this text quite apart from bliss; and this prattling text is then a frigid text" (5). This dizzyingly self-referential performance has its closest analog perhaps in André Gide's *Les Faux-monnayeurs* (1925), a favorite of "death of the author" critics because its hyperkinetic self-referencing functions not simply as a mirror held up against the artist's lifestyle but also, as Levin aptly phrases it, as a kind of hall of mirrors: "By writing his novel about a novelist writing a novel . . . [Gide] demonstrated that first-person narrative may become a double mirror reflecting infinity" (323). I would argue, however, that what goes on in Barthes and certainly in Gide reflects concerns that extend beyond formal pyrotechnics.

The "death of the author" branch of poststructuralism—we might also look to Jacques Derrida or Michel Foucault—represents as timeless cosmopolitanism a rhetoric of sexual and textual play that enters modernist literary discourse in a genre vehicle, the bohemian artist narrative, that is very much concerned with geographic and temporal specificity, at least with respect to representing the means of literary production. As we saw in the narratives of Johnson, Miller, and Hurston, *who, what, when,* and *where* matter; in fact, these criteria constitute the narrative. The blissful text, Barthes maintains, transcends the "text of grammarians, critics, commentators, [and] philologists" just as the blissful body transcends the "body of anatomists and physiologists" (16). Need we add cultural historians? "The pleasure of the text," he continues, "is that moment when my body pursues its own ideas—for my body does not have the same ideas I do" (17).[15] Where Barthes figures the solipsistic reading act as a bodily textual (and thus sexual) encounter, bohemian artist narratives imagine the social consequences of textual play by sexually charging the theme of literary production and consumption—"bliss" in such narratives rarely occurs in a social vacuum. Constant attention to sex and birth and rebirth motifs serves a larger political cause, dramatizing modernism's challenge to the literary institutions (including those killed off by "death of the author" criticism) engendered by modernization.

It is well worth noting that the Lost Generation, for all its masculinist posturing, remains perhaps the only literary generation birthed and reared by a lesbian couple, Gertrude Stein and Alice B. Toklas. Their efforts on behalf of figurative progeny—including painters, sculptors, writers, and soldiers—are chronicled in one of the earliest modernist literary memoirs, Stein's *The Autobiography of Alice B. Toklas* (1933), whose marketplace success spawned an avalanche of similar efforts to record life on the Left Bank and in other bohemian quarters.[16] As in most bohemian artist narratives, *The Autobiography* carefully dismantles and reconstructs Stein's artistic genealogy so that she can emerge as modernism's first authentic voice.[17] "Making herself into her own and everybody else's pseudomale precursor," Sandra Gilbert and Susan Gubar observe, "[Stein] definitively inherited the place of the father in order to put all the men she knew in their properly dependent places. From Freud's point of view, the 'masculinity complex' could be carried no further. The father had been turned into a fat-her" (1:188). Like Virgil Thompson, who described Stein as a "Founding Father of her century" (Stein, *Selected* xx), Gilbert and Gubar somewhat overstate the case; clearly, though, the "Gertrude" viewed through the eyes of the "Alice" persona engages the early-twentieth-century artworld from a paternalistic if not a fatherly standpoint; indeed, the complex landscapes of art exhibitions and galleries, of artists and buyers and go-betweens, are very much institutions of her own making. (It is no surprise then that Linda Wagner-Martin's recent biography of Stein is subtitled "Gertrude Stein and Her Family.")

Gertrude even exerts parental control where she feels least at ease, in the transatlantic literary marketplace. Throughout *The Autobiography,* key American writers, including the young Hemingway, seek her parental guidance and approval: "Gertrude Stein and Sherwood Anderson are very funny on the subject of Hemingway. The last time that Sherwood was in Paris they often talked about him. Hemingway had been formed by the two of them and they were both a little proud and a little ashamed of the work of their minds" (114). During the course of the narrative, Gertrude signals her pleasure and displeasure with her figurative son, and she never hesitates to upbraid him when he falls out of line: "Hemingway, after all you are ninety percent Rotarian" (220); "Gertrude Stein said, Hemingway, remarks are not literature" (219); "And that is Hemingway, he looks like a modern and he smells of the museums" (216). Gertrude can be far more generous, however, when she so chooses. Not only does Gertrude patronize such ultimately triumphant figures as Picasso and Matisse, but she and Alice invite them into their art-filled home, nourishing them with food and with less tangible but more lasting inspiration, including, in Hemingway's specific case, career advice ("if you keep doing newspaper work you will never see things, you will only see words and that will not do, that is of course if you intend to be a writer" [213]) and stylistic models ("in correcting [Stein's] proofs Hemingway learned a great deal and he admired all that he learned" [217]).

Alice describes her introduction in 1907 to life at 27 rue de Fleurus as encountering "the vie de Bohème just as one had seen it in the opera" (18), but her role in this drama unfolds as the dutiful and doting wife who enables the free range of Stein's "genius"—Alice is the woman behind the woman, so to speak. Just as lesbianism in *The Autobiography* is sublimated into domestic routine, and arguably into a routine defined by regressive gender role-playing,[18] so too is the analogy between sex and artistic production confined to strictly figurative relationships. The pseudo-fictive mode of narration in *The Autobiography,* however, renders incomplete any strictly figurative reading of the text; or I should say, we must read "figuratively" in the sense supplied by Paul Ricoeur: "The very expression 'figure of speech' implies that in metaphor, as in other tropes or turns, discourse assumes the nature of a body by displaying forms and traits which usually characterize a human face, man's 'figure'; it is as though the tropes gave to discourse a quasi-bodily externalization" (142). Stein's narrative ventriloquism in *The Autobiography* invites just such an analysis, for it requires the reader to jettison any heteronormative assumptions about the relationship between writing and sex and imagine the generative possibilities of a tranquil, same-sex domestic partnership. A number of critics have addressed the question of whether the narrator of *The Autobiography* more closely resembles the authorial voice of Stein or of Toklas, but Harriet Scott Chessman offers a more fitting alternative when she argues that Stein transfigures "the concept of single voice and authorship into a richly doubled authorial identity," that Stein prevents " 'one' from subverting the more utopian possibility of 'two' " (62). If by an act of textual ventriloquism Gertrude and Alice merge into a doubled authorial voice, so too can it be said that their bodies occupy the same figurative space—the space of the writer's kitchen or the cook's atelier—with the body of the wife blurring into the body of the genius in an almost coital relationship.

By dramatizing the conditions in which it was conceived and written, *The Autobiography* demonstrates how a relatively straightforward rendition (at least when compared to Stein's more experimental prose) of domestic life among the "wives of geniuses" (87) slips effortlessly into moments of hyper-involuted, metanarrative commentaries about the act of narration. Stein blurs the lines between the text's major characters, Alice and Gertrude, and suggests that a similarly indeterminate relationship exists between their "real life" counterparts, Toklas and Stein. In a scene aptly described by Margot Norris as an allegory for the "competition between fine art and domestic art staged as a marital quarrel" (91), Alice prepares a hot meal and calls Gertrude in from the atelier, where she has been busy at work, for supper. "She came in much excited and would not sit down," Alice writes (or says—the conversational tone makes the narrative difficult to categorize). "Here I want to show you something, she said. No I said it has to be eaten hot. . . . In spite of my protests and the food cooling I had to read. I can still see the little tiny pages of the note-book written forward and back. It was the portrait called Ada, the first in Geography and Plays. I began it and thought she was making fun of me and I protested, she says I protest now about my autobiography. Finally I read it all and was terribly pleased with it. And then we ate our supper" (114).

Much of the commentary on this passage centers on the question of Stein's capitulation to traditional gender roles and power relations, her "masculinity complex," as Gilbert and Gubar phrase it.[19] I would like to approach the scene from another angle by pointing out how this passage refuses to cooperate with any clear-cut ascription of roles, gendered or otherwise. Stein complicates already ambiguous pronominal relationships (to whom does "she" refer in a room with two women, where one masquerades as the other?) by superimposing disgust and pleasure onto the reading act: just as I am tempted to replace the many "she's" and "I's" in this short but tricky excerpt with [Gertrude] and [Alice], so too does Alice wish to read herself into the "Ada" portrait, to identify with a "fictional" character. Alice's protests against Gertrude's dismissive attitude toward the food laid out on the table are doubled by her protests against what she perceives as an unfair literary depiction (in "Ada"), which are doubled once more by her protests against the text (*The Autobiography*) in which the initial protests are represented. Stein's prose invites us into the kitchen, and we read over Alice's shoulder only to realize that a touching scene of domestic difficulty and reconciliation is taking place within arm's reach. If I were to replace the pronouns with character names, the most fascinating line in this passage would read: "Alice began 'Ada' and thought Gertrude was making fun of Alice and Alice protested, Gertrude says Alice protests now about Alice's *The Autobiography of Alice B. Toklas.*" The text invites us into the kitchen, but we are left with the questions, Who is the wife, and who the genius?

Who indeed? Gender and sexual role-playing in *The Autobiography* need not be located entirely on a twice-removed figurative level as I have thus far indicated. The final, quintessentially self-referential clause of Stein's narrative, " . . . this is it," issues from the same quirky Alice persona who begins the book with the quintessentially autobiographical gesture, "I was born . . . " (252, 3). In the last few paragraphs of the memoir, Stein finally exposes the "lie" that has governed the narrative from its beginnings; that is, Stein "outs" herself as the true author of the book and as the life partner of Toklas. Among the titles Gertrude proposes for the book Alice never writes (although Toklas did publish her own memoir, *What Is Remembered,* in 1963) are *My*

Life With the Great, Wives of Geniuses I Have Sat With, and *My Twenty-five Years With Gertrude Stein* (251), the latter a revealing indication of the pair's sexual orientation. *The Autobiography* concludes:

> When Ford Madox Ford was editing the Transatlantic Review he once said to Gertrude Stein, I am a pretty good writer and a pretty good editor and a pretty good business man but I find it difficult to be all three at once.
>
> I am a pretty good housekeeper and a pretty good gardener and a pretty good needlewoman and a pretty good secretary and a pretty good editor and a pretty good vet for dogs and I have to do them all at once and I found it difficult to add being a pretty good author.
>
> About six weeks ago Gertrude Stein said, it does not look to me as if you were ever going to write that autobiography. You know what I am going to do. I am going to write it for you. I am going to write it as simply as Defoe did the autobiography of Robinson Crusoe. And she has and this is it. (251–52)

Many critics seize upon Stein's comparison of *The Autobiography* and *Robinson Crusoe* as an open acknowledgment of the narrative's fictiveness, which certainly rings true—after all, both texts begin simply enough with "I was born." Others notice that Stein asserts her identity as a professional author by casting it against the backdrop of Toklas's mastery of domestic duties, which is also clearly the case. If we take the intertextual reference seriously, we might also recall Crusoe's tender (and even homoerotic) three-year relationship with "his man" Friday. And yet Stein significantly casts Toklas in the role of Crusoe, who according to the logic of Defoe's novel is "pretty good" at every enterprise he undertakes, from establishing a primitive economy to fending off hordes of cannibals to "authoring" what would become one of the most successful novels in the history of English literature. Stein's self-referentiality prohibits any simple ascription of textual ownership—it is, as this passage and the title of the book insist, Alice's autobiography. Stein's name does not even appear on the title page of the first edition. In the confusion engendered by textual play, in the rupture opened by authorial self-sacrifice, Stein envisions a literary birth: opposite "this is it" on the final page of the first edition, the book reprints the first page of her manuscript, which begins, of course, with "I was born." Improbably, Stein's lesbian life partnership begets *The Autobiography.*[20]

Another U.S. writer nurtured by Stein (in a manner of speaking) was Scott Fitzgerald, about whom she writes in *The Autobiography:* "Gertrude

Stein and Fitzgerald are very peculiar in their relation to each other. Gertrude Stein had been very much impressed by This Side of Paradise. She read it when it came out and before she knew any of the young american [*sic*] writers. She said of it that it was this book that really created for the public the new generation" (218). Upon its debut in April 1920, Fitzgerald's *This Side of Paradise* was read "generationally" to the extent that it exposed parents to such shocking behavior as premarital kissing and petting parties attended by youths "hipped on Freud," hardly the kind of bohemian revelry readers would come to expect by the time Stein's memoir appeared just over a decade later. "The book caused a shudder to run down the national spine," Frederick Lewis Allen observed. "It was incredible. It was abominable. What did it all mean? Was every decent standard being thrown over?" (75, 76). *This Side of Paradise* steps beyond the confines of midwestern debutante society to represent late-night Manhattan debauchery on the eve of Prohibition, and even refers directly to a statute (the Mann Act) designed to eradicate white slavery. Here, though, I will focus attention on another quasi-bohemian aspect of the novel, namely, its fascination with the relentless social posturing that takes place within Princeton's undergraduate dormitories. Fitzgerald specifically contrasts the homosocial world of Princeton aesthetes and decadents during World War I with "Philistine Princeton of two years before" (103). A key part of the artistic and political development of Amory Blaine, the novel's protagonist, is his extracurricular passion for "the misty side-streets of literature: Huysmans, Walter Pater, Théophile Gautier and the racier sections of Rabelais, Boccaccio, Petronius and Suetonius" (103).

Most of the educating in Fitzgerald's novel of education takes place in the dorm room rather than in the classroom, and important scenes within the utopian confines of "12 Univee" tacitly acknowledge the sexual dimension of pedagogical exchanges between social equals. Amory and his closest companion, Thomas Parke D'Invilliers—the characters are modeled after Fitzgerald and his Princeton classmate John Peale Bishop—spend much time discussing and reading aloud their own and others' literature in Tom's dorm room, which the two adorn in typical fin de siècle fashion: "Together they gilded the ceiling of Tom's room and decorated the walls with imitation tapestry, bought at an auction, tall candle sticks and figured curtains" (55). Amory and Tom first met at Joe's, a local diner that allows freshmen to escape "curious upperclass eyes," in a scene that very closely resembles a barroom pickup. There is one important difference, though: the young men's eyes and their conversation continually return to books: "By and by Amory's eyes wandered curiously to his fellow luncher's book"; "Moved to address his vis-à-vis he simulated interest in his book"; "'Are you referring to your bacon buns?' . . . 'No,' Amory answered. 'I was referring to Bernard Shaw' "; "They sallied into a discussion of poetry in the course of which they introduced themselves, and Amory's companion turned out to be none other than 'that awful highbrow,' Thomas Parke D'Invilliers, who signed the passionate love poems in the 'Lit' "; " 'Yes, that's the fella. I've just finished a book of his, 'The Picture of Dorian Gray,' and I certainly wish you'd read it. You'd like it . . . Don't you want to come up to the rooms? I've got a few other books' " (53, 54, 55). After carefully weighing how his new friendship will play out in the eyes of his classmates, including the "magnificent, exquisite Humbird" and other prep school alums, Amory is overcome by Tom's "undoubted attractions and value" (55) and follows Tom out of the diner and back to the dormitory, where he is introduced to Wilde and Swinburne, Keats and Chesterton, Yeats and Synge and the Savoy Operas.[21]

Significantly, Fitzgerald does not draw the line in this equation of reading and sex at sexually charged discussions between college mates; he further suggests that a similar relationship exists between the individual reader and the textual body. A character reading in *This Side of Paradise* does more than simply double the solipsistic act of an "actual" reader holding the novel; Fitzgerald's characters also dramatize the socially significant act of denying an inadequate literary paternity and replacing this with one truer to the shared ideals of a bohemian elite; that is, Amory and company choose their ancestors by reading them. In the course of Amory and Burne Holiday's sometimes heated and always disturbing discussion on "the matter of the bearing of physical attributes on a man's make-up" (122), Burne (a Marxian radical character based on another Princeton classmate, Henry Strater) tries to distill the ideal physiognomy from the photographs of his literary heroes. While Burne's methodology reeks of nineteenth-century pseudoscience—in important ways Burne is a thinking man's Tom Buchanan—Burne's reading list tends toward the bohemian, and his affections are unmistakably eroticized:

> "It's true," Burne agreed. "The light-haired man *is* the higher type, generally speaking. I worked the thing out with the Presidents of the United States once, and found that way over half of them were light-haired—yet think of the preponderant number of brunets in the race."
>
> "People unconsciously admit it," said Amory. "You'll notice a blond person is *expected* to talk."
>
> "And the large mouth and broad chin and rather big nose undoubtedly make the superior face."
>
> "I'm not so sure." Amory was all for classical features.

> "Oh yes—I'll show you," and Burne pulled out of his desk a photographic collection of heavily bearded, shaggy celebrities—Tolstoi, Whitman, Carpenter and others—
>
> "Aren't they wonderful?"
>
> Amory tried politely to appreciate them, and gave up laughingly.
>
> "Burne, I think they're the ugliest-looking crowd I ever came across. They look like an old men's home."
>
> "Oh Amory look at that forehead on Emerson; look at Tolstoi's eyes." His tone was reproachful.
>
> Amory shook his head.
>
> "No! Call them remarkable-looking or anything you want—but ugly they certainly are."
>
> Unabashed, Burne ran his hand lovingly across the spacious foreheads, and piling up the pictures put them back in his desk. (122–23)

This exchange—with dialogue in the tone of a lover's spat, and fraught with tension between the democratic idealism of Emerson and Whitman and the unabashedly racist elitism of Amory and Burne—suggests that the self-selected bohemian legacy can actually transfer phenotypic traits across time via the act of reading. That is, the more bohemian texts one encounters, the more that person bears a physical resemblance to her or his bohemian literary forebears. Burne does in fact grow more and more "shaggy" during the course of the novel. The solitary reading act thus functions as a means of genetic re-encoding, as if DNA could be transferred from the cells of (in this example) Whitman, onto the pages of *Leaves of Grass,* and into the cells of Burne.[22] *This Side of Paradise* eerily literalizes Whitman's injunction (in "Whoever You Are Holding Me Now in Hand") to his future readers: "thrusting me beneath your clothing, / Where I may feel the throbs of your heart or rest upon your hip, / Carry me when you go forth over land or sea / . . . And thus touching you would I silently sleep and be carried eternally" (271). For both Whitman and Fitzgerald, sexual relations can and do occur transgenerationally, in the appropriately seductive reading act.

Sexual and textual play rise to the narrative surface in Hemingway's posthumously published memoir, *A Moveable Feast* (1964). (He wrote a satiric precursor, "The Autobiography of Alice B. Hemingway," in the early 1930s [Tavernier-Courbin 7].) In the memoir's first chapter, "A Good Café on the Place St.-Michel," Ernest carefully outlines the manner in which he wrote "Up in Michigan," a story about a young woman's first sexual encounter that was collected in Hemingway's debut book, *Three Stories and Ten Poems* (1923). Over a café au lait and two rums St. James on a cold, wet autumn day,

Ernest, pencil in hand, transcribes the inhospitable Paris climate into his notebook: "I was writing about up in Michigan and since it was a wild, cold, blowing day it was that sort of day in the story" (5). As the rum penetrates "all through [his] body and [his] spirit," a pretty French girl enters the café and seats herself at a table nearby. "I looked at her," writes Ernest, "and she disturbed me and made me very excited. I wished I could put her in the story, or anywhere, but she had placed herself so she could watch the street and the entry and I knew she was waiting for someone. So I went on writing" (5). Ernest's desire to include the girl in his story not only introduces a gesture of self-referentiality but also mirrors the desires of a number of Hemingway's fictional heroes, who would take up the pencil and write—if only they could.

Each time he looks up at the girl, Ernest sharpens the embarrassingly phallic tool in his fingers, its shavings "curling into the saucer" on the table. "You belong to me," he thinks as he writes and looks at the girl, "and all Paris belongs to me and I belong to this notebook and this pencil" (6). Hemingway could scarcely be any more heavy-handed in equating writing with sexual intercourse:

> Then I went back to writing and I entered far into the story and was lost in it. . . . Then the story was finished and I was very tired. I read the last paragraph and then I looked up and looked for the girl and she had gone. I hope she's gone with a good man, I thought. But I felt sad.
>
> I closed up the story in the notebook and put it in my inside pocket and I asked the waiter for a dozen *portugaises* and a half-carafe of the dry white wine they had there. After writing a story I was always empty and both sad and happy, as though I had made love, and I was sure this was a very good story although I would not know how truly good until I read it over the next day. (6)

Donald Pizer comments on this scene: "The incident is beautifully apparent. The act of writing well, with one's sharpened pencil, is like the act of making love to an attractive girl" (174). Beyond mere appearances, though, this example from *A Moveable Feast* incorporates two key elements commonly found in bohemian artist narratives that deploy the motif of reading and writing as sex.

First, by suggesting a link between a "good man" and "good writing," Hemingway opens up the possibility that "bad men" produce "bad writing"; more precisely, his protean "good" sets up the analogy that good sex is to literature as bad sex is to pornography or pulp. Second, by aligning the successful writing act with a feeling of postcoital letdown, a sense of being "empty and both sad and happy" at once, Hemingway figures his story as a fluid cut loose from the body from which it issues (and later replaced with wine and oysters); the text is an organic entity entirely set apart from its creator—hence his need to "read it over the next day" to verify the story's literary merit. Ezra Pound had a similar idea in mind when, in the postscript to his 1922 translation of Remy de Gourmont's *The Natural Philosophy of Love* (1903), Pound surmised that the human brain originally grew out of "a sort of great clot of genital fluid held in suspense or reserve" (149).[23] In a typically Poundian instance of misogynistic mythologizing, the father of imagism equates "the power of the spermatozoide" with "the power of exteriorizing a form" (149). This mode of representing textual and sexual output often evolves into a related (and not necessarily sexist) motif common in bohemian artist narratives, in which writing and publishing are figured as childbirth.

By imagining reading and writing in terms of transhistorical sexual relations, the bohemian artist narrative sets itself in opposition to the mode of mass production and marketplace institutions upon which commercial literary success depends. To "conceive" of a text as a thing birthed and not as a thing made figuratively rescues art by freeing it from the burden of "practical" or "vulgar" responsibilities to society at large. Peter Bürger's critique of the modernization of literary institutions is particularly instructive on this point:

> Like the categories of genius and contemplation, the concept of the work of art as an organic totality is opposed to the principle of formal reason. The machine, not the organism, is the most advanced result of rational planning of production. Man is not able to create organisms. To consider the work of art as an organism, or an organic totality, means to separate it from the area of normal human production and to assign it to a quasi natural status. Here the categories of the organic work of art and the genius are linked. Only the genius is able to create objects totally different from those which can be produced by rationally planned human activity. ("Literary" 431–32)

In bohemian artist narratives, as in Bürger's analysis, artistic activity serves as the counterpoint to mechanistic production in the cacophony of modernization. The naturalization of literary creativity as birth or rebirth allows for the intersection of bohemianism's symbolic aggression toward bourgeois society with the bohemian clichés of sexual libertinism and social aloofness. Returning very briefly to Pound—whose goal in translating Gourmont was (no doubt) to unleash human sexuality in the English-speaking world from its Victorian garments—we encounter an almost implausibly schematic version of the organicist aesthetic outlined by Bürger. "Thought is a 'chemical process' in relation to the organ, the brain," Pound argues, adding, "creative thought is an act like fecundation, like the male cast of the human seed, but given that cast, that ejaculation, I am perfectly willing to grant that the thought once born, separated, in regard to itself, not in relation to the brain that begat it, does lead an independent life much like a member of the vegetable kingdom, blowing seeds, ideas from the paradisal garden at the summit of Dante's Mount Purgatory, capable of lodging and sprouting where they fall. And Gourmont has the phrase 'fecundating a generation of bodies as genius fecundates a generation of minds'" (152).

Bohemian artist narratives, to which Pound's pseudoscientific ramblings peripherally belong, modernistically sacrifice the author to an "interplay of signs" (as Foucault puts it ["What" 102]), but in so doing they reinforce the split between textual play and socially sanctioned (especially practical) writing. Into this chasm—the conceptual space between the bohemians and the philistines—we are forced to project authorial "genius." Pound and Bürger obviously share my fascination with etymology, so I will make explicit what they only suggest. The term "genius," with roots in the Greek verb for birth and becoming (γίγνομαι), derives more immediately from the Latin term for the guardian spirit present at childbirth, able to govern an individual's fortune and determine her or his lifelong character. The concept of the artistic genius, as Adorno points out in *Aesthetic Theory,* rose out of Kant's "fetishization of dirempted, abstract subjectivity," and it further "spawns the ideology of the organic and unconscious artwork" (170, 171). Moreover, Adorno illustrates how genius—as we saw in Stein's memoir—"suppresses the element of finite making, the τεκνη in artworks, in favor of their absolute originality" (170). Genius thus sits at the opposite end of the aesthetic spectrum from a "desolate, pedantic arts-and-crafts mentality devoted to tracing out stencils" (171). And yet the ideology of the genius partially surrenders the creative self in its insistence that the artwork exists apart from rationally planned human activity. Genius identifies the artist with the divine, but ironically her or his artwork, once in public circulation, "lives" an existence free from an artist's biography and (so the myth goes) independent of the public's whims. This is particularly true in bohemian artist narratives, which insist on reading and writing as sexually charged, and therefore inherently social, acts that direct antagonism against the larger social context in which reading and writing occur. In the next part of this chapter, then, I will examine how modernist writers put themselves in the figurative position of a text's begetter and guardian, and suggest why a writer would sacrifice the self for her or his book.

Birthing Books

In the fifth issue of *Contact,* published in June 1923, William Carlos Williams daringly compares the pages of the journal he co-founded with Robert McAlmon to a kind of honeymoon suite, or at least to the bed in that chamber. To read the little magazine, he suggests, approximates the sexual act: "When man or woman climbs into the pages of a magazine it should be with that same enlargement of the intelligence accessible to the young when they first climb into bed with each other." There can be no doubting what it means for a man and woman to climb into bed, but it remains unclear what it means to climb into the pages of a magazine. Does this metaphorize reading, writing, or publishing, or perhaps all three? "That time past," Williams adds, as though this quasi-erotic experience is shut off beyond a certain age, "men feel lesser things: less important magazines," and at this point the elliptical prose of Williams's sexually charged philosophy of reading evolves into poetry and back into prose again:

> the thing Lord Byron prolonged
> into banality —
> Spring
> Too long
> Gongola
>
> the thing, BEAUTY: climax of the intelligence. NOT truth. The thing that linked Shelley with Byron—which he (Shelley) too failed to identify when he coined his famous hyphenate: Intellectual-Beauty.
>
> ANYHOW—"A poet is a maker, as the word signifies: and he who cannot make, that is invent, hath his name for nothing." ("Glorious" n.p.)

The moment of intellectual "enlargement" akin to the sexual act represents for Williams a historical period come and gone; he relegates the "thing Lord Byron prolonged" to youthful indiscretion, and he finds the Keatsian (and Shelleyan and Byronic) romantic construct ("Beauty is truth, truth beauty") irrelevant these days because Williams overloads one-half of the chiastic crux ("beauty"), only to find the other half ("truth") irrelevant to modern art, including poetry.

Truth need not sully aesthetic judgment, Williams suggests; it is an unwelcome distraction because intellectual projection on the part of the poet, no matter how ornate (even gongoristic) the form, denies the "thingness" of the art object.[24] Byron's error of excess can be purged by the modernist preoccupation with formal self-sufficiency and self-reference: "What has happened has been a renewal, a reaffirmation, a reclarification of pure form in composition; a broadening of the field of choice among materials. The thing that has been said over and over again is that whatever the material (and this is the modern variant) all in the work must tend to relate to an intrinsic unity and not to anything outside itself." Nevertheless, Williams insists on a "practical attitude toward writing as against the front of 'pure aesthetics'" ("Glorious" n.p.). Williams's "thing" proves an unstable category precisely because an object's "thingness" remains contingent on historical and geographic specifics; to every age there is an appropriate "thing," whether this takes the shape of "Spencer's EPITHALEMION [*sic*]" or "Poe's ANNABEL LEE" (his examples in the essay).

Williams's logic reveals itself as much in the tendency toward internal rhyme and end rhyme in lines of poetry clipped at one, two, or three syllables as in the organicist aesthetic he offers with a tinge of reluctance. "Spring / Too long / Gongola" stands as a formal approximation of affective surplus—a modernist baby without the romantic bathwater—and the three lines strain to bear their (romantic) thematic weight in such a narrow (modernist) formal vessel. And yet here and elsewhere Williams invokes the notion that successful poetry creates a parallel universe ("an intrinsic unity") apart from the time and conditions with which poets and poetry come into contact, the "heterocosmic" aesthetic that M. H. Abrams identifies as central to romantic theory. Moreover, Williams adopts what I call the "birth-of-books motif" that first proliferated (as Margaret Helen Dupuis has shown) in Anglophone literature in early modern England, only to resurface in updated form in the early twentieth century; that is, he represents writing and publishing as a version of natural childbirth, with all its difficulties and its promise. In the pages of *Contact* alone, Williams frequently returns to the figure of artistic inspiration and creation as insemination, gestation, and birth.[25]

"In exploiting his position in America the artist, aware of the universal physical laws of his craft, will however take off only from the sensual accidents of his immediate contacts," Williams writes in the fourth issue of the journal, published in 1921. "The achievement of a *locus*, Contact has maintained, is the one thing which will put his work on a comparable basis with the best work created abroad. Before the approach to anything of a serious character there must be this separate implantation of the sperm in each case" ("Comment" 18). Earlier that year Williams held that in "begetting his poem" a poet "has drawn parallels, completed progressions, transferred units from one category to another, clipped here, modified there" ("Yours" 14), as though individual memories lived an independent existence until assembled into a larger, "begotten" mass. The creative capacities of a poet extend only as far as her or his ability to distill data with which he or she comes into contact, thus the title of the journal. Williams identified such contact in explicitly sexual terms ("implantation of the sperm") and imagined individual poems as the offspring of the "universal laws" of poetry and the "sensual accidents" of history and geography. One might say that Williams and McAlmon envision their roles as editors in terms of creative pandering between a writer and her or his materials as well as between writer and reader.

As much recent scholarship demonstrates, women editors and publishers also were instrumental in bringing modernist literature into contact with the reading public on both sides of the Atlantic, particularly within the institutional contexts of smaller presses and little magazines.[26] The myriad activities associated with the book and magazine trade have often been viewed as a form of midwifery, as though literary go-betweens such as Margaret Anderson and Harriet Monroe mirrored the strictly professional duties of Dr. William Carlos Williams (who in the course of a half-century medical career delivered over two thousand babies). Sylvia Beach, the American proprietor of Shakespeare and Company, the renowned Paris bookshop and home away from home for the Lost Generation, published James Joyce's *Ulysses* (1922) after it was declared obscene in both England and the United States. In her behind-the-scenes look at the novel's precarious start, detailed in her memoir *Shakespeare and Company* (1959), Beach describes how she selflessly relinquished the rights to the novel once its U.S. publication was secured, all for the benefit of Joyce's financial situation. "In the case of *Ulysses*," she informs us, "I gave Joyce leave to do whatever he wished. And, after all, the books were Joyce's. A baby belongs to its mother, not to the midwife, doesn't it?" (205). Beach thus invites comparisons between Joyce's creative struggles (including those with habitual poverty and failing eyesight) and the difficulties associated with maternal care. And while midwifery is a centuries-old tradition passed down matrilineally, its figurative application to the modernist literary marketplace similarly defies strict gender categorization.

In *The Big Sea* (1940), Langston Hughes's memoir of his early writing career, he extends the label "midwife" to two men and one woman who fostered African American literature during the Harlem Renaissance: "Jessie Fauset at the *Crisis*, Charles Johnson at *Opportunity*, and Alain Locke in Washington, were the three people who midwifed the so-called New Negro literature into being. Kind and critical—but not too critical for the young—they nursed us along until our books were born. Countee Cullen, Zora Neale Hurston, Arna Bontemps, Rudolph Fisher, Wallace Thurman, Jean Toomer, Nella Larsen, all of us came along about the same time. Most of us are quite grown up now" (218). Here we again witness the transgender identification of both literary midwives and mothers, in which the vocabulary of the nursery translates across gender *and* discourse lines. Hughes demonstrates how terminology associated with maternity ("nursed us along") intersects with trade jargon ("came along"), and he further suggests overlap between biological growth, career development, and the writing process. (Similar gender bending takes place elsewhere in Beach's memoir, when she relates how two male smugglers transported *Ulysses* from Canada into the United States by stuffing the book into their pants: "one [volume] in front and one behind; they must have looked like a couple of paternity cases" [87].)

The distinction between "organic genius" and the "arts-and-crafts mentality" identified by Adorno, latent in these last examples, becomes abundantly clear in a comparison of how the birth-of-books motif is deployed in Miller's *Tropic of Cancer* and in Hettie Jones's Beat Generation memoir, *How I Became Hettie Jones* (1990). During her seven-year marriage to LeRoi Jones, before the poet changed his name (to Amiri Baraka) and took up the black nationalist cause, the Joneses co-edited the avant-garde magazine *Yugen*, subtitled "a new consciousness in arts and letters" and one of the leading forums of Beat poetry.[27] Echoing the complex domestic politics of Stein's *Autobiography*, Hettie Jones records how, unable to afford professional printers, she "put together *Yugen* 3–6, and a couple of small books, on a drafting board propped on the kitchen table" (75). Jones further describes her editing and publishing efforts in terms of birthing a child, even setting up an analogy between the fate of the little magazine and the first pregnancy she carried to term (she previously had one abortion). Pregnant with the Jones's first child, Kellie Elisabeth, Hettie Jones relates how LeRoi and two colleagues gave birth, figuratively, to *Yugen 4* on the night of a publishing party:

> I've just come home from work, in the big black sweater I wear buttoned over an unzipped skirt. Although I always know it's there, I don't *think* about the baby much, most of the time I'm just living my life with it in me. Anyway tonight's a more imminent birth—*Yugen 4*. Something like the baby, its cover will be black with a white abstraction. Over the years every last issue will be sold, it will become, to the book trade, "rare." But now it's only corrugated boxes of reams of paper fresh from the outside doors. Then, with a great show of strength,

> and moans and exclamations, they're carried inside by three excited young men. (73)

In this example we see a positively inflected version of the birth-of-books motif: the Jones's figurative baby, like their biracial daughters (to whom the memoir is dedicated), is a labor of love, and although the journal drew a very small audience upon its initial release, its long-term value increased exponentially (as Jones points out) due to a limited circulation of handcrafted volumes. The party that evening proves a success in every way possible: the Joneses, together with the likes of Gilbert Sorrentino and Allen Ginsberg, piece together the fourth issue of *Yugen* over an intimate dinner of pasta, wine, illicit drugs, and playful nudity.

Both of these motifs—writing as sex and the birth of books—figure prominently in the numerous metaphors mixed by Diane Miller when she describes the craft of her father-in-law: "Henry strode across the page in all his brilliant audacity spilling his heart and his guts, his incisive mind cutting through anything that might even hint at dissembling. . . . And he loved the naked page or a naked woman because they were there for him to fill up with his vision, for him to plunge into, his own nakedness raw and sharp-edged as he gave birth to something greater than himself" (Gottesman 395). Such hyperbole is not uncommon in Miller criticism; nor is it uncommon for critics to figure Miller's career-long artistic project as an extended childbirth. For example, when French poet Blaise Cendrars wrote about *Tropic of Cancer* shortly after its publication by Obelisk Press, he more closely resembled a herald than a book reviewer: "Unto us is born an American writer—Henry Miller who has just written his first book, Henry Miller who has just published his first book in Paris" (Wickes 23). *Cancer*'s narrative occasions such analyses by rendering the birth-of-books motif in its sharp critique of modernization, including crass appeals to mass markets and otherwise vulgar forms of literary production. In the following excerpt Henry describes an encounter between his friend Van Norden, a sexually compulsive failed novelist (the character is patterned after American gossip columnist Wambly Bald), and a French prostitute. Henry is invited to watch, and he does so reluctantly at first:

> As I watch Van Norden tackle her, it seems to me that I'm looking at a machine whose cogs have slipped. Left to themselves, they could go on this way forever, grinding and slipping, without ever anything happening. Until a hand shuts the motor off. The sight of them coupled like a pair of goats without the least spark of passion, grinding and grind-

> ing away for no reason except the fifteen francs, washes away every bit of feeling I have except the inhuman one of satisfying my curiosity. The girl is lying on the edge of the bed and Van Norden is bent over her like a satyr with his two feet solidly planted on the floor. I am sitting on a chair behind him, watching their movements with a cool, scientific detachment; it doesn't matter to me if it should last forever. It's like watching one of those crazy machines which throw the newspaper out, millions and billions and trillions of them with their meaningless headlines. The machine seems more sensible, crazy as it is, and more fascinating to watch, than the human beings and the events which produced it. . . . The machine is better to watch. And these two are like a machine which has slipped its cogs. It needs the touch of a human hand to set it right. It needs a mechanic. (147–48)

Here we have the other, less fortunate half of the analogy Hemingway constructs in *A Moveable Feast:* "bad" sex is like pornography, or more accurately, dehumanized sex is like the empty headlines churned out by the billions and trillions on cheap newsprint. Birthing books in this case yields a deformed heap of words but no meaning. As Orwell noted, Miller's novel proceeds like a Whitman catalog in a depraved, unfeeling world: "[Van Norden is] like a machine throwing out newspapers, millions and billions of them every day, and the front page is loaded with catastrophes, with riots, murders, explosions, collisions, but he doesn't feel anything" (149).

A few of Miller's contemporaries, such as H.D. and Kay Boyle, also explore the sinister dimensions of the birth-of-books motif; they achieve a similar fusion of reproductive and creative failure by linking the physical and psychological scarring of an abortion with the trauma of identity formation in a society that demands absolute conformity from would-be writers who happen to be women.[28] In Hemingway's less enlightened memoir, sexual and artistic failure cross paths in the person of Hal, whose homosexuality functions as a symptom of his unproductive writing career (or vice versa). Hal suffers from writer's block, and he repeatedly interrupts and frustrates Ernest as he sits in a café, pencil in hand, trying to write. Ernest curtly dismisses Hal with: "Look, if you can't write why don't you learn to write criticism? . . . There will always be people who will help you and you can help your own people" (95). Even more pointed than this episode is Hemingway's dismissive attitude toward Stein, whom he portrays as a "pleading and begging" (118) lesbian, and toward Fitzgerald, who is described as a sexual bungler vilified by Zelda Fitzgerald for inadequate "measurements" (190). In these examples the evocative metaphor on which the birth-of-books motif depends—the resemblance between literary and biological production—seemingly develops beyond the artist's control into a thing of inhumane terror, abject suffering, or snide disregard. But always the birth-of-books motif, even when it goes awry like this, retains an edge of cultural critique. Each of these cases insists on its redemptive alternative.

Cancer, for example, gives us the other half of the bad-sex, bad-writing analogy, the regenerative palimpsest outlasting mass-produced, obscene literature. Miller also utilizes the birth-of-books motif in an uncynical fashion, as in this self-referential description of Henry pregnant with his novel: "As I say, the day began gloriously. It was only this morning that I became conscious of the physical Paris of which I have been unaware for weeks. Perhaps it is because the book has begun to grow inside me. I am carrying it around with me everywhere. I walk across the streets big with child and the cops escort me across the street. Women get up to offer me their seats. Nobody pushes me rudely any more. I am pregnant. I waddle awkwardly, my big stomach pressed against the weight of the world" (26–27). Miller establishes a polar relationship between the two modes of the birth-of-books motif: on one hand, the motif represents a mechanistic panorama of the worst the twentieth century has to offer, fifteen francs of tawdry sex and numbing headlines; on the other hand, the motif positions Henry at a special remove from such banalities, since the common decency of Paris society allows the writer and his work to range freely if awkwardly. Quite simply, the people of Paris get it, they appreciate Henry's deserved place as a writer carrying the burden of his book, *The Last Book,* and Henry thus sees Paris in an entirely fresh light. Bohemian Paris stands in clear opposition to the dehumanizing, mechanized metropolis of bourgeois New York in Miller's novel: "Paris is simply an obstetrical instrument that tears at the living embryo from the womb and puts it in the incubator. Paris is the cradle of artificial births. Rocking here in the cradle each one slips back into the soil" (29).

This sudden appreciation of the new in the everyday, an almost epiphanic phenomenon, no doubt drew Williams to Miller and his work.[29] However, while Miller viewed America as an "air-conditioned nightmare" (the title of his 1941 U.S. travel narrative), Williams viewed it as *the* place—and its history as *the* history—that must be explored fully to revitalize American literature. In his study of avant-garde tendencies in Williams's poetry, John Lowney argues that Williams shared the European avant-garde's "goal of integrating art into the praxis of life," but he also points out that "Williams articulated his commitment to the local and the quotidian, especially in his use of working class speech types and other discourses traditionally excluded from lyric poetry, as a distinctly American anti-elitist response to modernization" (18).

What Lowney fittingly labels a "'localist' avant-gardism, which correlates indigenous diction and forms with the rejection of European aesthetic models" (18), also applies to Williams's prose, from his *Contact* manifestos to his more extensive meditation on American cultural history, *In the American Grain* (1925). The book consists of twenty-one chronologically arranged chapters, each one centering on a significant figure in the cultural history of the Americas, from Eric the Red to Hernando de Soto to Cotton Mather to Abraham Lincoln. Williams crafted his narrative by arranging historical documents collected with the help of his wife, Florence, in the New York Public Library Reading Room—journals, letters, history textbooks—and by interpolating his own thoughts with these in order, as he puts it in the book's preface, "to rename the things seen, now lost in a chaos of borrowed titles, many of them inappropriate, under which the true character lies hid. . . . [I]t has been my wish to draw from every source one thing, the strange phosphorous of the life, nameless under an old misappellation" (n.p.).

Bryce Conrad argues that Williams departs from masculinist versions of literary descent (such as those offered by T. S. Eliot and Harold Bloom) and replaces these with an androgynetic version of literary history. "Minds beget minds," Williams once wrote to an Australian journal editor, "there's no use denying that. Newton begat Einstein just as Newton himself was got androgynously out of Archimedes" (qtd. in Conrad 106). Williams stages androgynous literary production most thoroughly in *In the American Grain,* in which male figures from American cultural history (in the hemispheric sense) repeatedly attempt to inseminate a New World imagined as a sometimes resistant, sometimes docile woman. The last chapter, on Lincoln, even describes the sixteenth president as "a woman in an old shawl—with a great bearded face and a towering black hat" (234). In a chapter on Poe, Williams suggests that "one is forced on the conception of the New World as a woman" (220), although he steers well clear of tradition in his application of the centuries-old trope of the New World as a woman. Conrad observes: "The New World is not a passive woman upon whose body the male inscribes his narrative. She resists inscription within history—history, that is, as represented by the rigidly fixed literary forms that Williams associates with the 'father to father' sterility of Europe's ruling literary canons. Indeed, it is her power to rupture those forms that makes her a supplying female, the one who fertilizes the male. That is the founding mythos of *In the American Grain*—the birth of a poet out of the fertilizing contact with the female body" (107). We thus witness how Williams's notion that literature begotten of poetry's "universal laws" and history's "sensual accidents" serves an American cultural nationalist mythology.[30] All of the major world religions and myth systems represent the origin of language and of writing as divine gifts bridging humanity's humble origins with its subsequent place in historical time.[31] Williams updates this religiocentric pattern by arguing that literature represents humanity's gift to itself, that poetry is born out of a well-grounded historical and geographic sensibility; from this awareness proceeds "a renewal, a reaffirmation, [and] a reclarification of pure form in composition."

While the theme of the rebirth of a national literature out of fecund contact with the local spirit pervades *In the American Grain,* it is perhaps most clear in "Descent," a chapter ostensibly about the career of Samuel Houston, but Williams makes extensive use of the many possibilities built into the title: a person's lineage, a downward slope, an invasion. Williams argues that "Houston was one of the few men of his time suited mentally, morally, physically for dominant achievement" (212), but he devotes just a few lines to describing the trajectory of the official career for which Houston is now remembered: "Governor of Tennessee, 1829. . . . [D]efeated Santa Ana at San Jacinto and received the soubriquet 'Sam Jacinto,' Governor of Texas, U.S. Senator during a long term, several times mentioned for the presidency, married again, several children, when in deep thought whittled pine sticks, tigerskin vest, blanket, sombrero, joined Baptist Church, opposed secession of southern states, lived to have Lincoln recognize him by offer of a Major-Generalship, which he refused" (212; 215). The snide tone that creeps into this description betrays the real concern that drew Williams to Houston, namely, the conditions that auspiciously announced tremendous promise for the backwoods statesman but resulted instead in petty careerism. Houston had it in him to escape the trappings of lineage (one type of "descent") by submerging himself in the mysteries of the landscape and the Cherokee way of life (a different but related "descent").

"The primitive destiny of the land is obscure," Williams comments, "but it has been obscured further by a field of unrelated culture stuccoed upon it that has made that destiny more difficult than ever to determine. To this latter nearly all aesthetic adhesions of the present day occur. Through that stratum of obscurity the acute but frail genius of the place must penetrate. The seed is tough but the chances are entirely against a growth" (212). Williams metaphorizes U.S. cultural evolution as an accretion of dead layers plastered over the living landscape, a man-made barrier preventing genetic transmission (the "genius" has difficulty planting the "seed") and cultural flowering. The imported artifice of America's colonial legacy, Williams continues, literally invades (a third kind of "descent") the once-fertile New World in the form of postcolonial anxiety:

> The instigation to invasion is apparent: ready profit. The excuse also is apparent: progress. The refusal of these things is like feathered darts on armor. We are tyros in what we are glad to believe are the fundamentals of artistic understanding. We crave filling and eagerly grab for what there is. The next step is, floating upon cash, we wish to be *like* the others. Now come into the Universities, the conformists of all colors from the arch-English to the Italian peasant and his goats.
>
> It is imperative that we *sink*. But from a low position it is impossible to answer those who know all the Latin and some of the Sanskrit names, much French and perhaps one or two other literatures. Their riposte is: Knownothingism. (214)

Williams will have nothing to do with the likes of T. S. Eliot ("those who know all the Latin and some of the Sanskrit names") and what Eliot stands for. Williams compares academic literature, and the commercialism he perceives to be its near cousin, to an invading colonial army decked in impenetrable armor. The amateur darts of the native prove no match against the overwhelming force of "profit" and "progress."

Williams is almost willing to admit defeat—"I would rather sneak off and die like a sick dog then [*sic*] be a well known literary person in America" (215)—but he recognizes that the promise of Houston's life, Houston's willingness to descend "once more, to the ground" (213) with his adopted Cherokee family, is figuratively doubled by moments of poetic flowering in the likes of Poe and Whitman, who represent a triumphant nativist, primitivist literary emergence: "Poe can be understood only in a knowledge of his deep roots. The quality of the flower will then be seen to be normal, in all its tortured spirituosity and paleness, a desert flower with roots under the sand of his day. Whitman had to come from under. All have to come from under and through a dead layer" (213). Poe and Whitman stand for fruition—they inseminate the earth and occasion a literary rebirth in spite of layers of desiccated culture—where Houston represents merely conventional success, a dubious triumph in Williams's eyes. Houston's "ascent" in the world of politics forms the bourgeois counterpart to Poe's and Whitman's bohemian "descent" into the nourishing undergrowth of American history.

Throughout *In the American Grain,* Williams projects a bohemian awareness of spatial and cultural difference onto a hemispheric scale to lay the groundwork for an American renaissance. There are bohemians and philistines in the narrative, to be sure, particularly in the chapter on "Père Sebastian Rasles" (which takes place in Valéry Larbaud's Paris salon), but more often than not Williams replaces these with American Indians and New England Puritans: "The Puritan, finding one thing like another in a world destined for blossom only in 'Eternity,' all soul, all 'emptiness' then here, was precluded from SEEING the Indian. They never realized the Indian in the least save as an unformed PURITAN" (213). No renaissance here; rather, an "abortion of the mind" (112). The bohemian is thus transformed into a geographically and historically ubiquitous figure, the "vanishing" American. This is not to say that Williams does not find the time ripe for a rebirth of American literature, provided, of course, that the wider culture opens itself to the possibility of such an event. "It is an extraordinary phenomenon that Americans have lost the sense," Williams tells Larbaud during their lengthy conversation about American colonial history, "being made up as we are, that what we are has its origin in what *the nation* in the past has been; that there is a source in AMERICA for everything we think or do" (109). America, Williams continues at a later point in the discussion, struggles against the pull of its puritan past, its self-denial, its blindness: "Lost, in [puritan tenets] (and its environments) as in a forest, I do believe the average American to be an Indian, but an Indian robbed of his world—unless we call machines a forest in themselves" (128). What would America and its literature look like if it were to emerge from its machine-age forest? How does a writer celebrate rebirth? In the next chapter I demonstrate that the key step, the only one necessary, really, is that a literature define itself and its readership as a new generation.

4
The Modernist Generation
Growing Up in the American Race

> I have done what you wanted to do, Walt Whitman,
> Allen Ginsberg, I have done this thing,
> I and the other women this exceptional
> act with the exceptional heroic body,
> this giving birth, this glistening verb,
> and I am putting my proud American boast
> right here with the others.
>
> Sharon Olds, "The Language of the Brag" (1980)

The previous chapter traced the genealogy of not one but two varieties of bohemian narrative: on the one hand are explicitly autobiographical memoirs, a genre that emerged as a publishing industry staple during the twentieth century; on the other hand are autobiographical novels, a genre with thinly disguised characters and plot elements based on writers' lives. Bohemian artist narratives blur the line between fact and fiction even while they insist on maintaining clear boundaries between social types; a memoir like Gertrude Stein's *The Autobiography of Alice B. Toklas* (1933) depends upon obviously fictional elements, and a novel such as Scott Fitzgerald's *This Side of Paradise* (1920) represents many of the writer's actual experiences at Princeton. Henry Miller's *Tropic of Cancer* (1934) tries to render the distinction between fact and fiction irrelevant with its richly suggestive epigraph, borrowed from Emerson's *Journals:* "These novels will give way, by and by, to diaries or autobiographies—captivating books, if only a man knew how to choose among what he calls his experiences that which is really his experience, and how to record the truth truly" (iii). *Cancer* lives up to this framework by measuring its success according to the subversive standard of slanted truth telling and by metafictively highlighting the drama of its composition: "This is not a book. This is libel, slander, defamation of character" (2). Miller's defiant posturing anticipates Jack Kerouac's spontaneous prose, and nothing, Miller insists, will steer him from his course: "I have made a silent pact with myself not to change a line of what I write," Henry narrates. "I am not interested in perfecting my thoughts, nor my actions. . . . There is only one thing which interests me vitally now, and that is the recording of all that which is omitted in books. . . . The age demands violence, but we are getting only abortive explosions" (11). Spontaneous, unadulterated, angry: we know that Miller fine-tuned his manuscript during two or so years of writing and revision, but we accept Henry's rhetoric of authenticity as part of the tacit agreement between the writer and the reader of bohemian artist narratives. No, we demand it.

Miller's sentiment—that the modern novel assigns itself the painful task of truth telling, that it in effect aspires to confession—has evolved in recent years into a truism of modernist studies. As William C. Spengemann observes, "the modernist movement away from representational discourse toward self-enacting, self-reflexive verbal structures and the critical studies that have been devised to explain this movement conspire to make the very idea of literary modernism seem synonymous with that of autobiography" (13). Miller's claim "not to change a line" of what he writes thus serves the end of "recording . . . all that which is omitted" from prior literature: narrative involution and personal introspection, he suggests, are two sides of the same modernist coin.

In this chapter I explore how the bohemian artist narrative depends upon generational rhetoric to manufacture fictions of authenticity. Virtually every bohemian artist narrative positions itself as a *roman à clef,* or more precisely as a *Künstlerroman à clef,* an artist novel with a key—and possession of this key determines insider status within a generational social structure. Like Miller's novel, bohemian artist narratives demand to be read autobiographically, authentically; what is more, they typically have been so read, although not without some extraliterary prodding in this direction. The publishing industry and the academy together advance autobiographical readings by exposing a rather obvious lie: like Emerson's *Journal* entry, literary institutions affirm that truthful fictions rest on factual foundations.

In part because the *roman à clef* requires specialized knowledge in the form of a historical key to actual persons and events, bohemian artist narratives instruct the reader and, in a manner parallel to the evolution of the narratives' bohemian protagonists, induct the reader into previously closed-off social circles. It might even be said that bohemian artist narratives and literary critical apparatuses (including this study) guide the reader unfamiliar with a generation's particular mode of self-understanding and expression, allowing her or him to navigate a text's semifictive universe. Whether true or not, bohemian artist narratives insist that they are best read by bohemians. Insider status is a privilege acquired in ritualistic acts of reading (of texts and cultural patterns simultaneously), and generational location is signified as immersion primarily into linguistic subcultures. Language codes in bohemian artist narratives assume many shapes and borrow from a variety of marginal discourses that specify identitarian difference.

For present purposes, though, I will focus on argots arising out of musical performance and appreciation, and specifically jazz culture, since this category constitutes the single most important measure of belonging within specifically American subcultures during the twentieth century.[1] I argue that this specialized lingo announces the birth of an "American race": the strategy of the bohemian artist narrative might be described as an aestheticized naturalism, in which biological and intellectual drives compete and ultimately fuse in the course of self-discovery and self-expression. Jazz represents the epitome of this process; its celebration and aestheticization of inherited personal traits and compulsive instincts function as part of a larger strategy of symbolic aggression against the "artificial" expectations of bourgeois society, the cartoon version of the American dream according to the bohemian scheme of things. Charlie Parker, this logic insists, speaks and shapes a more American idiom than, say, Lawrence Welk. Thus, although the bohemian artist narrative has its origins in nineteenth-century European fiction—indeed, transatlantic influence in both directions remains a constant to the present day—the genre nevertheless advances the cause of American literary nationalism precisely because the rhetoric of generational membership follows the pattern of ethnogenesis and nationalist emergence.

How to Record the Truth Truly

Maurice Beebe, in his study of the *Künstlerroman* in Europe and the United States, distinguishes between the genre's two modes of signifying artistic emergence. The "Sacred Fount" tradition, he argues, "tends to equate art with experience and assumes that the true artist is one who lives not less, but more fully and intensely than others. Within this tradition art is essentially the re-creation of experience" (13). He opposes this with what he calls the "Ivory Tower" tradition, which "exalts art above life and insists that the artist can make use of life only if he stands aloof" (13). Beebe locates bohemian artist narratives as a subcategory of the Sacred Fount tradition and identifies three major waves of bohemian popularity in nineteenth- and twentieth-century literary history: the first of these is ushered in by Henri Murger's *Scènes de la Vie Bohème* (1851); the second by George Du Maurier's *Trilby* (1894); and the "third major wave of popularity came in the 1920's, and books like Ernest Hemingway's *The Sun Also Rises* [1926] kept the tradition of the Latin Quarter alive for a new generation of aspiring artists. That the Bohemian tradition is still powerful is shown by the 'beatnik' vogue of our time which, like all previous manifestations of Bohemianism, seems rooted in the Romantic concept of art as experience" (78). Beebe positions Hemingway's novel about American expatriate life in France and Spain as the third-generation successor of Murger's and Du Maurier's more strictly European narratives, taking for granted the bohemian credentials of Hemingway's American characters, as though they belong on a genealogical chart with Murger's French and Du Maurier's British artists. Beebe also reads *The Sun Also Rises* as a Sacred Fount novel—that is, as a narrative that above all aspires to the re-creation of intense experience.[2] This is not such a surprise, though; after all, Hemingway once proclaimed that a "writer's job is to tell the truth" (qtd. in C. Baker, *Writer* 48).

Both *Scènes* and *Trilby* occasioned several contemporary articles, and at least a few books, devoted to unraveling the "who's who" mystery built into each narrative. More recently, similar approaches have been applied to the work of (for example) Scott Fitzgerald and Jack Kerouac; even lesser-known bohemian writers such as H.D. and John Rechy have inspired *roman à clef* criticism. But for better or for worse, no text has been more extensively analyzed in this fashion than *The Sun Also Rises.* A recurring theme of Hemingway criticism, in fact, has been pinpointing the relationship between Hemingway's novels and his "true" experiences, and in particular the relationship between his characters and the actual persons on which these are based. When *The Sun Also Rises* was first published in late 1926, a number of reviewers emphasized the quickly decoded truth in the novel. "For those who know the stamping ground of the American expatriates in Paris," wrote Herbert S. Gorman in his November 1926 *New York World* review, "it will become speedily patent that practically all of these characters are directly based on actual people" (Stephens 38). The following month Cleveland B. Chase informed the readers of *Saturday Review* that "anyone who is acquainted with the habitués of the cafés of the Boulevard Montparnasse will recognize most of the characters at once. Not one of them, I think, is the product of the author's imagination. Even the fishing trip about which the story centers is an actual event that took place, if my memory is not at fault, in the spring of 1924" (Stephens 42). In his *New York Sun* review of November 1929, Burton Rascoe gauged Hemingway's success as a realist—his facility with setting and dialogue—by holding up fact against fiction ("Americans familiar with the Dome and Rotondo [*sic*] in Paris appear in the novel in the thinnest of disguises, and remarkably true to character" [Stephens 35]); meanwhile the editors of the *Dial* took the same approach in January 1927, only to arrive at a less favorable conclusion: "If to report correctly and endlessly the vapid talk and indolent thinking of Montparnasse café idlers is to write a novel, Mr. Hemingway has written a novel" (Stephens 45). A tone of self-confident, cosmopolitan sophistication informs each of these reviews—"those who know"; "anyone who is acquainted"; "Americans familiar." Together they claim what sociologist Robert K. Merton describes as "privileged access" to knowledge, and thus they claim insider status within a seemingly closed-off bohemian enclave.

A similar mode of analysis informs Hemingway studies inside the academy. While Merton defines "Insiders and Outsiders . . . as categories in a social structure, not as inside dopesters or the specially initiated possessors of esoteric information" (337)—he has in mind distinctions based on race and ethnicity—within scholarly discourse privileged access usually reveals itself on a level somewhere between "inside dopesterism" and academic jargon. One result of this tonal positioning is that privileged knowledge can be shared and insider status can be transferred to outsiders. Carlos Baker, whose pathbreaking scholarship made Hemingway's fiction accessible to the generation of students who came of age during World War II, stands as an early example of what I am referring to.[3] In his first Hemingway study, Baker provides the standard view of the early and ongoing commercial success of Hemingway's debut novel; note, however, a tone that casually but assertively distinguishes between insider and outsider:

> Of *The Sun Also Rises,* Robert Littell brightly remarked [in 1927] that it "won the *succès de scandale* of a *roman à clef* floated on *vin ordinaire.*" One immediate cause of its success was that if you knew something about the Montparnassians who frequented the Dôme, the Rotonde, the Select, the Deux Magots, the Napolitain, the Dingo Bar, or Zelli's during the period 1923–1925, you were alleged to own a key which would admit the bearer to the "real" identities of the fictional people. As Model-T jokes helped early Fords to fame, so the international guessing-game of who was who in *The Sun Also Rises* assisted with the word-of-mouth promotion of the book. (*Writer* 77–78)

Here the technical language of literary scholarship meshes with the urbane, inside dopesterism of the novel's earliest reviews, an approach invited, I would like to suggest, by *The Sun Also Rises* itself. Baker's explanation of the novel's early rise to fame further illustrates how a hermetic intellectual community (which communicates by "word-of-mouth") freely circulates across national borders (the "guessing-game" is of course "international")—a description that replicates Hemingway's bohemian narrative in important ways.

Baker's efforts as Hemingway critic and biographer helped ensure that the novel's status in the marketplace translated into the academy, where numerous Hemingway biographies have joined dozens of reminiscences determined to set the record straight about "the way it was" (the title of Harold Loeb's 1959 memoir) in Paris and Pamplona.[4] Bertram D. Sarason, for instance, edited an entire collection of material by and about the persons after whom the novel's characters are patterned. Such studies yield a now-familiar list of the novel's characters and their real-life counterparts: Brett Ashley is Duff Twysden; Jake Barnes is Ernest Hemingway; Braddocks is Ford Madox Ford; Mike Campbell is Pat Guthrie; Robert Cohn is Harold Loeb; Frances Clyne is Kitty Cannell; Juanito Montoya is Juanito Quintana; Robert Prentiss is Glenway Wescott; Pedro Romero is Niño de la Palma; and Bill Gorton is two parts Bill Smith and one part Donald Ogden Stewart rolled into a single character. It is quite common for a *roman à clef* to signify a relationship between a character and a historical person by altering a name only slightly; an obvious example here is Braddocks, which rhymes with Madox, although Pedro Romero was a famous eighteenth-century matador with whom Niño de la Palma was regularly compared. Other "characters" not directly involved in the narrative (such as Spider Kelley, the Princeton boxing coach, and writers like W. H. Hudson and H. L. Mencken) are mentioned by their actual names.

Michael S. Reynolds records how in early drafts of the novel Hemingway used the real names on this list, but as the plot began to unfold along lines unflattering to his friends and associates, the author was forced into fictional substitutions. "As soon as he saw what he was writing," Reynolds argues, "Ernest knew he could not use real names, nor could he use all the people from Pamplona. Hadley disappeared completely; Bill Smith and Don Stewart melded into Bill Gorton. Pat Guthrie changed to Mike Campbell; Loeb to Gerald and then Robert Cohn, while Duff stayed Duff until the end of the first draft. The most significant change was the disappearance of 'Hem' who metamorphosed into a new narrator, Jake Barnes" (*Hemingway* 307).[5]

Surprisingly, none of the individuals recognized as characters in *The Sun*

Also Rises took legal action against Hemingway or his publishers,[6] despite the fact that the novel provoked intense feelings of betrayal. Loeb and Cannell were especially hurt, and Twysden did not immediately forgive Hemingway for her depiction in the novel.[7] Perhaps with the threat of a lawsuit in mind, Jonathan Cape, the English publisher of the novel (brought out in 1927 with the title *Fiesta*), included a now standard disclaimer inside the book's title page: "No character in this book is the portrait of any actual person." Most legal precedent suggests that a publisher's disclaimer has little bearing on the outcome of a suit brought against an author or publisher (or, in England, a printer, who is another potential target in a libel case). Legal scholar Philip Wittenberg writes: "Frequently there is inserted in the beginning of a book the legend: 'The characters in this book are fictitious; any resemblance to living persons is purely coincidental.' The phrase is probably meaningless in the event of a suit based on material contained in the book, if a real person is intended" (216). Parties can sue for libel even if they are differently named in a text—as in a *roman à clef*—if the complainants can prove that reasonable persons would identify them as the individuals described in fiction, and further that public injury resulted from the publication.[8]

The first U.S. edition of *The Sun Also Rises,* published by Scribner's, did not include a disclaimer. But Hemingway did write an apology for what he had done; it was simply omitted from the published version of the novel. After the manuscript was complete, but before the novel went to press, Hemingway composed a sketch, again based on an actual event in his life, "in which Jake Barnes encounters Brett and Mike in the Dingo Bar and attempts to reassure himself that he has done no lasting harm to Brett by publishing his novel" (Fleming 34). What interests me about the sketch is its impulse toward both personal introspection and narrative self-reflexivity: it is a text about a writer who wishes to atone for a text he has written. Hemingway's unpublished postlude meshes seamlessly with the published novel precisely because a desire for narrative authenticity informs *The Sun Also Rises* both thematically, with its recurring attention to "real" expression, literary and otherwise, and formally, with its sharp focus on the mechanics of reproducing "real" expression. Even if we were born decades after Hemingway, the novel invites us to *read* ourselves into his generation.

The Mechanics of Generational Identity in *The Sun Also Rises*

The Sun Also Rises thematizes literary authenticity in countless ways, but it inevitably returns to the question of a writer's lifestyle. According to the logic of the novel, one is either a bohemian who writes (authentic) or a would-be writer who dabbles in fashionable bohemianism (inauthentic). One works, the other talks. A character like Robert Cohn falls short of this standard not so much because he is Jewish—at least not in the eyes of Jake, the ultimate arbiter of literary merit—but because Cohn's ideas are derivative, arrived at secondhand via the washed-up criticism of Mencken (49) or the quixotic travel narratives of Hudson (17).[9] At one point in the novel, Harvey Stone says of Mencken, "He's written about all the things he knows, and now he's on all the things he doesn't know" (50). Elsewhere, Jake says of Cohn's infatuation with Hudson:

> "The Purple Land" [1885] is a very sinister book if read too late in life. It recounts splendid imaginary amorous adventures of a perfect English gentleman in an intensely romantic land, the scenery of which is very well described. For a man to take it at thirty-four as a guide-book to what life holds is about as safe as it would be for a man of the same age to enter Wall Street direct from a French convent, equipped with a complete set of the more practical Alger books. Cohn, I believe, took every word of "The Purple Land" as literally as though it had been an R. G. Dun report. (17)

Bill Gorton, in a quip-filled conversation with Jake during their Irati River valley fishing trip, takes time out from his witticisms to meditate on the bohemian "lostness," or inauthenticity, of American expatriate writers: "You're an expatriate. You've lost touch with the soil. You get precious. Fake European standards have ruined you. You drink yourself to death. You become obsessed by sex. You spend all your time talking, not working. You are an expatriate, see? You hang around cafés" (120). Any number of back-to-the-soil U.S. cultural nationalists, from Sherwood Anderson to William Carlos Williams, could have uttered these faintly familiar lines.[10] Indeed, for the duration of the novel he narrates, Jake is little more than a failed novelist—and yet the materiality of the first-person novel indicates that Jake emerges, in the end, as a genuine bohemian and a successful literary artist, a *real* writer. He abides by the rule, usually unspoken but revealed by an embittered Frances Clyne, that it is a writer's duty "to get material for a new book" (57) from the shattered lives of those nearby, to write, in effect, a *roman à clef.* That Jake moves so freely in and out of disparate social circles—that he reports truthfully about the Left Bank café set, about Spanish *aficionados* and French cyclists, and most important for his artistic development, about literary texts (including Turgenieff's) that get it "right" (153)—allows the narrative to rehearse several modes of authenticity over and over. His expatriate status and wide-ranging interests notwithstanding, Jake never mimics; not once does he wallow in decadence in spite of his seeming excesses. Jake's solid, authentic expression stands out against Cohn's fretful inauthenticity like a dark silhouette cast upon a bare white wall. Of the two, Jake is the *real* American writer.

Walter Benn Michaels thus correctly points out that *The Sun Also Rises,* among other "great American modernist texts" of the 1920s, "must be understood as deeply committed to the nativist project of racializing the American" (13); however, Michaels ignores important textual cues when he characterizes Hemingway's "nativist project" as racist in the heavy-handed mode of, say, Lothrop Stoddard's *The Rising Tide of Color* (1920). After all, the novel's most unabashedly racist character, Bill Gorton, is at best a drunk who is fiercely loyal to his drunken friends, including Jake, a Catholic. And the most authentic character by almost all measures is the mild-mannered Pedro Romero, a native of the fifteenth-century Moorish stronghold, Ronda, near Gibraltar, whose "face was very brown" (179). Ironically, Jake must travel from Paris to Pamplona for us to recognize his authenticity fully, for it is with the Spanish *aficionados* that his authenticity comes under intense scrutiny. Jake's acceptance among the *aficionados* is less a performance of racialist solidarity (as Michaels asserts [27–28]) than an induction into a quasi-religious order of true believers:

> Aficion means passion. An aficionado is one who is passionate about the bull-fights. . . . Somehow it was taken for granted that an American could not have aficion. He might simulate it or confuse it with excitement, but he could not really have it. When they saw that I had aficion, and there was no password, no set questions that could bring it out, rather it was a sort of oral spiritual examination with the questions always a little on the defensive and never apparent, there was this same embarrassed putting the hand on the shoulder, or a "Buen hombre." But nearly always there was the actual touching. It seemed as though they wanted to touch you to make it certain. (136; 137)

The Hotel Montoya thus serves as a secular double of the cathedrals Jake visits in order to pray or to seek penance; the priestly "Montoya could forgive anything of a bull-fighter who had aficion. . . . For one who had aficion he could forgive anything" (137). The hotel provides sanctuary for those with *aficion,* passion, the semantic equivalent in the novel's ubiquitous Spanish for authenticity. *Aficion* sets apart the "buen hombre" ("all the good bull-fighters" [136] stay at Montoya's) from those who practice false flattery, or, even more damning, indulge in showy, "false aesthetics" (219). To discuss authenticity in terms of aesthetics (or an "oral spiritual examination") is no accident: aficion may be a difficult code, but it can be learned. *The Sun Also Rises* suggests that cultural practices do not depend on what one *is*—if an American can show *aficion,* anyone can—but rather on what one believes in with passion.

Describing Hemingway's strategic use of translation, Michaels observes:

> In bullfighting . . . reality is called *aficion,* and, even though Americans are thought at best to "simulate" it, Jake has it. In writing, it is the vocabulary of experience, of words which serve not to represent the experience but to testify to its authenticity. (Hugh Kenner describes Hemingway as the "recorder of authenticities.") Thus, although the usual procedure of *The Sun Also Rises* is to translate French dialogue into idiomatic English, it is sometimes translated with a bizarre literality (as in the concierge's reference to Brett as "a species of woman") and sometimes not translated at all (as in the concierge's later description of Brett as "gentille"). (73)

Michaels offers the additional, provocative claim that these modernist gestures insist on the "phenomenological authenticity" of the sign, that "the claim of authenticity for the writer's experience asserts at the same time the primacy of the sign's materiality" (73). What cannot be translated simply *is,* because a sign cannot signify; it can only *be.*

However, *The Sun Also Rises* does in fact "translate" various non-English phrases by providing an interpretive context for the terms introduced. Each time Jake explains to his compatriots a technical term drawn from the vocabulary of bullfighting—and these terms are almost always in Spanish—he simultaneously provides a kind of practical gloss for the reader, much as Hemingway added an "explanatory glossary" to *Death in the Afternoon* (1932). When, for instance, Jake and a bullfight critic explain to Pedro Romero the English terms for his sport, they provide a glimpse into the workings not only of the Spanish language but also of Spanish culture. "He was anxious to know the English for *Corrida de toros,* the exact translation. Bull-fight he was suspicious of. I explained that bull-fight in Spanish was the *lidia* of a *toro.* The Spanish word *corrida* means in English the running of bulls—the French translation is *Course de taureaux.* The critic put that in. There is no Spanish word for bull-fight" (177). While no exact translation for "bullfight" may be available, Hemingway nevertheless offers a kind of inexact translation for the term, one that unfolds with the conversation. More precisely, he suggests that the Spanish have no need for the word "bullfight," so ingrained is the ritual in the wider culture. (Showy critics, meanwhile, speak French.) This translingual didacticism, so common in Hemingway's fiction, could easily be called a form of instruction, or initiation, or induction, but for now let us call it simply translation. Indeed, the *Oxford English Dictionary* incorporates more than three hundred quotations from Hemingway's work, including such words as "bal musette" (a "popular dance-hall") and "quite" (the "action of distracting the bull") that were first introduced into the English language by *The Sun Also Rises.*[11] Surely this testifies to Hemingway's success as a translator.

The foremost element of generational identity—speaking a figurative language available only to a select few, being "hip to the lingo," so to speak—resembles the pattern established when "foreign" words or phrases are brought into a second language. Returning very briefly to Karl Mannheim's theory of "generational location," let us recall that by defining a "generation" as a "particular kind of identity of location, embracing related 'age groups' embedded in a historical-social process" (367), Mannheim suggests that individuals might read themselves into a larger, generational social structure built into a narrative. He identifies an "actual generation" as a group of age cohorts who "participate in the characteristic social and intellectual currents" (379) of their time and place, events such as war or technological change. Finally, "generation units" are members of an actual generation who share an ideological position (such as conservative or liberal) on definitive contemporary issues; they "work up the material of their common experiences" (379) to create the bonds of kinship in support of a common cause. "The profound emotional significance of a slogan," Mannheim writes, "of an expressive gesture, or of a work of art lies in the fact that we not merely absorb them as objective data, but also as vehicles of formative tendencies and fundamental integrative attitudes, thus identifying ourselves with a set of collective strivings" (380). Generational location, in other words, provides the interpretive context in which individual utterances take place. Mannheim proposes that we read beyond discrete cultural expressions for the "tendencies" and "attitudes" they encode. Generations are like a panorama before which literary texts are brought into focus. Signs can therefore never simply *be;* they must also *mean* in accordance with history and social structures.

Nowhere in *The Sun Also Rises* is the contextual basis of generational identity and expression more clear than in the "induction" of the Englishman Harris into the bohemian circle composed of Jake and Bill during their fishing trip to the Irati River valley. This episode, which immediately precedes Jake's analysis of "aficion," demonstrates how individuals who share the same "generational location" dramatize their solidarity as a "generation unit," the level of social organization at which generational identity intersects with aesthetic practice. From the start all three characters exhibit features that would place them, in Mannheimian terms, within the same actual generation: they speak the same language and, while they are very closed about the subject, all were profoundly affected by the Great War, easily the signal event for generational location during the early twentieth century. As their chance encounter in Spain would indicate, they even enjoy many of the same leisure activities.

However, what truly sets them apart as a generation unit is the way in which they develop, in a remarkably short time, a vocabulary that is theirs alone. Bill transforms a rather pedestrian verb, "utilize," and imbues it with an aura of mock solemnity. As he and Jake lunch beside the river, Bill begins sermonizing with: "'Let us rejoice in our blessings. Let us utilize the fowls of the air. Let us utilize the product of the vine. Will you utilize a little, brother?'" (127). Before long, Jake follows Bill's lead as he passes along a bottle of wine: "'Here,' I said, 'Utilize a little of this'" (127). After two days of fishing with Jake and Bill, the Englishman joins in on the word game: "'I say,' said Harris, 'let's utilize [the pub].' He had taken up utilizing from Bill" (133); "'I say. You know this does utilize well'" (134).

A generational code is embedded in a single word ("utilize") that operates as a part-for-whole substitute for a shared system of values. Foremost of these is the desire to "utilize" whenever and wherever possible, the more the better.[12] This value system is further embedded in the irony of a sermon about (let's face it) the spiritual significance of debauchery, as though Bill were mistranslating a biblical injunction originally written in Hebrew or Greek. Hemingway signals total mastery of the generational code by allowing Harris to translate a transitive verb into an intransitive one ("this does utilize well") and additionally by allowing Jake's narration to translate the verb into its gerund form ("utilizing"). The trio's collective strivings, Mannheim might say, have generated an endlessly adaptable vehicle for generational expression, and if we read carefully, if we listen with young ears, we can pick up in everyday conversation where Jake, Bill, and Harris left off. The remainder of this chapter explores in greater detail how generational dynamics provide twentieth-century American literature with additional "vehicles of formative tendencies and fundamental integrative attitudes," even when these common bonds are expressed negatively, in terms of generational revolt. Generational coding and decoding—in literary studies this equals writing and reading—call attention to themselves as such when codes advertise their secrecy, whether this assumes the shape of racial insiderism or social outlawry.

Writes of Passage: The Sacred Letter

By the time we arrive at the publication of John Clellon Holmes's *Go* in 1952 we have reached a moment when even the publisher's disclaimer participates in what can be described as a generational in-joke. The first edition of the Beat novel, published by Scribner's, includes the familiar notice inside the title page, but with an important twist to the standard legalese: "The characters and events depicted in this novel are imaginary and any resemblance to persons, living or dead, and happenings, past or present, is purely coincidental." As with Hemingway's novel, the mere existence of such a disclaimer is a tacit wink in the direction of the reader, who will easily decode the "real" persons inhabiting Holmes's *roman à clef* because character names are virtual anagrams for their Beat Generation counterparts: Paul Hobbes is John Holmes; Gene Pasternak is Jack Kerouac; David Stofsky is Allen Ginsberg; Hart Kennedy is Neal Cassady; John Waters is William Burroughs; Albert Ancke is Herbert Huncke; and as Holmes points out in his preface to a 1977 reprint edition, "some of the girls are amalgams of several people" (xviii). These "characters" would find their way into Holmes's later fiction and into the work of the real-life Pasternak, Stofsky, and Waters. Holmes, for instance, reappears in Kerouac's novels as Tom Saybrook (*On the Road* [1957]), Baliol Mac Jones (*The Subterraneans* [1958]), James Watson (*Book of Dreams* [1961]), and Tom Wilson (*Visions of Cody* [1972]). Just as important, the disclaimer itself functions as a code to be deciphered by the reader privy to inside information, by someone hip to the "happenings"—from impromptu poetry readings to more thoroughly staged avant-garde gatherings—that were beginning to flourish in Greenwich Village cold-water flats and similar bohemian locales.[13]

Among the "happenings" described in *Go* is a watershed event in twentieth-century American letters, the emergence of Ginsberg (Stofsky in the novel) as prophet of the Beat Generation. (*Go* is the text that first popularized the phrase "Beat Generation," although Holmes always scrupulously attributed its coinage to Kerouac. Kerouac, meanwhile, gave credit to Huncke.) The narrative's focus, with one important exception, hovers for the entire novel around Hobbes, whose reported thoughts tend toward detached, skeptical inquiry, with a hint at times of sociological categorizing. During the final chapter in "Days of Visitation," the first of three sections in the novel,[14] *Go*'s narrative focus shifts to Stofsky, who is visited, as he insists in the face of Hobbes's lingering doubts, by a profound vision. "I've decided to believe in God!" Stofsky declares to Hobbes one day, "I've come to realize that all coldly conceptual thinking—like psychoanalysis and sociology, even some religions —are just masks that give reality an intellectual order by making a selection of observations from it" (65). Stofsky also believes it his duty to demonstrate the importance of love to a cynical age. He arrives at his transcendental conclusions, we soon learn, after a frenzied night of reading Blake, whose poetry he occasionally recites for Hobbes, or for anyone else who will listen. Hobbes warns Stofsky to "take it easy on the reading. You know, eye strain can bring about perfectly credible hallucinations" (69), but Stofsky pays no head.

Instead, Stofsky returns to his New York cold-water flat, located at York and Seventy-eighth,[15] where he resumes his studies of Blake ("He had been reading Blake for over an hour without once looking up, even, it seemed, without blinking" [81]) and, in inspired fits, composes a few lines of poetry. In a daze but determined to continue his investigations, Stofsky wanders to the Columbia Book Store, where he plans to lift a complete edition of Blake's work. While there he reads various poems, mostly from *Songs of Experience:*

> Lines kept on pulsing through his head and, when staring at a page, before his eyes as well:
>
> "The look of love alarms . . .
> The weeping child could not be heard . . .
> And her thorns were my only delight . . . "[16]
>
> Then, without warning, it happened for the first time. . . . A student, moving lazily toward him with idle interest in his eyes suddenly seemed to be contorted with fear; his features, as he gazed inflexibly into the book before him, twisted with a crude animal terror. . . . He gaped at the student, now almost in front of him, into the wide, flat face still, in his eyes, rigid with that cloying fear as it perused the book.
>
> Just then, however, the face raised itself to his and abruptly dissolved into an alarmed sneer:
>
> "Well, whaddya see?"
>
> Stofsky ran out of the place, shaking with wonder and apprehension. He walked out without a thought of direction, pushing through crowds of students, his mind snarled with thoughts and images.
>
> A vision! A vision! The words kept stinging into his consciousness like quickening waves of fever. As he went on, almost running now, he

> found himself haunted by the odd uprush of pity and rage that had taken control of him during the moment in the book store. It was love! he cried inside himself. A molecular ectoplasm hurtling through everything like a wild, bright light! (82–83)

After experiencing this Blakean vision, Stofsky tries "poem after poem as if they were the key" (85) to some hidden knowledge, and he enjoys a whole new relationship with his surroundings, with his friends and acquaintances, and even with literary history. Soon the "flickering, disembodied voices" of Blake and Melville and others are "calling to him" (87) as in a dream, and Stofsky takes over their prophetic voices. With this vision Stofsky gains access to a whole new language, and the conversion is complete when he shares the vision with Hobbes and his other Beat Generation friends, whom he tries to convert in turn.

Künstlerromane typically describe the evolution of an inquisitive, usually introspective personality (more Stofsky than Hobbes) in generational terms, as a growing sense of alienation from family and other significant social ties that impede artistic flowering. Beebe argues that "narrative development in the typical artist-novel requires that the hero test and reject the claims of love and life, of God, home, and country, until nothing is left but his true self and his consecration as artist. Quest for self is the dominant theme of the artist-novel" (*Ivory* 6). Books serve as a way station along this path toward self-discovery, and in bohemian artist narratives they are a passport to acceptance within bohemian enclaves. Conversion experiences engendered by profound reading experiences, like Stofsky's described in *Go*, thus form a regular feature of bohemian artist narratives (although they are rarely depicted in such intricate detail). As we saw in the previous chapter, bohemian artist narratives thematize literary influence—they literally interrupt narrative progress while recounting intricate literary genealogies—to indicate separation from an artist's philistine contemporaries and reconstruct her or his more deep-rooted bohemian family tree. Sometimes these conversions are expressed with almost compulsive intertextual references, including exhaustive lists of titles and authors read by a developing artist, and modernist texts such as James Branch Cabell's *Jurgen* (1919) and Saul Bellow's *The Adventures of Augie March* (1953) anticipate the postmodernist extremism of Ishmael Reed's *Mumbo Jumbo* (1972), which includes a 104-item "partial bibliography" (listing everyone from Freud and Jung to "Zoran" Hurston). At other times we encounter texts like Thomas Wolfe's *Look Homeward, Angel* (1929), which in the course of hundreds of pages traces the artistic emergence of Eugene Gant in terms of linguistic acquisition stages, like those schematized by psychologist Jean Piaget (a maneuver learned, no doubt, from James Joyce's seminal artist novel). Bohemian artist narratives of all stripes regularly return to a small and predictable group of influential authors and titles when describing reading-induced conversions: Murger, Whitman, Pater, Wilde, Proust, and surprisingly few others. These are the heralds (and models) of cultural renewal for all subsequent ages. Since the 1950s, though, one text stands out above all others as a rite of passage into bohemian sensibilities and subcultures: Ginsberg's generational jeremiad, *Howl* (1956).

Ginsberg's "Blake-light tragedy" (as he puts it in the poem), like most bohemian literature, refers to a number of actual experiences in the poet's life, including persons and texts that nourished literary growth during the early stages of his career. (Ginsberg authenticates the hard facts of his life story in over twenty pages of notes appended to the thirtieth-anniversary "final" edition of the poem.) The "overt intention of this mystical name-dropping," the poet explains, "was to connect younger readers, Whitman's children already familiar with Poe and Bop, to older Gnostic tradition. Whitman dropped such hints to his fancied readers" (126 n. 19). Ginsberg debuted *Howl* in a famous reading with five other Beat Generation poets—Philip Lamantia, Michael McClure, Kenneth Rexroth, Gary Snyder, and Philip Whalen—on 7 October 1955 at the Six Gallery in North Beach, the so-called Latin Quarter of San Francisco. As Ginsberg and Gregory Corso describe the event, "a group of six unknown poets in San Francisco, in a moment of drunken enthusiasm, decided to defy the system of academic poetry, official reviews, New York publishing machinery, national sobriety and generally accepted standards of good taste" (Ginsberg 165). In an instant, the Six Gallery reading, Ginsberg's first before a public audience, acquired mythical status, and almost as quickly it achieved fictional status.

Kerouac's *The Dharma Bums* (1958) re-creates in fiction Ginsberg's emergence as a generational prophet with only the slightest changes to factual details. "It was a great night, a historic night in more ways than one," comments the novel's unnamed narrator. "[Japhy Rider] and some other poets . . . were scheduled to give a poetry reading at the Gallery Six in town." Japhy Rider, a character modeled after Gary Snyder, is the novel's hero even though he "didn't look like a poet." However, a cast of familiar characters do look the part: "The other poets were either hornrimmed intellectual hepcats with wild black hair like Alvah Goldbrook [Allen Ginsberg], or delicate pale handsome poets like Ike O'Shay [Mike McClure] (in a suit), or out-of-this-world genteel-looking Renaissance Italians like Francis DaPavia [Philip Lamantia] (who looks like a young priest), or bow-tied wild-haired old anarchist fuds like Rheinhold Cacoethes [Kenneth Rexroth], or big fat bespectacled quiet booboos like Warren Coughlin [Philip Whalen]" (10–11). Although the narrator, obviously based on Kerouac, cannot be found on the evening program, he and Alvah together launch a whole new movement in American letters:

> Anyway I followed the whole gang of howling poets to the reading at the Gallery Six that night, which was, among other important things, the night of the birth of the San Francisco Poetry Renaissance. Everyone was there. It was a mad night. And I was the one who got things jumping by going around collecting dimes and quarters from the rather stiff audience standing around in the gallery and coming back with three huge gallon jugs of California Burgundy and getting them all piffed so that by eleven o'clock when Alvah Goldbrook was reading his, wailing his poem "Wail" drunk with arms outspread everybody was yelling "Go! Go! Go!" (like a jam session) and old Rheinhold Cacoethes the father of the Frisco poetry scene was wiping his tears in gladness. (13–14)

In this passage, Kerouac—whom Ginsberg credits for the title of *Howl*—does not hesitate to superimpose the theme of generational succession (in which Rexroth represents the proud father figure) over the motif of literary emergence as childbirth (including his adoption of the "San Francisco Renaissance" tag, which began circulating widely in the fall of 1955). Soon the stiff-standing audience warms up to the performance and loses itself in Ginsberg's chant, punctuated at the end of each line with Kerouac's shouts of "Go!"—or so the legend goes. And the audience finds itself, too, realizing its pent-up generational potential in a moment of inspired clarity of vision. Descriptions of Ginsberg, in both fiction and nonfiction, repeatedly stress his role as a generational prophet; in this example, Ginsberg functions as a bohemian Christ figure, "wailing . . . with arms outspread." And almost without fail, descriptions of first encounters with *Howl*—whether at a public reading, as depicted in *The Dharma Bums*, or with the print version, part of the Pocket Poets Series published by Lawrence Ferlinghetti's City Lights Books—recuperate a healing, generational solidarity from Ginsberg's otherwise bleak poem.

Beat poet Ed Sanders, in his *Tales of Beatnik Glory* (1975), a memoir of artistic life in Greenwich Village during the 1950s and 1960s, recounts how his discovery of *Howl* in 1957 crystallized the alienation he felt toward his family, his high school, and the expectation that he would pursue a conventional career in law or business. During a high school excursion to nearby State U., Sanders purchases a copy of *Howl and Other Poems,* which he pockets while attending a fraternity rush party. Little does he expect what comes next:

> When he got back home, he read *Howl* and was stunned. Here was a young man whose family had prepared a map of life for him that included two avenues, either a) law school (like his uncle Milton), or b) to work in his father's dry goods store. *Howl* ripped into his mind like the tornado that had uprooted the cherry tree in his backyard when he was a child. He began to cry. He rolled all over the floor of his bathroom crying. He walked down the stairs in the middle of the night to wake his parents and read it to them. His mother threatened to call the state police. His father went to work an hour early the next morning. (281)

The generation gap that Sanders here metaphorizes as deracination, an uprooting brought about by Ginsberg's tempestuous verse, is felt more immediately as an inability to communicate with his parents. It is as if, after reading *Howl,* Sanders now speaks a language foreign to his mother and father, which is true in a sense, since they make no attempt to understand the dramatic changes visiting their son. After spending a day away from school reading the poem to himself, over and over as though reciting an incantation, Sanders attempts reintegration into society so that he might convert it as he was converted. The disciple has turned prophet: "When he returned to school the next day he was a changed person." (Most chapters in the memoir are narrated in the third person.) "'Holy holy holy holy holy holy,' he must have chanted that word, in long continuous singsong sentences, at least four or five thousand times a day. . . . He read the poem to anybody who would listen to him and he got into trouble almost immediately" (282). The high school principal expels Sanders for three days when he recites *Howl* in shop class and woodburns the first line of the poem onto a spice cabinet—an artist's act of symbolic aggression against mere artisanry. Rather than join Sanders's cause, his classmates mock the performance. And when an English teacher later throws him out of class because his *Howl*-inspired poem, "Springtime Shriek," contains a vulgar phrase ("*They screwed.*" [285]), Sanders gives up on his provincial, midwestern hometown: "I'm going to New York to become a poet" (286), Sanders tells his best friend. Thus ends the first volume of the memoir, and begins a foray into the bohemian underworld of Greenwich Village.

The psychic alienation and physical uprooting that *Howl* brings into focus for Sanders can also be found in Diane Di Prima's *Memoirs of a Beatnik* (1969), although for Di Prima the generation gap takes the shape of a free-floating paranoia permeating the wider U.S. culture. Distrust saturates both sides of the line dividing Beat from Square in the memoir. By the end of her bohemian artist narrative, Di Prima and her fellow Greenwich Villagers struggle "through the horror of the 1956 election" (which returned former general and Columbia University president Dwight D. Eisenhower to the White House) and "the horror of the Rosenberg executions and the Hungarian revolution." The beatniks wander through life "paranoid, glued to the radio, and talking endlessly of where [they] could possibly go into exile" (124). Di Prima's efforts to publish little magazines, to produce avant-garde theater, and otherwise to engage in aesthetic resistance to middle-class American culture are drowned out by pressures to conform to bourgeois expectations; "neo-fascist city planning" (125) thwarts her bohemian enclave. "As far as we knew," she despairs, "there was only a small handful of us—perhaps forty or fifty in the city—who knew what we knew: who raced about in Levis and work shirts, made art, smoked dope, dug the new jazz, and spoke a bastardization of the black argot. We surmised that there might be another fifty living in San Francisco, Chicago, New Orleans, etc., but our isolation was total and impenetrable, and we did not try to communicate with even this small handful of our confreres" (126). It would seem that Di Prima and her circle view themselves at this point as an "actual generation," but they remain a generation in theory only; the disorganized bohemians have yet to express themselves with the common slogan needed before they might emerge as a "generation unit." They quietly share a look and an argot but dare not speak their beliefs in public.

That is, until Di Prima encounters *Howl* for the first time that fall. Significantly, Di Prima's conversion experience resembles the sacrament of Holy Communion, beatnik priest and all; she describes a bohemian reenactment of the Last Supper (although perhaps "First Supper" better describes it):

> Then one evening—it was an evening like many others, there were some twelve or fourteen people eating supper, including Pete and Don and some Studio people, Betty McPeters and her entourage, people were milling about, drinking wine, talking emphatically in small groups while Beatrice Harmon and I were getting the meal together—the priestly ex-book-thief arrived and thrust a small black and white book into my hand, saying, "I think this might interest you." I took it and flipped it open idly, still intent on dishing out the beef stew, and found myself in the middle of *Howl* by Allen Ginsberg. Put down the ladle and turned

> to the beginning and was caught up immediately in that sad, powerful opening: "I saw the best minds of my generation destroyed by madness . . ." . . . The phrase "breaking ground" kept coming into my head. I knew that this Allen Ginsberg, whoever he was, had broken ground for all of us—all few hundreds of us—simply by getting this published. I had no idea yet what that meant, or how far it would take us. (126–27)

Ginsberg is Di Prima's messiah, *Howl* her Eucharist and New Testament rolled into one—up to a point: Di Prima makes certain to secularize the prophet and apply his insights to worldly matters. She reasons that "if there was one Allen there must be more"; he simply represents the "vanguard of a much larger thing" (127). Di Prima and her generation, who previously waited bitterly, cynically "for man's era to draw to a close in a blaze of radiation—all these would now step forward and say their piece. Not many would hear them, but they would, finally, hear each other. I was about to meet my brothers and sisters" (127). Di Prima recognizes that "we had come of age," and where in the past the beatniks "clung instinctively to the easy, unselfconscious Bohemianism we had maintained at the pad," defiant but "alone in a strange world," now they find themselves "buried under a sweeping sense of exhilaration, of glee; someone was speaking for all of us, and the poem was good. I was high and delighted. I made my way back to the house and to supper, and we read *Howl* together, I read it aloud to everyone. A new era had begun" (127). Here the narrative vacillates between the first-person singular and plural to project the private consequences of the solitary reading act onto the larger social structures in which reading and writing practices are embedded. Di Prima's "I" and "we" are interchangeable because reading is experienced as a community-building, boundary-maintaining ritual.

Memoirs of a Beatnik ends with a scene symbolizing Di Prima's newly acquired generational identity, depicted in an absurdly pornographic fashion (fitting for a largely pornographic narrative): after a long night of wine and marijuana and poetry reciting with Ginsberg (whom she contacted after reading *Howl*), Kerouac, and two others, Di Prima finds herself enmeshed in a "strange, nondescript kind of orgy." Her generational identity expresses itself as bohemian aggression against philistine values, and moreover the cultural construct (the Beat Generation) rehearses the fiction of its biological origins; that is, Di Prima recognizes a generation as related age groups whose members are allowed to mate (if not marry). Again, Ginsberg provides a kind of Whitmanesque inspiration: "Allen set things going by largely and fully embracing all of us, each in turn and all at once, sliding from body to body in a great wallow of flesh" (131). (It is not necessary to describe the orgy in any more detail except to say that eventually Ginsberg wanders away with two male companions while Di Prima pairs off with Kerouac.) A few weeks but only one page after this night of poetry and sex with her new Beat Generation "brothers," Di Prima concludes the memoir in a richly symbolic way: "And when the full moon shone on the fire-escape again, I didn't get my period as I should have. And as the moon waned, my breasts grew and became sore, and I knew I was pregnant. And I began to put my books in boxes, and pack up the odds and ends of my life, for a whole new adventure was starting, and I had no idea where it would land me" (134). The child, Di Prima's first, is not Kerouac's, but that is a minor factual detail; the memoir, Di Prima's figurative child, belongs as much to Kerouac and Ginsberg as it does to the many other bohemian artists who wander in and out of her life.

Although Di Prima does not identify her project in these precise terms, her memoir records the transformation of what is often called the "Silent Generation"—a group of age cohorts noted for its passivity and conformity to the expectations of Cold War society—into the narrower but more famous Beat Generation. Joyce Johnson, a novelist and sometime lover of Kerouac, analyzes this generational emergence (from Silent to Beat) in a much more self-evident way in *Minor Characters* (1983), a memoir focusing on the women (especially the wives and girlfriends) regularly overlooked by informal and academic studies of the Beat movement. (In Kerouac's *Desolation Angels* [1965], a novel she often cites, Johnson is Alice Newman, "an interesting young person, a Jewess, elegant middle-class sad and looking for something" [293–94].) At the center of the memoir is a question Johnson recalls asking herself after reading Holmes's *New York Times Magazine* article "This Is the Beat Generation" (1952): "Could we be somehow more a part of the Beat Generation than of the Silent one we'd been born into chronologically?" (71). Johnson had read *Go* earlier that year and recognized David Stofsky as Allen Ginsberg, her best friend Elise Cohen's poet lover. "'Allen is my intercessor,' [Elise] says" a few weeks after their first date. "For Elise, it was Allen who became the holy figure who could intercede in her behalf with a wrathful God" (76). Ultimately Ginsberg proves unable to live up to this billing, at least when it comes to Elise, who takes her own life after years of painful, seemingly futile hanging on. However, Ginsberg does reach Johnson, and *Minor Characters* describes an important ritual ceremony confirming Johnson's status as a member of the Beat Generation: a public reading of *Howl* at a "small makeshift theater in Berkeley" (115) in May 1956.

Johnson describes the event with thick detail: she notes the crowd, "young people, mostly—poets and students, wives and girlfriends of the same"; she describes the theater, dark but with just enough light to reveal line drawings "of two naked men, Allen Ginsberg and Peter Orlovsky, in acts of love"; and she observes the cool detachment of the audience, "unshockable . . . [o]r if there is shock, it's the shock of recognition" (115). When Ginsberg chants the litany of charges against modern industrial society, personified in the poem as Moloch, the Canaanite fire god—a section added to the poem since the Six Gallery reading the previous fall—Johnson records the spectators' "boos and hisses." The poet "captures the crowd," she continues, "like a prophet of a coming revolution," and Ginsberg concludes the performance "in a rainbow razzmadazzle of the colored stage lights" (116). Johnson's future lover, Kerouac, is also there, and again he is drunk, and again he cajoles the young audience into participation. But Johnson adds an unexpected detail: "One curious thing is that despite appearances this reading in May is not a starting point but a reenactment. The same poets, the audience arriving knowing what to expect, and thus part of the performance themselves. The ritual of a movement that's less than a year old but maturing" (116). Everyone has a copy of the script, it seems, and each knows her or his role in the evening's affairs. Even more amazing, Johnson later reveals that she was not actually present at the Berkeley performance. At this point in her life, she reminds us, she is still working for the MCA literary agency in New York, the firm that once represented the young Kerouac (at least until Ginsberg barged into the office demanding the return of Kerouac's unpublished manuscripts). Johnson learned about the Berkeley reading a full four months after the event took place, from Richard Eberhart's September 1956 *New York Times Book Review* article, "West Coast Rhythms."[17] In other words, Johnson *wished* herself into the audience, she *read* herself into the Beat Generation.

Johnson thus represents her private initiation into the bohemian underworld as an entry into what Benedict Anderson labels an "imagined community"; that is, a kinship group whose members "will never know most of their fellow-members, meet them, or even hear of them, yet in the minds of each lives the image of their communion" (6).[18] Anderson's most lasting contribution to the study of nationalism is the insight that the proliferation of modern print technologies and genres (especially the newspaper and the novel) allows ever larger numbers of men and women "to think about themselves, and to relate themselves to others, in profoundly new ways" (36); that is, by participating in discrete cultural rituals—by simultaneously reading a specific body of texts in roughly the same manner—individuals recognize that they share both time (secular, serial) and space (bounded, bureaucratized). It is, of course, the mission of the bohemian artist narrative to challenge the logic of nation building and the economic and political interests nations serve. As with most bohemian artist narratives, Johnson portrays the bohemian challenge to the established order as the agonistic cry of youthful art against utilitarian age; but throughout *Minor Characters* she thematizes the textual dimension of bohemian social encounters and community formation. As a girl, Johnson discovers what awaits her in college from Fitzgerald novels. While working at MCA, she becomes acquainted with Kerouac and falls in love with him by reading *The Town and the City* (1950), his first novel. She reads the proofs to a *Mademoiselle* magazine article about the San Francisco Renaissance as a "map to a revolution" (119) taking place in North Beach bookstores, coffeeshops, and jazz joints. In all Johnson records only a handful of actual encounters with Kerouac, Ginsberg, and the rest of her generation, but she supplements lived experience by citing dozens of Beat Generation novels and memoirs (directly or indirectly) as though consulting her own private journals.

Imagined communities do not as a matter of natural course fulfill national destinies, but they can, and often do, articulate racialist desires, particularly when the mechanics of group communion simultaneously exclude those who fall outside the community's imagination. The ideal of group purity, unattainable though this fiction may be, inevitably gropes for self-validating species markers, the more obvious the better. In bohemian artist narratives this mechanism is always present, and quite simple: they define and maintain community primarily with an artistic argot (although this is supplemented with shabby fashion accessories). Murger writes that "Bohemians speak amongst themselves a special language borrowed from the conversation of the studios, the jargon of behind the scenes, and the discussion of the editor's room. . . . [It is] a slang intelligent, but unintelligible to those who have not its key, and the audacity of which surpasses that of the freest tongues. This Bohemian vocabulary is the hell of rhetoric and the paradise of neologism" (xliii). *Scènes de la Vie Bohème,* then, like all bohemian artist narratives, takes us behind the scenes; it gives us the key to intelligent slang. Twentieth-century U.S. writers would add to Murger's list of bohemian discourses the argots arising out of drug culture, motorcycle gangs, the gay underworld, hippie communes, African American and immigrant ghettos, and most of all, jazz, a language Kerouac once called the "new bop generation way of speaking" (*Subterraneans* 7). In the remainder of this chapter I will reveal how "jazz" continually reemerges as the formal device and thematic category through which the U.S. bohemian artist narrative becomes synonymous with American cultural nationalism.

Sex, Drugs, and Jelly Roll: An American Language

When it came time to describe the murky origins of ragtime music, James Weldon Johnson, in his preface to *The Book of American Negro Poetry* (1922), felt comfortable with a literary cliché: "The earliest Ragtime songs, like Topsy, 'jes' grew'" (xi).[19] The same can be said of ragtime's younger cousin, jazz. Indeed, cultural historians will likely delve into and debate for generations to come both the genealogy of the musical genre and the etymology of the word itself. At least since the early part of the twentieth century, writers have speculated about the roots of jazz, producing some intriguing (and even far-fetched) results. When Robert Haven Schauffler asked in *Collier's* magazine "Who Invented Jazz?" (the title of his 1925 essay), he jocularly responded: Beethoven. Schauffler went so far as to cite specific movements from the composer's oeuvre as evidence of proto-jazz music. The following year in the same magazine, Rebecca Hourwich more seriously offered that jazz stems "directly and indirectly from the music of Africa. If you could hear the native music makers and watch their dances, you would easily recognize the strange lyric bond that links the Dark Continent with the New World" (14). Hourwich goes on to trace the putative diaspora of jazz from Africa to Moorish Spain, into Latin America during the colonial era, and finally to the U.S. South, where the genre was steadily renewed through the years by the African slave trade.

Never mind whence the music derives; it is difficult enough to get a secure handle on the source of the word itself.[20] Legend has it that the term derives from the name of a turn-of-the-century African American musician. A fairly typical example of the legend is spun by journalist J. A. Rogers in "Jazz at Home," his contribution to *The New Negro* (1925):

> The origin of the present jazz craze is interesting. More cities claim its birthplace than claimed Homer dead. New Orleans, San Francisco, Memphis, Chicago, all assert the honor is theirs. Jazz, as it is to-day, seems to have come into being this way, however: W. C. Handy, a Negro, having digested the airs of the itinerant musicians referred to [Mississippi River piano players], evolved the first classic, *Memphis Blues.* Then came Jasbo Brown, a reckless musician of a Negro cabaret in Chicago, who played this and other blues, blowing his own extravagant moods and risqué interpretations into them, while hilarious with gin.

> To give further meanings to his veiled allusions he would make the trombone "talk" by putting a derby hat and later a tin can at its mouth. The delighted patrons would shout, "More, Jasbo. More, Jas, more." And so the name originated. (Locke, *New* 218–19)

In other versions of this tale the principal character goes by the name of Jack, Jasper, Jess, Razz, or Chas. (an abbreviation of Charles), to name just a few. One variation claims that "jazz" is an abbreviated form of the "Jassacks Band" (an inversion of "Jackass"), a trio from the Deep South. Jazz performance—much as we saw in literary depictions of *Howl* readings—demands a fine balance between individual improvisation and communal participation to be considered a success; therefore the legend almost always mentions that Jasbo (by whichever name) plays his trombone (or saxophone or drums) under the influence of a potent liquor, usually gin; the crowd as well tends to be gin-fueled, a detail leading to the kind of uninhibited verbal interaction described by Rogers, thus dissolving the convention-imposed barrier between entertainer and audience.

Much more solid evidence suggests that "jazz" derives from a translinguistic source, although the precise details are a matter of further debate. A number of writers during the 1910s and 1920s cite Lafcadio Hearn's *Two Years in the French West Indies* (1890) to trace the origins of the word to the languages of West Africa (even though Hearn nowhere mentions the term). Walter Kingsley probably set this theory in motion when in 1917 he wrote in the *New York Sun:*

> The word is African in origin. It is common on the Gold Coast of Africa and in the hinterland of the Cape Coast Castle. In his studies of the creole patois and idiom in New Orleans Lafcadio Hearn reported that the word "jaz," meaning to speed things up, to make excitement, was common among the blacks of the South and had been adopted by the creoles as a term to be applied to music of a rudimentary syncopated type. In the old plantation days when the slaves were having one of their rare holidays and the fun languished some West Coast Africans would cry out, "Jaz her up," and this would be the cue for fast and furious fun. (6)

Some writers describe the word as Arabic in origin, while still others attempt an etymological compromise by asserting that it is both West African and Arabic or that it is a New World creole concoction. Then there are those who believe "jazz" to have been spontaneously coined or to be an onomatopoetic approximation of an African drum sound. Perhaps the best evidence, at least judging by the written record, suggests that "jazz" derives from the French *jaser,* which means "to chatter" or "to gossip" as well as (colloquially) "to possess carnally." It seems that at some point during the late eighteenth or early nineteenth century *jaser* was imported into the language from France by multilingual speakers, including slaves, in either England or the U.S. South, or both.[21] However, it is impossible to determine precisely where the term comes from, and it will probably remain so, because "jazz" was in circulation orally well before it came into print, at least as it has been applied to musical culture.

In his influential study of the "American language," Mencken writes: "The effort to trace [jazz] to Africa failed, though it was used by the Negroes in the Mississippi river towns long before it came into general use. But the meaning they—and most white Southerners, too—attached to it was that of sexual intercourse. Its extension to the kind of music it now designates would not be unnatural. Perhaps *jazz,* as we know it, is the resultant of several etyma" (235). Significantly, "jazz" and its various associations (the *OED* lists ragtime dance, syncopated Negro music, energy, empty talk, and sexual intercourse) and supposed etymologies have been regarded as the stuff of low (or popular) culture, not worthy of serious study (Mencken being one of the rare early exceptions). Lawrence W. Levine observes that both "jazz" and "culture" (in the Arnoldian sense of redeeming "high" cultural production) came into general usage at roughly the same time—1900, give or take a few years—and that the two terms helped define each other in their structural opposition: "One could understand what Culture was by looking at the characteristics of jazz and reversing them" ("Jazz" 7). This feature of the early rhetoric surrounding jazz was regularly transformed into an asset by writers and critics (the musicians seem not to have cared) interested in redefining American arts and letters in contrast to European civilization, much as we saw with the contemporaneous development of American renaissance rhetoric. Jazz departs from European aesthetic standards and, therefore, marks an evolutionary step away from European origins. So much the better if it was an Englishman denouncing jazz.

In September 1921, Bloomsbury art critic Clive Bell waded into the controversy with his *New Republic* essay "Plus de Jazz," in which he sounds the death knell of the jazz movement that "bounced into the world somewhere about the year 1911 . . . headed by a band and troupe of niggers, dancing" (93). Bell was, of course, tremendously off the mark in declaring that "jazz is dead, or dying at any rate, and the moment has come for someone who likes to fancy himself wider awake than his fellows to write its obituary notice" (93). What is most ironic about his harsh critique of jazz, though, are the symptoms Bell records in diagnosing its impending demise. Jazz—and with this term Bell includes not just music but also painting and poetry—is dying, he contends, because "impudence is its essence—impudence in quite natural and legitimate revolt against Nobility and Beauty: impudence which finds its technical equivalent in syncopation" (93). Improbably, Bell argues that jazz is dying because it is "very young: like short skirts, it suits thin, girlish legs, but has a slightly humiliating effect on gray hairs" (93). Usually quite accurate in his description of the cultural situation, Bell nevertheless devalues jazz by stressing its youth and vigor as well as its unpredictability. For instance, he smartly points out that jazz "manifests itself both formally and in content," inspiring a nervous distrust of traditional aesthetic hierarchies. The theme of generational revolt manifests itself formally, where the "distinctive characteristic" of jazz "is the familiar one—syncopation. It has given us ragtime literature which flouts traditional rhythms and sequences and grammar and logic" (94). As a finale, Bell unfurls a list of opposites that might well be labeled "Culture versus Jazz": "Thought rather than spirits is required, quality rather than color, knowledge rather than irreticence, intellect rather than singularity, wit rather than romps, precision rather than surprise, dignity rather than impudence, and lucidity above all things: *plus de Jazz*" (96). Sniffing in his finest French, Bell thus dismisses jazz as a passing fad, a phase to be outgrown.

Bell's almost Cartesian analysis of jazz aesthetics—his fascination with the genre's grip on the body—finds its way into wider, socially attuned analyses of jazz and its place in modern life. Donald Davidson offers one of the more subtle critiques of jazz by a writer of any nationality in his contribution to the recrudescent Agrarian manifesto, *I'll Take My Stand* (1930). Davidson, who seems to forget that jazz was originally a southern export, laments the dulling influence of all mass-produced art, including jazz, as well as the estranging effects of labor in an advanced capitalist economy: "The shopgirl does not recite Shakespeare before breakfast. Henry Ford's hired hands do not hum themes from Beethoven as they go to work. Instead, the shop-girl reads the comic strip with her bowl of patent cereal and puts on a jazz record while she rouges her lips. She reads the confession magazines and goes to the movies" (35). For an unreconstructed southerner like Davidson, as for certified European leftists such as Maxim Gorki and Theodor Adorno, jazz represents either a prurient surrender to wasteful passions or a prefabricated, predigested commodity, a soul-sapping diversion—but in no way do they view jazz as a vehicle for meaningful expression. In his comments on "The Music of the Degenerate," which the *Dial* published in translation in 1928,

Gorki describes the jazz that disturbs his peaceful night in southern Italy as an "insulting chaos of mad sounds . . . submitted to an imperceptible rhythm." After "listening for one, two minutes to those wails," he continues, "one begins unwillingly to imagine that this is an orchestra of maniacs, stricken with sexual mania and directed by a man-stallion who brandishes a huge genetic member" (483). Adorno offers the now-familiar Frankfurt school lament that in "our present society the masses themselves are kneaded by the same mode of production as the arti-craft material foisted upon them. The customers of musical entertainment are themselves objects or, indeed, products of the same mechanisms which determine the production of popular music" ("Popular Music" 38). Too weary to think critically about serious art music at the end of a long day, Adorno maintains, the masses opt instead for "pseudo-individuated" jazz tunes.

Even as ardent a supporter of jazz as Gilbert Seldes—who in *The Seven Lively Arts* (1924) calls jazz America's "characteristic expression" (83)—dismissed its African American artists as "wayward, instinctive, and primitive geniuses" (98). He extends the patronization when he claims that "so far in their music the negroes have given their response to the world with an exceptional naïveté, a directness of expression which has interested *our* [white] minds as well as touched our emotions; they have shown comparatively little evidence of the functioning of *their* intelligence" (98). Seldes captures in a single sentence the most heavy-handed, and in many respects the most troubling, facet of early-twentieth-century jazz criticism: both anti- and pro-jazz crusaders imagine a vast split between mind and body, between intellect and instinct—between white and black.[22] Vocal critics of jazz proliferated in the United States during the early twentieth century, both in and out of print, and most revert to the crude racial calculus found here; locating examples such as these presents little challenge. *Etude*, a Philadelphia-based trade journal for music instructors, ran an entire series about jazz, mostly dismissive in tone, in 1924. Major U.S. newspapers ran dozens if not hundreds of editorials and op-ed pieces denouncing jazz and what it represents throughout the period that we now call the Jazz Age.

It is just as easy, however, to locate those who celebrate jazz for its spirits, color, irreticence, singularity, romps, surprise, and impudence. This list of invectives reads precisely like the early-twentieth-century cultural nationalist prescription for what ails American literature; the categories represent for twentieth-century U.S. writers both the challenges and the promise ushered in by modernity, and jazz might be viewed (in retooled Arnoldian terms) as a version of measured anarchy. Indeed, Carl Van Doren, speaking at the famous Civic Club dinner in March 1924, exclaimed that "what American literature decidedly needs at the moment is color, music, gusto, the free expression of gay or desperate moods" ("Younger" 145). Seldes averred that in "words and music the negro side [of jazz] expresses something which underlines a great deal of America—our independence, our carelessness, our frankness, our gaiety" (95). Jazz is the language of airplanes and electric streetcars, at least figuratively; quite literally it is the language of radio and talking pictures. And with T. S. Eliot and James Joyce as Bell's prime examples of "ragtime literature"—just months before the publication of *The Waste Land* and *Ulysses*—it is no wonder that Fitzgerald would claim the modernist mantle of unofficial Jazz Age spokesperson. In his *Scribner's* essay "Echoes of the Jazz Age" (1931), Fitzgerald extends the list of jazz writers by adding (for example) Sherwood Anderson, Michael Arlen, D. H. Lawrence, and of course himself (*Crack-Up* 16 ff.). By the time Scribner's published Fitzgerald's *Tales of the Jazz Age* (1922), the collection that coined the period marker "Jazz Age" and heralded the birth of jazz literature, the "genre" would be dubbed the quintessential form of American expression, a natural outgrowth, like Topsy, of the rich soil of the South, transplanted to the sordid nightclubs of the urban North. James Weldon Johnson, a jazz musician and lyricist in his own right, argues in *The Book of American Negro Poetry* that "as for Ragtime, I go straight to the statement that it is the one artistic production by which America is known the world over. It has been all-conquering. Everywhere it is hailed as 'American music'" (x).[23] During the last decade of the nineteenth century, Czech composer Antonín Dvořák, while teaching in the United States, predicted that "negro melodies . . . must be the real foundation of any serious and original school of composition to be developed in the United States" (qtd. in Levine, "Jazz" 9). Extending the list of Cartesian oppositions, we quickly move beyond mind/body and white/black to European/American.

For at least a century, then, writers and critics have seized upon the referential instability, or more precisely the referential surplus, of "jazz" to assess the health of American culture and to outline a vision for its future. As Ann Douglas points out, "the term 'jazz' was used loosely in New York and elsewhere in the 1910s and 1920s to cover everything from ragtime to Eliot's *Waste Land*, from Tin Pan Alley tunes to what we now think of as jazz proper—the music of Duke Ellington and Louis Armstrong and their peers" (74). "Jazz" has consistently served as the discursive site of choice where succeeding generations have articulated—in generational terms—the emergence of an "American race." That is, "jazz" provides U.S. writers with an illustration of what is assumed to be a racial connection between American identity and American cultural expression; to paraphrase both James Weldon Johnson and Walter Benn Michaels, it is only once we know who we are, *American*, that we will be able to tell what we should do, *jazz.* Several music historians have already addressed the place of jazz music in the wider U.S. culture and, fulfilling Johnson's dream, world culture.[24] I do not wish to reproduce their efforts here; rather, I will confine myself to a handful of key moments in twentieth-century literary history in which U.S. writers investigate the complex relationship between jazz, literary expression, and American identity.

A number of U.S. writers have taken advantage of jazz culture's marginal social status to comment on the relative inhibition of the American mainstream, and it is quite simple to dismiss such efforts as facile primitivism. In *The Great Gatsby* (1925), for example, Fitzgerald contrasts the fecundity of jazz at a wedding reception, punctuated by "intermittent cries of 'Yea—ea—ea!'" (135), with the strained conversation of the novel's protagonists, who sit uncomfortably in an upstairs hotel room. Daisy Buchanan drives home the point when she comments, "We're getting old. . . . If we were young we'd rise and dance" (135). (*Gatsby* anticipates this racialized dichotomy between fertile youth and barren age when Nick Carraway observes a funeral hearse traveling in one direction while "three modish Negroes, two bucks and a girl" [73] travel by limousine in the other.) In Willa Cather's *My Antonia* (1918), the jazz pianist Blind d'Arnault represents the "only . . . break in the dreary monotony" (181) of March after a "stale and shabby, old and sullen" (180) winter season. The musician kindles in Jim Burden, the novel's narrator, something of the passion he feels for Antonia Shimerda. She is a literal bohemian, an immigrant actually from Bohemia, while Blind d'Arnault is a figurative one. Jim tries, unsuccessfully, to reconcile Blind d'Arnault's "soft, amiable negro voice, like those [he] remembered from childhood" (184), with the pianist's more threatening musical abilities. While at the keys Blind d'Arnault resembles "some glistening African god of pleasure, full of strong, savage blood" (191). Jim isolates Blind d'Arnault's prodigious gifts and views them as distinct from sanctioned musicianship; Cather's novel presents us with a clear case of authenticity versus artifice, jazz versus culture: "He was always a negro prodigy who played barbarously and wonderfully. As piano-playing, it was perhaps abominable, but as music it was something real, vitalized by a sense of rhythm that was stronger than his other physical senses" (189). Then of course there is the Montmartre "nigger drummer" in *The Sun Also Rises.* Rather than attempt dialect, Hemingway simply replaces the drummer's jazz song with a series of ellipses: "'. . . . . .' the drummer chanted, then returned to his sticks" (70); "'. . . . . .' the drummer sang softly" (71); "'. . . . . .' the drummer shouted and grinned at Brett" (71). It is a reality so real that it isn't even there.

Before dismissing these examples as mere capitulations to a Jazz Age vogue, it is necessary to contextualize their jazz rhetoric with the dovetailed discourses of American modernism and primitivism. There can be no better way to begin such an inquiry than with an examination of Claude McKay's *Home to Harlem* (1928), a novel that is "American" in a loose sense only (since McKay was a Jamaican-born immigrant who never felt at home in the Harlem Renaissance); however, *Home to Harlem* is without question a bohemian artist narrative. A month after the novel's publication, in an April 1928 letter, Harold Jackman asked McKay if he thought "colored people feel as primitive as so many critics describe them as feeling when they hear jazz." Jackman wanted to know because the truth was distorted, as he put it, by the "hokum and myth about the Negro these days (since the Negro Renaissance, as it is called)" (Lewis 224). McKay's answer was surely, "Yes, they do," at least judging by the following excerpt from *Home to Harlem*. In this example the third-person narrator follows Ray—McKay's alter ego in the novel, a West Indian leftist intellectual and would-be novelist—into a house party where a "slim yellow youth was playing a 'blues'" (190):

> The piano-player had wandered off into some dim, far-away, ancestral source of music. Far, far away from music-hall syncopation and jazz, he was lost in some sensual dream of his own. No tortures, banal shrieks and agonies. Tum-tum . . . tum-tum . . . tum-tum . . . tum-tum. . . . The notes were naked acute alert. Like black youth burning naked in the bush. Love in the deep heart of the jungle. . . . The sharp spring of a leopard from a leafy limb, the snarl of a jackal, green lizards in amorous play, the flight of a plumed bird, and the sudden laughter of mischievous monkeys in their green homes. Tum-tum . . . tum-tum . . . tum-tum . . . tum-tum. . . . Simple-clear and quivering. Like a primitive dance of war or of love . . . the marshaling of spears or the sacred frenzy of phallic celebration.
>
> Black lovers of life caught up in their own free native rhythm, threaded to a remote scarce-remembered past, celebrating the midnight hours in themselves, for themselves, of themselves, in a house in Fifteenth Street, Philadelphia. (196–97)

McKay's back-to-the-jungle jazz rhetoric resembles on a very superficial level the nativist politics of the back-to-Africa movement, but ironically it does so with an intertextual reference to the Gettysburg Address, echoing Lincoln's resonant "of the people, by the people, for the people." And yet McKay borrows from the foundational American text much more for its pulse—its "free native rhythm," as it were—than for its ideological content; after all, the novel makes it abundantly clear that in important ways all men are *not* created equal. Besides indulging in flights of imagistic fancy, recorded in purple prose matched only by Ray's cocaine-induced visions (157 ff.), this passage unhinges narrative from any strict adherence to realist convention; Clive Bell might point out that McKay "flouts traditional rhythms and sequences and grammar and logic." These rules are abandoned as adjectives and whole clauses are stacked one atop another, leveling syntactic hierarchies between disparate elements, even between reality and fantasy. Because it was the first Negro (if not African American) novel to reach the best-seller lists, *Home to Harlem* attracted much notice from the Harlem Renaissance intelligentsia, although little of this attention delved beyond the novel's "mischievous monkeys" or its many "tum-tum"s.

Although he does not mention *Home to Harlem* by name, Allison Davis, in his August 1928 essay for *Crisis,* "Our Negro 'Intellectuals,'" lists McKay among the young writers (including Countee Cullen, Langston Hughes, and Rudolph Fisher) of the "'jazz age' following the war" who wish "to bring fresh and primitive forces to a jaded age" (268). Davis, an anthropologist who later went on to a distinguished career in the field of child development, argues that "the cabaret has been an unhealthy obsession for these youths, who in their naïveté imagine that there is something profoundly stirring about the degradation of these habitués" (268). Davis contextualizes the African American literary production he decries by pointing out that "Mr. Waldo Frank, Mr. Scott Fitzgerald, and a host of other white authors were at the same time popularizing the jazz complex" (268), and perhaps with McKay's novel in mind Davis also attacks the confessional prurience of D. H. Lawrence and James Joyce. In *Home to Harlem,* Ray "had been startled" by Joyce and "fascinated" by Lawrence; indeed, Ray "wondered if there was not a great Lawrence reservoir of words too terrible and too terrifying for nice printing" (227). Rather than shy away from the response Lawrence and Joyce trigger, as Davis would have it, Ray instead decides that "literature . . . [has] little interest for him now if thought and feeling did not wrestle and sprawl with appetite and dark desire all over the pages" (227–28).[25]

Critics who early on grappled with the question of why McKay, or any writer for that matter, would feel the need to explore "appetite and dark desire" along with "thought and feeling" tended to shift the debate from the self-referential terms supplied by the novel to the pressures exerted by a literary marketplace dominated by white readers and publishers—in other words, they shifted the debate from text to context, from modernism to primitivism. "In this mad rush to make the Negro exhibit his sensational and primitivistic qualities," Davis complains, "our young writers did not lack white support" (268). In "Negro Authors Must Eat," published in the *Nation* in 1929, George W. Jacobs distinguishes between two types of Harlem fiction writers, neither of which he approves: "One type subscribes unapologetically to the sensational. The other type subscribes no less unapologetically to a solitary contemplation of a black savage dropped bodily into white culture. The prostitute is the high priestess of the first type. Negro primitivism is the creed of the second. Extremists both" (710). Jacobs attributes such extremism, not surprisingly, to what he calls the "shackles" of white patronage. Alain Locke, in a 1937 review of McKay's career up to that point, describes the Jamaican as "still spiritually unmoored" because he continues to address himself "to the gallery of faddist Negrophiles" ("Spiritual" 81, 85) who ruined things for the Harlem Renaissance. And W. E. B. Du Bois, in his review of *Home to Harlem* for the *Crisis,* alleged that "McKay has set out to cater for that prurient demand on the part of white folk for a portrayal of Negroes of that utter licentiousness which conventional civilization holds white folk back from enjoying." Du Bois argues that McKay supplies the demand of "a number of New York publishers," and not only satisfies them but on top of this adds "much for good measure. He has used every art and emphasis to paint drunkenness, fighting, lascivious sexual promiscuity and utter absence of restraint in as bold and bright colors as he can" ("Two" 202).

In that same review, Du Bois famously quips that *Home to Harlem* "for the most part nauseates me, and after the dirtier parts of its filth I feel distinctly like taking a bath" (202). This dismissive attitude toward McKay has often been cited as a symptom of Du Bois's propagandistic approach to art, or as the genteel response of a Talented Tenth crusader. One might also call it a case of the older generation upbraiding the younger, for its own sake, of course. Each of these goes a long way to explain why Du Bois would describe the reading experience in terms of bodily illness or an unseemly, begriming activity. The novel's proletarian hero, Jake, on the other hand, enjoys Harlem largely for its less pristine offerings, and when he first returns there after deserting the U.S. army in France, the narrator, approaching Jake's point of view for a moment, describes Harlem's pleasures as (among other things) a contagion: "Oh, to be in Harlem again after two years away. The deep-dyed color, the thickness, the closeness of it. The noises of Harlem. The sugared laughter. The honey-talk on its streets. And all night long, ragtime and 'blues' playing somewhere, . . . singing somewhere, dancing somewhere! Oh, the contagious fever of Harlem. Burning everywhere in dark-eyed Harlem. . . . Burning now in Jake's sweet blood" (15). McKay valorizes Harlem for its urban density and the continuous sensual assault this provides, including the night's nonstop ragtime and blues. Elsewhere in the novel McKay extends the trope of infectious jazz in the service of a related figurative device: he imagines Harlem as the point of origin of the "jazz fever" that sweeps downtown, across the continent, and finally across the ocean, like an out-of-control epidemic, much more potent than the army abandoned by Jake. One night at the home of Madame Suarez, an upscale Harlem buffet flat (part of the "strange un-American world where colored meets and mingles freely with white" [106]), a girl "curiously made up in mauve" plays a popular ragtime song on the piano: "Broadway was wild about [the song] and Harlem was crazy. All America jazzed to it, and it was already world-famous. Already being jazzed perhaps in Paris and Cairo, Shanghai, Honolulu, and Java" (107). No place on earth, it seems, is immune to the effects of jazz.

Home to Harlem thus inverts the nativist fear that massive waves of immigration and overcrowding in the cities would devastate the native U.S. population with infectious disease. As Michael North points out, this nativist paranoia extended into language policy and aesthetic doctrine, in which "art and the body politic reproduce one another so closely that an invasion of one is an invasion of the other, and both depend for their health on order, unity, and homogeneity." According to the nativist view of arts and letters, North writes, "difference is indistinguishable from disease" (132). It is quite common, however, to encounter almost palindromic reversals of this nervous logic in jazz rhetoric: as in McKay's novel, cultural critics regularly describe jazz as a disease spreading vigor and exuberance wherever its carriers emigrate and its germs take hold. Locke, in *The Negro and His Music* (1936), insists that "it would be truer to characterize jazz as an epidemic than as a revolution. The vogue spread so rapidly that the original source was hardly traceable" (81). So quickly and so thoroughly was U.S. culture "inoculated with the new spirit and tempo" (81), he continues, that Americans soon forgot what life was like before the Jazz Age. Rogers extends this view when he refers to jazz as a "transplanted exotic"; its element is the "humble native soil wherever the modern unsophisticated Negro feels happy and sings and dances to his mood." It therefore "follows that jazz is more at home in Harlem than in Paris, though from the look and sound of certain quarters of Paris one would hardly think so. It is just the epidemic contagiousness of jazz that makes it, like the measles, sweep the block. But somebody had to have it first: that was the Negro" (Locke, *New* 216).[26]

"Jazz fever" is more than just a convenient metaphor to explain the turbid origins of the genre or to describe the worldwide sweep of its popularity; it is also a useful way to define the floating relationship between *Home to Harlem*'s narrator and its two principal characters, Jake and Ray. Although both are Negro, they are worlds apart by virtually all other measures. Ironically, each envies the other and wishes he could trade places: "Chappie, I wish I was edjucated mahself" (272), the instinctive Jake tells Ray; the intellectual Ray responds to this confession by telling Jake, "You're happier than I as you are. The more I learn the less I understand and love life" (274). The narrator's voice, while closer to Ray's throughout the novel, nevertheless betrays the dualistic tension embodied in the two friends: the narrator wants to be Ray until it grows weary of this introspective mask; the narrator wants to be Jake, too, but unexamined hedonism will not sustain an entire novel's worth of prose.[27] Only when jazz fever envelops the narrator and controls the narrative do both voices register in chorus: "Oh, 'blues,' 'blues,' 'blues.' Black-framed white grinning. Finger-snapping. Undertone singing. . . . 'Blues,' 'blues,' 'blues.' Red moods, black moods, golden moods. Curious, syncopated slipping-over into one mood, back-sliding back to the first mood. Humming in harmony, barbaric harmony, joy-drunk, chasing out the shadow of the moment before" (54). The narrative frequently slips over into one mood and backslides into another; a jazz-inspired moment like this allows McKay to advertise the "curious, syncopated" mechanics of his novel. Jazz is the contagion gladly shared by both characters.

In spite of such moments of modernist self-reflexivity, *Home to Harlem,* thematically if not formally, racializes the connection between jazz and Afrodiaspora identity. Performers in the novel tap into "dim, far-away, ancestral" musical sources. Jazz provokes synaesthetic representations of sound that displace musical explication in favor of powerful flavors ("sugared laughter"; "honey-talk") and even more powerful, primitivist visual images ("black youth burning naked in the bush"; "love in the deep heart of the jungle"). It is easy to forget that McKay does not represent "primitive" life in the novel as, say, an anthropologist would; he is rather unfolding primitivist language experiments in lieu of jazz music. Here is no "honorary modernism," the phrase North uses to describe the typical manner in which McKay's conventional poems have been received (McKay's sonnets, for example, are traditional in form but thematically modern because they deal with anger and alienation, rage and race). Metaphorical substitutions in *Home to Harlem* are so heavy-handed that their artifice becomes self-evident, and McKay's quest for the perfect jazz rhythm ("tum-tum . . . tum-tum"; "in themselves, for themselves, of themselves") obviates any literalist reading of the text at these crucial junctures. Or to put it another way, McKay's novel becomes "more self-reflexive as it [becomes] more outrageously provoking" (North 120). Writing about jazz, McKay suggests, is like painting about the color blue: a modernist inquiry into the nature of representation and an exploration of the means and conditions that must be in place for artistic expression to occur. Because jazz literature inevitably raises figurative approximation to the narrative surface—because, as Eric J. Sundquist reminds us, language is either embarrassed or inspired (or both) whenever it tries to match African American dialect or music—jazz rhetoric necessarily admits its linguistic and cultural constructedness.

Jazz rhetoric also thematizes jazz culture's transmission across social and cultural boundaries—in times of epidemic, jazz knows no bounds. "The vocabulary of the jazz addict is largely identical with that of the jazz performer," Mencken writes. "He himself is a *hepcat, alligator,* or *rugcutter.* . . . When he encounters swing that really lifts him he says that he has been *sent down to the very bricks,* an experience comparable to suffering demoniacal possession" (741). If Mencken's examples of jazz lingo seem hopelessly out of date, this is only natural; after all, he also observes that "this slang of the adolescent burgeons very quickly, and just as quickly becomes as passé as a yearling egg" (741). It is for this reason that early attempts in fiction to explain such words and phrases as "cool" or "hip," especially when these are set off by quotation marks, achieve an unintended comedic effect almost immediately.[28] The lexical cutting edge quickly goes dull, but the ease with which jazz argot passes into and out of style indicates that jazz rhetoric can be instantly replenished with an entirely new set of terms. This rhetorical flexibility announces the cultural constructedness of jazz, suggesting that it can be taught and mastered regardless of racial, class, or gender divisions (although some are more equal than others when it comes to the culture industry). This is very much the point of Norman Mailer's *Dissent* essay "The White Negro" (1957), in which he comments on the connection between jazz culture's interracial dynamics and its avant-gardism: "The presence of the Hip as a working philosophy in the sub-worlds of American life is probably due to jazz, and its knifelike entrance into culture, its subtle but so penetrating influence on an avant-garde generation—that postwar generation of adventurers who (some consciously, some by osmosis) had absorbed the lessons of disillusionment and disgust of the twenties, the depression, the war" (340). Among the many reasons jazz has, since its inception, been linked with modernity—why jazz proper defines the Jazz Age—is its ability to capture alienation and angst in the "blues" as well as its gift for improvisation and adaptation. If jazz is an epidemic, then its virus mutates at a rate that far exceeds any one person's ability to combat its effects. One jazz addict begets more of the same until their numbers are legion and words like "hip," "square," "swing," and "go" (each of which Mailer defines in context) sweep across the land.

At the very center of *Go,* Holmes explores in fiction how and why jazz can emerge as the language not just of an isolated audience but also of an entire generation. Hobbes enters a subterranean Times Square nightclub, the Go Hole, where the "sound built slowly from an eerie, hesitant geometry of ensemble phrases to the wild tumult of some tenor sax solo" (161). As in a religious revival, the music is punctuated with the "thud-thud-thud of stamping feet" and the occasional cry of "go!" (161). The narrator pauses to reflect on what he witnesses: "In this modern jazz, they heard something rebel and nameless that spoke for them, and their lives knew a gospel for the first time. It was more than a music; it became an attitude toward life, a way of walking, a language and a costume; and these introverted kids (emotional outcasts of a war they had been too young to join, or in which they had lost their innocence), who had never belonged anywhere before, now felt somewhere at last" (161). Jazz supplies the generation about which Holmes writes, the Beat Generation, with the specific material from which (to paraphrase Mannheim once again) an integrative attitude can be fashioned—it is the "rebel and nameless" language of their unitary strivings, the sound representing their collective disillusionment and disgust, learned, as Mailer indicates, at key turning points in history. The intricate cultural and social distinctions embedded in the term provide more than adequate context for "jazz" to function as a starting-off point for generational expression. Or as Mailer puts it, the "life-view of the Hip . . . raises its argot above the passing whimsies of the bohemian or the lumpenproletariat" (353).

Go thus wears the theme of generational identity formation on its narrative sleeve. It can also be said that the moment of jazz-induced awakening described by Holmes, in which "introverted kids" discover their collective voice, parallels in miniature the overall narrative arc of the novel, which traces the epiphanic Blakean vision of Stofsky and the more measured development of Hobbes as a novelist. Very little distance separates the jazz enthusiasts in the audience from the musicians onstage: while some in the crowd shout "go!" others nearby "become totally 'gone' and start to babble and laugh" (161), as much a part of the performance as the saxophone or trumpet player. The same can be said of the ever-shrinking distance between the jazz musician and the bohemian artist narrator, or so Holmes would have us believe. All share a vocabulary that translates across discourses (musical, literary, and otherwise) because jazz requires a leap of hermeneutic faith: one either gets it and acts accordingly, or one silently admits defeat. One is either hip or square. The rules of grammar and syntax are made up along the way, supplied by the cultural and social context of one's generational location. As I mentioned at the beginning of this chapter, jazz is not the only discourse from which bohemian artist narratives draw to signify generational solidarity and literary emergence, it is simply the one most consistently viewed as "American." In the words of Wittman Ah Sing, the narrator of Maxine Hong Kingston's *Tripmaster Monkey: His Fake Book* (1989), jazz is "our ain't-taking-no-shit-from-nobody street-strutting language" (27).

Jazz is the juke-joint language of synaesthetic surplus in Zora Neale Hurston's *Their Eyes Were Watching God* (1937): "All night now the jooks clanged and clamored. Pianos living three lifetimes in one. Blues made and used right on the spot. Dancing, fighting, singing, crying, laughing, winning and losing love every hour. Work all day for money, fight all night for love. The rich black earth clinging to bodies and biting the skin like ants" (125).

Jazz is Langston Hughes's language of Whitmanesque contradictions in "The Blues I'm Playing" (1934), first published in *Scribner's* and later collected in *The Ways of White Folks:* "And [Oceola's] fingers began to wander slowly up and down the keyboard, flowing into the soft and lazy syncopation of a Negro blues, a blues that deepened and grew into rollicking jazz, then into an earth-throbbing rhythm that shook the lilies in the Persian vases of Mrs. Ellsworth's music room" (122). Oceola's patron asks, "Is this what I spent thousands of dollars to teach you?" (122), and receives this reply: "'No,' said Oceola simply. 'This is mine. . . . Listen! . . . How sad and gay it is. Blue and happy—laughing and crying. . . . How white like you and black like me. . . . How much like a man. . . . And how like a woman'" (122).

Jazz is Whitman's language of "the age transfigured," of that "which gives similitude to all periods and locations and processes and animate and inanimate forms," his language of "vagueness and infiniteness in the swimming shape of today" (23). Jazz is the language "for ages and ages in common and for all degrees and complexions and all departments and sects and for a woman as much as a man and a man as much as a woman" (24).

Jazz is the language of Maya Angelou, Dorothy Baker, James Baldwin, Ted Berrigan, Toni Cade Bambara, Donald Barthelme, Gregory Corso, Jayne Cortez, Hart Crane, E. E. Cummings, John Dos Passos, Ralph Ellison, William Faulkner, Michael S. Harper, Oscar Hijuelos, Lawson Inada, Bob Kaufman, Vachel Lindsay, Anita Loos, Mina Loy, Toni Morrison, Frank O'Hara, Dorothy Parker, Ann Petry, Thomas Pynchon, Ishmael Reed, Josef Skvorecky, Terry Southern, Gertrude Stein, Wallace Stevens, Lorenzo Thomas, Jean Toomer, Alice Walker, Eudora Welty, and Richard Wright.

Plus de jazz, indeed!

Epilogue
Good-bye, Jazz Age

> And Emerson sang:—"Good-by, proud world." The hill
> of sun-burned Uncle Sam
> Is a citadel set for ten thousand years yet, far from the
> scrabble and cram.
>
> His homestead the State, the Hearth, the Hope, The Star
> Spangled Banner of Power.
> Good-by, Jazz Age. I'm going Home. "The Clock on the
> Stair" strikes the hour.
>
> Vachel Lindsay, "The Jazz Age" (1930)

In the summer of 1957, Richard Chase, a member of the faculty of Columbia University, published his thoughts on "The Fate of the Avant-Garde" in the *Partisan Review*, by then one of the few remaining bastions of left criticism in the United States. To anyone already exposed to *The American Novel and Its Tradition*, which was published that same year, his argument must have had a familiar ring to it. Chase contends that the "avant-garde tradition," allowing temporarily for the oxymoron, extends well back in American cultural history and took firm root in the United States because America's is a culture of contradictions:

> By comparison with America England is an organic and continuous culture. What has not been sufficiently seen is that American culture shows far more enduring contradictions and discontinuities than does English culture—or if this has been seen, its consequences have not yet

> been understood. American civilization, happily similar to English in many ways and particularly in its political character, tends, in the quality of its cultural movements, to resemble French and Russian civilization, at least in the sense that it shows very disparate extremes of taste and opinion. (366)

Chase analyzes the twentieth-century version of America's Manichaean cultural contradictions in terms of a vast rift between "highbrow" and "lowbrow" sensibilities; but more important than this, at least for the cultivation of an avant-garde, are the pressures exerted by "middlebrow" culture. The undifferentiated democratic masses constantly threaten to drown out opposing voices, Chase complains, and against this threat the avant-garde must steel itself: "In America especially, official middle-class opinion is always relegating its avant-garde to the ash can." "But," he hopefully adds, "the phoenix rises again" (364).

Still, it is hard not to detect a tone of genuine worry (if not quite defeat) in what Chase has to say about America's cultural past and its prospects. He admits that, in the wake of high modernism—a period of "resurgence" he identifies as taking place from 1912 to roughly 1950—the avant-garde was for the most part marginalized within the academy, or else relegated to a handful of right-minded journals and publishers. "As for the future," Chase concludes, "one can only believe that the end of the present interim period will be marked by a new resurgence from the uneasy subliminal depths of our culture, in the classic manner of avant-garde action—provided, that is, that 1950 marks the end of a phase of American culture as we have known it, and not the end of culture itself" (375). Chase calls for yet another American renaissance, but he refuses to outline its precise shape.

I would like to believe that Chase took some solace when his article was published that summer, for it was preceded almost immediately in the *Partisan Review* by "Sonny's Blues" (1957), James Baldwin's short story about two brothers alienated from one another by a significant age gap and, more important, by radically divergent styles of life. "The seven years' difference in our ages lay between us like a chasm," the unnamed narrator muses; "I wondered if these years would ever operate between us as a bridge" (333). The narrator of the story, a respectable Harlem schoolteacher, strains to comprehend his younger brother Sonny, a talented jazz pianist and recovering heroin addict. "Sonny's Blues" thematizes misreading on the part of the narrator; the story is, in effect, about the narrator's inability to understand his brother's (and his own) troubles. In the words of Keith E. Byerman: "The source of this inability is [the narrator's] reliance on a language that is at once rationalistic and metaphoric. . . . Even in the description of his own emotional states, the verbal pattern overshadows the experience. Whenever the message is delivered, he evades it through language; he creates and then reads substitute texts, such as the messenger, or distorts the sense of the message by changing it to fit his preconceived ideas" (199). What remains, then, is an artistically transfigured expression of mental anguish, as though the pain of narrative can be sublimated into poetic forms.

Baldwin thus transfers the drama of the story from its various plot elements, the most important of which are relayed in flashbacks, onto the level of narrative unfolding. In a series of partial disclosures, the narrator reveals various misfortunes, various "blues"—Sonny's struggles with heroin and troubles with the law; the senseless murder of the narrator's uncle; the tragic death of the narrator's daughter, a victim of polio. The first indication of trouble comes in the form of a newspaper story; this is followed by a word-of-mouth revelation from Sonny's friend, a fellow heroin addict; in a flashback we learn, from the narrator's mother, that tragedy, like the misfortune that visited the narrator's uncle, strikes without warning and without explanation; and finally comes a moment of epiphanic revelation during Sonny's performance at a Greenwich Village nightclub, with which the story ends.

At the center of this nightclub scene we find a famous passage about the nature of language and its relation to the nonverbal mode of expression offered by music:

> All I know about music is that not many people ever really hear it. And even then, on the rare occasions when something opens within, and the music enters, what we mainly hear, or hear corroborated, are personal, private, vanishing evocations. But the man who creates the music is hearing something else, is dealing with the roar rising from the void and imposing order on it as it hits the air. What is evoked in him, then, is of another order, more terrible because it has no words, and triumphant, too, for that same reason. And his triumph, when he triumphs, is ours. (356)

Most critics rightly point out that this somewhat wide-open description of musical performance and appreciation also functions as a metanarrative commentary about the act of writing fiction; the passage betrays, in other words, an acutely modernist sensibility on the part of Baldwin, the consummate modernist. What is more amazing, in my view at least, is that during the last forty-five or so years of American literary history, academic criticism caught up to, and kept pace with, the complex dynamics of Baldwin's narrative. "Sonny's Blues" has since 1957 become one of the most frequently reprinted works of twentieth-century American literature (it appears in over twenty-five anthologies), and Baldwin's work has generated a considerable amount of critical discussion in recent years (the MLA Bibliography currently lists almost five hundred citations about the author). The story itself may not be avant-gardist in any obvious way, but critics now apply their insights about jazz music and culture to uncover a wealth of experimental possibilities in the seemingly straightforward narrative.

Several critics, for instance, point out that Baldwin's references to Louis Armstrong ("I'm not talking about none of that old-time, down home crap" [342], Sonny fumes about Armstrong at one point) and to Charlie "Bird" Parker ("He's just one of the greatest jazz musicians alive" [342]) summarize a fierce debate going on at the time, which pitted jazz traditionalists against the upstart avant-gardism of bop musicians. Suzy Bernstein Goldman demonstrates how the formal narrative evolution of "Sonny's Blues" parallels the structural development of a jazz song: "Four time sequences [including flashbacks] mark four movements while the leitmotifs of this symphonic lesson in communication are provided by the images of sound. . . . This story about communication between people then reaches its climax when the narrator finally hears his brother's sorrow in his music, hears, that is, Sonny's blues" (231). Donald C. Murray reveals that implicit in this "blues framework" is a cyclic vision of historical evolution; in other words, the blues community recognizes that in the past lies the future, and in the future the past. Jon Panish, meanwhile, makes a persuasive case that the song that inspires the narrator's moment of temporary understanding, the Tin Pan Alley classic "Am I Blue," functions as a subtle reference to the larger social dynamics in which the scene is embedded. "A popular song of the sort that musicians during the bop era loved to perversely and purposefully twist into all sorts of unconventional harmonic and rhythmic shapes," Panish writes, "'Am I Blue' is given an 'almost sardonic' treatment by the quartet. The musicians take this hollow standard (the 'void') which has co-opted the basic element of African American music in its title—the blues—and transform it into, return it to, that very African American form (the 'order'). Moreover, by reappropriating this song Sonny and the band make the music—both the whitened version of the blues and the blues itself—theirs" (83–84). And Baldwin makes the song "ours" as well, interweaving at this climactic moment in the story third-person-singular narration (as in the title, it is "Sonny's blues") and first-person-plural narration. "And his triumph, when he triumphs, is ours."

The critical history of "Sonny's Blues" thus reenacts on a grand scale the inner dynamics of its narrative: a constant linguistic vacillation between revelation and concealment, between the individual and the collective. And these properties of the story reveal in miniature the larger course of twentieth-century American literary history: like the give-and-take of a virtuoso jazz performance, America's various generations and renaissances, not to mention its other literary movements, maintain a delicate balance between invention and convention, tradition and avant-gardism. Baldwin's unique place in U.S. letters makes him perhaps the ideal spokesperson for the national culture in which he existed so precariously, so creatively. "As [Baldwin] observed, perhaps like Joyce's Stephen Daedalus, he could not escape the nightmare of history because he was trapped in history and history was trapped in him," suggests Baldwin biographer Horace A. Porter. "Baldwin as a writer and as a man observed America from an unusual position of denial and high fulfillment; he was thus privileged to offer special testimony on the American vision as it works itself out in tragedy and triumph" (171). A member of neither a generation nor a renaissance, Baldwin nevertheless embodies both metaphors precisely because his critical distance from American culture allows him to express what is terrible and what is triumphant about American life. More than that: about life.

By 1931, Scott Fitzgerald believed that the Jazz Age he had first identified a decade earlier had already drawn to a close, but that if one listened closely enough, echoes could be heard, rumbling in the distance like thunder. "Sometimes . . . there is a ghostly rumble among the drums," he nostalgically mused, "an asthmatic whisper in the trombones that swings me back into the early twenties when we drank wood alcohol and every day in every way grew better and better" (*Crack-Up* 22). I would like to believe that Fitzgerald was woefully premature in declaring the end of the Jazz Age; if this study has demonstrated anything, I think we can safely say that our age is still in full stride.

Notes

Introduction

1. As Matthiessen informs us, this quotation does not actually belong to Emerson; rather, it is drawn from the Emersonian oration of Robert Bartlett, who addressed the Harvard commencement of 1839.

2. I realize that my loose treatment of the period marker will upset those committed to identifying a sharp break between modernism and postmodernism; however, I wish to foreground continuity between the early and late twentieth centuries, because modernist and avant-garde movements throughout the 1900s rely on a small and repetitive set of identity labels. As I hope to demonstrate, this overlap reflects common, though by no means identical, ideological and aesthetic concerns.

3. See Baraka, "Social Change and Poetic Tradition" (1997), Kingston, *Tripmaster Monkey* (1989), and H. Baker, *Modernism and the Harlem Renaissance* (1987).

4. "The name [modernism] . . . is clear," write Malcolm Bradbury and James McFarlane, "the nature of the movement—the where, when, why and what of it—is much less so" (22). Astradur Eysteinsson, meanwhile, admits that modernism "has come to serve a crucial function in criticism and literary history," even though the concept "may seem intolerably vague" (1).

5. While the science is anything but precise, here is one statistical indication of the trend I am describing: Quest, the Trinity University electronic library catalog, lists 125 titles under the heading "Modernism (Literature)—United States." Of these, the majority have been published since 1995, and only 8 (6.4 percent) were published before 1990.

6. The concept of a *habitus*, a dispositional "structured structuring structure," is elaborated at length in Bourdieu, *Outline of a Theory of Practice* (1977).

Chapter 1

1. At least in this example. Elsewhere, Emerson is just as likely to deploy the rubric of ages and epochs. Indeed, it would be difficult if not impossible to pin him down to any single view of historical periods.

2. Willa Cather and William Faulkner, each of whom spent considerable time overseas and published disaffected war novels, provide interesting examples. Their subsequent positioning as regionalists seems to have won out in their assignment to a place in literary history.

3. Mannheim invokes the notion of a "problem" in the discursive (or philological) sense to rehabilitate the term for use by the human sciences. His choice of title was no doubt influenced by Wilhelm Pinder's *Das Problem der Generationen in der Kunstgeschichte Europas* (1926).

4. A more recent variation of this approach can be seen in countless studies of immigrant generations, which utilize the rubric of first-, second-, and third-generation declension to explain or predict language loss/acquisition and assimilation to mainstream culture.

5. The field of literary history tends to rely on a synthesis of the positivist and the romantic-historical formulations of the problem of generations. For example, we frequently encounter "positivist" literary historical models based on the fact of monarchic succession, which gives us the Elizabethan and Victorian eras, even though it remains difficult to define with any precision Elizabethan or Victorian literature. Still, it is possible to adopt a romantic-historical posture and speak of Nella Larsen and Walter White as "Victorian" novelists or, more abstractly, to describe the "postmodern" tendencies of Elizabethan writers.

6. The Spanish philosopher José Ortega y Gasset (who believed that generational thinking represents modernism's most important contribution to the history of ideas) agrees with Mannheim when he argues that competing subgroups of the same age share a "generational sign of identity": underneath even the "violent opposition of 'pros' and 'antis' it is easy to perceive a real union of interests. Both parties consist of men of their own time; and great as their differences may be their mutual resemblances are still greater" (15).

7. The phrase "younger generation," at least according to the *OED,* dates only to the middle of the nineteenth century, when it found its way into a wide range of discourses. The earliest usage can be found under the entry for "gradual"; E. B. Pusey's *Crisis in the English Church* (1842) is the specific reference cited. The earliest cited reference to a literary "younger generation" is George Bernard Shaw's *Our Theatres in the Nineties* (1896), found under the entry for "younger." Additional examples from this entry include Leonard Woolf's *Wise Virgins* (1914), Roy Campbell's *Georgiad* (1931), and T. S. Eliot's *Family Reunion* (1939).

8. Although the overall U.S. population has historically grown older on average (due to decreasing birthrates and improved medical care), during the latter half of the nineteenth century the distribution of young persons (those below twenty years of age) extended from the eastern seaboard across the Great Plains and, especially since the 1890s, the West Coast (Taeuber and Taeuber 30, 34–35, 43). According to demographers Conrad and Irene B. Taeuber, "In the years from 1890 to 1910 numbers of children under 5 years of age increased 39 percent for the Nation as a whole, but rates of increase in the divisions extended from 12 percent in the West North Central

division to 119 percent in the Mountain division and 103 percent in the Pacific division" (41).

9. According to education historians Wayne J. Urban and Jennings L. Wagoner Jr., Congress forced southern states to amend their constitutions to provide for a system of free public schools (161). For a nuanced and critical view of the common school movement, see Joel Spring, *The American School, 1642–1996* (1997).

10. Until the mid-twentieth century, the literacy rate among nonwhite and foreign-born Americans lagged behind that of their white counterparts. In 1900 the illiteracy rate among the foreign-born population was 12.9 percent; among nonwhites it was 44.5 percent (Kaestle et al. 25). See also Lee Soltow and Edward Stevens, *The Rise of Literacy and the Common School in the United States* (1981).

11. Tom Woods, Robert Wohl, and Marc Dolan have each contributed to this area of research.

12. Pfemfert's phrase in its original context reads: "Deutschland ist in seiner Entwicklung auf einem toten Punkt angelangt. Es geht bergrab. Vergeblich tastet eine verlorene Generation nach Halt und Rettung" ("Unsere" 1). Malcolm Bradbury and James McFarlane point out that by World War I, writers in Germany came to regard the term "modern" as a "sign of all that was old-fashioned and bourgeois, a term the connotations of which suggested nothing so much as exhaustion and decay" (39).

13. Pfemfert urges in the original: "Seid weder 'radikal' im Sinne der Tagespolitik noch seid 'deutschnational.' Seid jung! Streitet um das Recht des Jungseins gegen eine verknöcherte Welt!" ("Jugend" 1).

14. Keys also wrote on the war for the *New Republic* and on English literature for the *North American Review* and the *Yale Review. Return,* a novel about an American expatriate poet, was published posthumously in 1954.

15. After the novel's second printing, Ecclesiastes 1:2 ("Vanity of vanities . . . all is vanity") was omitted from the epigraph. *The Lost Generation* was also the original title of Malcolm Cowley's *Exile's Return,* although it is unclear why Cowley abandoned this choice (McAlmon, *McAlmon* 370).

16. Cowley elaborates: by the end of 1927, the "pretty girls from Smith and Vassar and wherever," young flappers during the war, "were learning to talk about 'our own' generation, which they contrasted with 'your lost' generation." Not too long thereafter, the "Smith College girls in New York were modeling themselves after Lady Brett in *The Sun Also Rises.* Hundreds of bright young men from the Middle West were trying to be Hemingway heroes, talking in tough understatements from the sides of their mouths" (*Exile's* 224, 225–26).

17. Stein does mention that Fitzgerald's *This Side of Paradise* "really created for the public the new generation" (218). Perhaps the most "generational" aspect of *The Autobiography* is Stein's and Alice B. Toklas's godmotherly relationship with Allied soldiers of all nationalities.

18. Dorothy Parker gave the Hemingway myth a memorable dash of her wry humor in a 1929 essay, "The Artist's Reward": "I have heard of him, at various times

and all in one great bunch, that he is so hard-boiled he makes a daily practice of busting his widowed mother in the nose; that he dictates his stories because he can't write, and has them read to him because he can't read; that he is expatriate to such a degree that he tears down any American flag he sees flying in France; that no woman within half-a-mile of him is a safe woman; that he not only commands enormous prices for his short stories, but insists, additionally, on taking the right eye of the editor's face; that he has been a tramp, a safe-cracker, and a stockyard attendant; that he is the Pet of the Left Bank, and may be found at any hour of the day or night sitting at a little table at the Select, rubbing absinthe into his gums; that he really hates all forms of sport, only skis, hunts, fishes, and fights bulls in order to be cute; that a wound he sustained in the Great War was of a whimsical, inconvenient, and inevitably laughable description; and that he also writes under the name of Morley Callaghan. About all that remains to be said is that he is the Lost Dauphin, that he was shot as a German spy, and that he is actually a woman, masquerading in man's clothes. And those rumors are doubtless being started, even as we sit here" (583–84).

19. See chapter 4 for more on the generational dynamics of the *roman à clef.*

20. In "This Is the Beat Generation" (1952), John Clellon Holmes describes the origin of the phrase "Beat Generation" (popularized by his novel *Go,* published earlier that year) and attempts to outline some of its major tenets. He does so largely in contrast to the myth of the Lost Generation.

21. See Mizener, "Lost Generation."

22. Poggioli writes: "The proverb says, 'one finds what one looks for,' and nothing is easier to find than an enemy, even if you do not go far to look. In an analogous way, though in a direction opposite to that followed by political radicalism, aesthetic radicalism often expresses itself by opposing that special category of society (in both the large and the limited sense of the word) called the old generation, the generation of the fathers" (34).

Chapter 2

1. According to the *OED,* "Words formed with the prefix *re-* first make their appearance in English about the year 1280. . . . Towards the end of the 16th c. *re-* begins to rank as an ordinary English prefix, chiefly employed with words of Latin origin, but also freely prefixed to native verbs, a practice rare before this period, though Wycliff, Trevisa, and others have *renew* (after L. *renovare*). Such formations, however, are common in Elizabethan writers: Shakespeare has *recall, regreet* (frequent), *relive, requicken, resend, respeak, restem, retell* (thrice), and *reward,* and many others occur in contemporary literature, as *rebuild, recast, refind, reflow, regather,* etc." (*OED,* "re-"). A conspicuous absence from Shakespeare is "renaissance," which did not enter the language until the mid-nineteenth century (although "renascence" dates to the early eighteenth century).

2. There are too many important studies of the "American Renaissance" and the "Harlem Renaissance" to list here. Major studies of the "Chicago Renaissance" in-

clude Bernard I. Duffey, *The Chicago Renaissance in American Letters* (1954), and Dale Kramer, *Chicago Renaissance* (1966). Arthur Frank Wertheim produced the most comprehensive study of the "Little Renaissance," although he confines his discussion to the New York scene. (During the movement's heydey in the 1910s it was known as the "American Renaissance," and the Midwest was as central to its development as New York.) Richard King's *A Southern Renaissance* (1980) now stands as the definitive study of the movement first identified by Hershel Brickell in 1927 ("The Literary Awakening of the South") and Howard Mumford Jones in 1930 ("Is There a Southern Renaissance?"). Michael Davidson's *San Francisco Renaissance* (1989) is the most extensive analysis of that subset of the Beat Generation. Philip D. Ortego, who first identified a Chicano Renaissance in a 1971 article bearing that title, and Kenneth Lincoln, who published *Native American Renaissance* in 1983, were both inspired by the contemporaneous resurgence in interest in the Harlem Renaissance. Most recently, Robert McRuer added his provocative title *The Queer Renaissance* (1997) to this seemingly endless list of "modernist" movements.

3. An ethical system of "wholesome provincialism" was developed by Josiah Royce, professor of English and philosophy at the University of California and Harvard. Werner Sollors (*Beyond* 174 ff.) and George Hutchinson (*Harlem* 79 ff.) have dealt at some length with his impact on U.S. cultural history.

4. On the postcoloniality of nineteenth-century U.S. literature see Lawrence Buell, "American Literary Emergence as Postcolonial Phenomenon" (1992).

5. While the designation of an "early modern" period in cultural history indicates some slight unease with the less objective term "renaissance," most critics feel comfortable using the two interchangeably. In fact, the debate over whether a renaissance even occurred in early modern Europe, and what dates it might have covered, has largely subsided since the 1960s.

6. Charlene Avallone argues that the emergence of "American renaissance" criticism over the past century produced a formalist critical legacy at the expense of women writers. "In the struggle to determine what counts in the American cultural field, who adjudicates that field, and what validations are given lasting and representative significance," she writes, "the language of renaissance serves to maintain male preeminence" (1102). Avallone relates "the consignment of women writers to a separate, subordinate sphere" to "the institution of formalist reading strategies . . . in current renaissance models" (1104). I would counter that Avallone does not give due credit to the role played by women in nineteenth- and twentieth-century renaissances—and nowhere near the credit due their critics—particularly with respect to the Irish, Little, and Harlem Renaissances. And of the critics mentioned by Avallone, only F. O. Matthiessen can safely be labeled a formalist critic. Matthiessen stumbled upon his title *American Renaissance* almost by accident: the working title of his study was *American Masterwork: Language and Art in the Age of Emerson and Whitman* (following Ezra Pound's notion of art history as the history of masterworks), although in the final draft he crossed this out in favor of *From Emerson to Whitman: The Great Age of American Literature* (Francis Otto Matthiessen Papers,

box 2, Houghton Library, Harvard University). Matthiessen's final title choice, which seems so incidental as to be an accident of critical history, invokes the transhistorical renaissance worldview suggested to him by André Malraux: "Every civilization is like the Renaissance, and creates its own heritage out of everything in the past that helps it to surpass itself" (qtd. in Matthiessen, *American* xv n.).

7. Before Matthiessen's study, the "American Renaissance" of the nineteenth century was universally called the "New England Renaissance." Meanwhile, from roughly 1915 to 1940 the phrases "American Renaissance" and "American Poetry Renaissance" were used to describe a perceived flowering of American literary culture, not always but usually limited to poetry. Matthiessen's American canon extends beyond New England (to include Whitman and Melville), which explains the more expansive title of his book, although many subsequent critics apply "American Renaissance" to the New England scene only. After Matthiessen published his study in 1941, the "American Poetry Renaissance" became known as the "Little Renaissance," perhaps to explain the proliferation of little magazines or to identify American modernism as a "second flowering," but mostly to avoid confusion.

8. Pierre Bourdieu is instructive on this point: "The demiurgic ambition of the artist, capable of applying to *any* object the pure intention of an artistic effort which is an end of itself, calls for unlimited receptiveness on the part of an aesthete capable of applying the specifically aesthetic intention to any object, whether or not it has been produced with aesthetic intention. This demand is objectified in the art museum; there the aesthetic disposition becomes an institution. Nothing more totally manifests and achieves the autonomizing of aesthetic activity vis-à-vis extra-aesthetic interests or functions than the art museum's juxtaposition of works" (*Distinction* 30). Unlike William Hazlitt or Thomas Carlyle, who helped popularize in England the ideal that art collections approximate the pinnacle of human expression, Emerson believed that the masterpiece transforms the spectator into an active creator by revealing the artistry latent in the natural world. All objects, according to this logic, can be viewed as *objets d'art*. For a succinct analysis of museum culture's transformation of the cultural field during the nineteenth century—not coincidentally titled *Musée Imaginaire*—see Malraux.

9. I say "third generation" because the transcendentalists are preceded by a Golden Age first generation and a Dark Age second generation. This pattern is common to all renaissances, although generations play a particularly important role in New World cultural history.

10. Osgood writes: "Those names [Klopstock, Winckelmann, Lessing, Herder, Goethe, Schiller, Kant, Fichte, Schelling, Hegel] may not be fully matched by our American authors, but they have had essentially their counterparts here, and surely our New England view of the universe may be made to illustrate Christianity as well as the German Weltanschauung which is before us now" (761).

11. Richardson has in mind Arnold's discourse on "Numbers," the first in his collection. In the United States, as in England, Arnold finds little more than a barbarian aristocracy and a philistine middle class, Emerson being one of the rare exceptions.

12. The most comprehensive biography of Wendell to date is Robert T. Self, *Barrett Wendell* (1975).

13. Renan's essay was made widely available in English in 1896 and again in 1910. Although Renan, ethnically a Breton, places the Golden Age of Celtic poetry during the Middle Ages, he measures poetic influence in terms of military conquest and even reverse imperialism, much like Burckhardt a few years later: "Especially it is forgotten that this little people, now concentrated on the very confines of the world, in the midst of rocks and mountains whence its enemies have been powerless to force it, is in possession of a literature which, in the Middle Ages, exercised an immense influence, changed the current of European civilization, and imposed its poetical motives on nearly the whole of Christendom" (2). In his later and better-known lecture delivered at the Sorbonne, "What Is a Nation?" (1882), Renan argues for the modernity of the nation-state by deemphasizing race, language, and religion and instead emphasizing the cultural constructedness of nationality.

14. Weygandt taught and wrote about the Irish Renaissance for a broad audience. He is perhaps best known for his study of *Irish Plays and Playwrights* (1913), which begins with a chapter on the "Celtic Renaissance." For more on the relationship between Pound and Yeats, see James Longenbach, *Stone Cottage* (1988), and Robert M. Crunden, *American Salons* (1993).

15. See esp. Tracy Mishkin and George Bornstein, *The Harlem and Irish Renaissances* (1998). For a more sobering account of anti-black Irish American racism, see Noel Ignatiev, *How the Irish Became White* (1995).

16. Lyons provides a concise distinction between the Yeatsian and Hydean branches of the Irish Renaissance: "For Yeats and his friends, it cannot be too often repeated, the true ambition was to create an Irish literature in English, which would take its place as a part of European civilization. But for Hyde and *his* friends, though art was not negligible, far more important was the propaganda for cultural nationalism which the Gaelic League existed to promote" (47). Still, in the American press the two were generally recognized as the co-founders of a single Irish Renaissance, for as Lyons again points out, "it is hardly too much to say that for most of the nineteenth century English culture was the most effective unifying force in Ireland, disguising for many decades—indeed, very nearly destroying—the underlying diversity which was an essential element in the life of the country" (7).

17. Mary K. Ford, in a 1906 article for the *North American Review,* dismissed Yeats's writing and his lectures in the United States as "represent[ing] the latest intellectual fad" (773) and lumped him together with "the many writers who are connected with the Celtic Revival" (775) and who likewise lack the simple charm of "authentic" Irish literature. Her model for authentic folk expression is an interesting one: Ford asks "whether the so-called 'Celtic Renaissance' is, like the plaintive music of negro slavery, the emotional expression of a suppressed nationality, or merely a modern, conscious, and complex form of writing, ill-adapted as a garment for the Irish sentiment it is meant to clothe" (771).

18. There were at least eight Celtic studies programs in the United States by 1915.

Brief surveys of the institutional history of Celtic studies in North America can be found in John L. Gerig, "Celtic Studies in the United States" (1916), and Roland Blenner-Hassett, "A Brief History of Celtic Studies" (1954).

19. Most of Yeats's American essays, which provided much-needed financial support during the early part of his career, were collected as *Letters to the New Island* (1934).

20. Examples of Irish Renaissance articles drawn from Anglo-American literary magazines between 1890 and 1920 include Katherine Tynan Hinkson, "The Literary Revival in Ireland" (1894); Lady Aberdeen (Isabel Gordon), "The Present Irish Literary Revival" (1895); Walter Lecky, "The American Celt and His Critics" (1896); M. A. O'Byrne, "How the Celtic Revival Arose" (1896); A. Lang, "The Celtic Renaissance" (1897); Justin McCarthy, "Revival of Irish Language and Literature" (1901); T. O'Donnell, "The Gaelic Revival in Ireland" (1901); "The Gaelic Revival in Literature" (1902); Stephen Gwynn, "The Gaelic Revival in Literature" and "The Revival of a Language" (1902); J. D. Miller, "Celtic Renaissance" (1903); "The Irish Literary Revival" (1903); L. McManus, "The Irish Literary Revival" (1904); Frank Weitenkampf, "The Irish Literary Revival" (1904); Cornelius Weygandt, "The Irish Literary Revival" (1904); Charles Leonard Moore, "The Celtic Revival" (1906); Moira L. Ray, "The Irish Literary Revival and Its Gaelic Writers" (1906); Edward Wright, "A Celtic Renaissance of the Past" (1907); J. J. O'Shea, "Gaelic Revival Pioneers" (1910); K. L. Montgomery, "Some Writers of the Celtic Renaissance" (1911); and Ernest Boyd, "The Irish Renaissance—Renascent" (1919). A handful of writers took issue with the idea of an Irish Renaissance, questioning the validity of the rebirth metaphor, and even questioning its "Celtic authenticity," including J. P. Mahaffy, "The Recent Fuss about the Irish Language" (1899); and Mary K. Ford, "Is the Celtic Revival Really Irish?" (1906).

21. Early-twentieth-century radicalism inverted both cultural archetypes, invoking the puritan and pioneer legacies to account for negative aspects of U.S. civilization. On the dismantling of the puritan myth, see John Higham, *Strangers in the Land* (1955). For a similar account of the pioneer myth, see Gerald D. Nash, *Creating the West* (1991).

22. According to Dowling, "When Yeats wished to contrast Ireland's literary situation with England's, he would thus emphasize the artificiality and exhaustion of the English literary medium, taking literary Decadence at its word. When, on the other hand, he wished to advance the claims of the new visionary art he believed was springing up both in England and Ireland as well as on the Continent, he became more scrupulous with the term, exchanging the aggressively polemical 'Decadence' for the phrase 'autumn of the body' " (247).

23. Paul Elmer More, one of the so-called New Humanists to whom the pejorative label "genteel" was regularly affixed, represents one of the few American critics to take issue with Yeats's movement, which he interpreted as a far cry "from the virile passion and pathos, [and] the action" (178) of its Celtic sources. More gives the Irish Renaissance a prominent place in the first series of his *Shelburne Essays* (1904), but

the "mysticism" and "loose revery" of Yeats's "Celtic phantasmagoria" (a phrase borrowed from the Irishman) sound a "flaccid note" (178, 179, 181) to More's ear.

24. Tate was one of the first writers to identify a "Southern Renaissance" in his 1945 essay on "The New Provincialism." (Herschel Brickell was probably the first, in his essay on "The Literary Awakening in the South" [1927], written in response to Mencken's caustic description of the South as a "Sahara of the Bozart.") While the Southern Renaissance could be profitably studied in comparison with other American renaissances, particularly the Harlem Renaissance, its regionalist politics tended to emphasize the less progressive aspects of southern cultural history. Tate wrote in the later essay, "With the war of 1914–1918, the South re-entered the world—but gave a backward glance as it stepped over the border: that backward glance gave us the Southern renascence, a literature conscious of the past in the present" (292). The alternative spelling, "renascence," is common in writers of the southern movement, perhaps to emphasize difference from the Harlem Renaissance.

25. A similar strain of primitivist nativism informs D. H. Lawrence's *New Republic* essay "America, Listen to Your Own" (1920), in which Lawrence implores U.S. artists to reevaluate that "which was so abhorrent to the Pilgrim Fathers and to the Spaniards, that which was called the Devil, the black Demon of savage America"; in other words, "Americans must take up life where the Red Indian, the Aztec, the Maya, and the Incas left it off. They must pick up the life-thread where the mysterious Red race let it fall" (69).

26. According to the *Norton Anthology of African American Literature,* in 1904 the *A.M.E. Church Bulletin* similarly called for a "New Negro Renaissance" (Gates and McKay 2617). However, this is not entirely correct. In fact, in that journal W. H. A. Moore admits that "the New Negro Literary Movement is not the note of a reawakening, it is a halting, stammering voice touched with sadness and the pathos of yearning. Unlike the Celtic revival it is not a potent influence in the literature of today; neither is it the spirit of an endeavor to recover the song that is lost or the motive of an aspiration to reclaim the soul-love that is dead" (49). During the previous year, in 1903, Frazelia Campbell did explain to the *A.M.E. Church Review* readership that "it is left to the 20th [century] to bring about a moral and political Renaissance, which shall crush the lingering remnant of the Middle Ages, in an unreasoning class prejudice and which shall award to all—Gypsy, Chinese, Jew, American Negro, the right due to each" (39).

27. Braithwaite is referring to Thomas's *The American Negro* (1901).

28. Schoell's impressive and universally overlooked study, which approaches book length at over forty densely printed pages, follows a now familiar line of discussion, as evidenced by its section titles: "Situation des Noirs après la Guerre"; "L'industrialisation des États du Sud"; "Urbanisation des Noirs"; "Vers une classe moyenne noire"; "La Presse noire"; "Le Nègre à la mode. L'art nègre"; "Littérature négro-américaine"; "Énlargissement de l'horizon des Nègres. Préoccupations africaines"; "Vues d'avenir."

29. The final section of George Hutchinson's *The Harlem Renaissance in Black and White* is by far the most complete and up-to-date study of *The New Negro.* It includes a rich publishing history of the anthology and a brief interpretation of its contents.

30. In Du Bois's oft-cited review of the anthology, his art-versus-propaganda rift with Locke largely boils down to a matter of semantics: "With one point alone do I differ with the Editor. Mr. Locke has newly been seized with the idea that Beauty rather than Propaganda should be the object of Negro literature and art. His book proves the falseness of this thesis. This is a book filled and bursting with propaganda but it is a propaganda for the most part beautifully and painstakingly done; and it is a grave question if ever in this world in any renaissance there can be a search for disembodied beauty which is not really a passionate effort to do something tangible, accompanied and illumined and made holy by the vision of eternal beauty" ("Our Book" 141). The question of art and propaganda in the Harlem Renaissance, which can be seen in microcosm in the ongoing debate carried out between Du Bois and Locke, has been treated at some length by a number of critics (see esp. Huggins, Johnson and Johnson, and Lewis). Still, it is hardly enough to say that Locke preaches the virtues of art and Du Bois the need for propaganda. Well before his review of *The New Negro,* Du Bois wrote that "The New Crisis" would "stress Beauty—all Beauty, but especially the beauty of Negro life and character; its music, its dancing, its drawing and painting and the new birth of its literature" (8). And in late 1928, Locke would write in "Art or Propaganda?" that "our espousal of art thus becomes no mere idle acceptance of 'art for art's sake,' or cultivation of the last decadences of the over-civilized. . . . Propaganda itself is preferable to shallow, truckling imitation. . . . After Beauty, let Truth come into the Renaissance picture" (12).

31. McKay, however, describes his entrance into the Harlem Renaissance scene as that of a generational interloper: "I was an older man and not regarded as a member of the renaissance, but more as a forerunner. Indeed, some of them had aired their resentment of my intrusion from abroad into the renaissance set-up" (*Long Way* 321). Thurman read this "generation" even more figuratively, arguing in "Negro Poets and Their Poetry" (1928) that "Countee Cullen is the symbol of a fast disappearing generation of Negro writers. In him it reaches out its literary apogee. On the other hand Langston Hughes announces the entrance of a new generation, while Claude McKay, glorious revolutionary that he is, remains uncatalogued" (559).

32. Charles S. Johnson put his finger on the disconnect between Hughes and Schuyler in an anonymous *Opportunity* editorial, published just weeks after the debate took place: "For neither does Mr. Schuyler mean that there is no beauty in Negro life, nor Mr. Hughes that Negroes are contentedly inferior creatures with amusing peculiarities. When one of them is talking about art forms the other is discussing art content; one is thinking of the Negro bourgeois, the other of intellectual parvenus; one of art, the other of artists. When Mr. Schuyler is thinking of unconscious folk art of the past, Mr. Hughes is thinking of individual Negro artists of the present, and when Mr. Schuyler is thinking of individual Negro artists of the past like Pushkin

and Dumas, Mr. Hughes is thinking about the sable Babbitts of the present. And both discuss art as if they were thinking of culture" ("American Negro Art" 238).

Chapter 3

1. Schermerhorn's examples of such symbolic elements include "kinship patterns, physical contiguity (as in localism or sectionalism), religious affiliation, language or dialect forms, tribal affiliation, nationality, phenotypical features, or any combination of these" (12). A "dominant group," in contrast, is defined as "that collectivity within a society which has preeminent authority to function both as guardians and sustainers of the controlling value system, and as prime allocators of rewards in the society" (12–13).

2. Murger's novel was originally published serially as *Scènes de la Bohème* between 1845 and 1849 in the *Corsaire-Satan*, a Paris newspaper devoted to literature and politics. In 1849 Murger (with Théodore Barrière) adapted the series for the stage as *La Vie de Bohème*. Two years later, after a successful stage run, the various sketches were collected as a novel by the Paris publisher Michel Lévy.

3. In "A New Theory of Bohemians," published in the *Knickerbocker* in 1861, Bristed altered his view of bohemianism and even suggested that he belonged to that camp. "Certainly I do claim to be a Bohemian," he writes, "as a literary man by profession and (after a fashion) practice, and as never having been out of debt but twice since the age of sixteen" (316). (In the article Bristed defines a bohemian very simply as "a man with literary or artistic tastes, and an incurable proclivity to debt" [312].)

4. According to book historian Emily Jenkins, *Harper's* circulation grew by 100,000 between the first and second installments of the novel. Of *Trilby* in book form, she adds: "*Harper's* originally ordered 6,500 copies of the manuscript printed in book form, but American advance orders were so great the number was changed to 10,000, then 25,000, then 35,000. The *Sun* reported a first edition totaling 90,000. One hundred thousand copies sold in two months" (229).

5. See also Parry (100 ff.) and Jenkins (235 ff.).

6. These were written by John G. Hawley and James Schönberg.

7. This description also borrows from the legend of *la belle dame sans merci*, a theme also explored in Johnson's frequently anthologized poem "The White Witch."

8. On the obscenity trials following the U.S. publication of *Tropic of Cancer*, see Earl R. Hutchinson, Tropic of Cancer *on Trial* (1968), and Charles Rembar, *The End of Obscenity* (1968).

9. Sollors quotes from Margaret Mead's *And Keep Your Powder Dry*, which was published the same year as Hurston's memoir: "Washington does not represent the past to which one belongs by birth, but the past to which one tries to belong by effort. . . . Washington is not that to which Americans passionately cling but that to which they want to belong, and fear, in the bottom of their hearts, that they cannot and do not" (qtd. in *Beyond* 229).

10. The only bohemian narratives to which Hurston refers specifically in *Dust*

Tracks are O. O. McIntyre's cynical essays (43). Largely forgotten today, during the Jazz Age he covered the pretenses of Manhattan society in a regular column for *Cosmopolitan.*

11. Much of Hurston's self-censoring has been attributed to the pressure she felt from Bertram Lippincott and others at the publishing firm, particularly after the U.S. entrance into World War II. One Lippincott editor, for example, noted on Hurston's manuscript: "Suggest eliminating international opinions as irrelevant to autobiography" (qtd. in Howard 165). Following the publication of *Dust Tracks,* Hurston spent many years writing about race issues for such magazines as *American Mercury, Reader's Digest,* and *Saturday Evening Post.* For more on this politically ambiguous period in Hurston's life, see Hemenway (esp. ch. 11).

12. Autobiographical readings of *Brown Buffalo* include Genaro M. Padilla, "The Self as Cultural Metaphor in Acosta's *Autobiography of a Brown Buffalo*" (1984), and Kimberly A. Kowalczyk, "Oscar Zeta Acosta: The Brown Buffalo and His Search for Identity" (1988). Satiric/ideological readings include Héctor Calderón, "To Read Chicano Narrative: Commentary and Metacommentary" (1982), and Ramón Saldívar, *Chicano Narrative* (1990).

13. On the neocolonial rhetoric of three Beat Generation writers, see Robert Holton, "Kerouac among the Fellahin" (1995), and Manuel Luis Martinez, "'With Imperious Eye'" (1998).

14. In "A Note on the Text" to the U.S. edition of *Le Plaisir du texte,* Richard Howard writes that "Roland Barthes's translator, Richard Miller, has been resourceful, of course, and he has come up with the readiest plausibility by translating *jouissance* . . . as 'bliss'; but of course he cannot come up with 'coming,' which precisely translates what the original text can afford. The Bible they translated calls it 'knowing' while the Stuarts called it 'dying,' the Victorians called it 'spending,' and we call it 'coming'; a hard look at the horizon of our literary culture suggests that it will not be long before we come to a new word for orgasm proper—we shall call it 'being'" (v–vi).

15. The recent groundswell of titles shedding critical light on discursive formations of the "body" outstrips my ability to keep track of the latest developments in this rapidly expanding area of literary studies. Surely, though, it is no accident that this trend in historicist revisionism follows in the wake of poststructuralist "death of the author" criticism, which plumbs the myriad relationships among reading, writing, and sexual intercourse as it undermines received modes of registering literary authority (especially so-called Old Historicist concerns with biography).

16. An abridged version of *The Autobiography,* published in four issues of the *Atlantic Monthly,* paved the way for the book's U.S. success, which included selection by the Book-of-the-Month Club.

17. As in Miller's and Hurston's narratives, Stein reconstructs her early childhood reading experiences (74 ff.) and apprentice years at Radcliffe College and Johns Hopkins University (77 ff.), only to conclude that *The Making of Americans* (1925) was "really the beginning of modern writing" (215).

18. On Stein's representation of lesbianism in *The Autobiography,* see Catherine R.

Simpson, "Gertrude Stein and the Lesbian Lie" (1992). Sylvia Beach, in her memoir *Shakespeare and Company* (1959), offers a less flattering account of the public performance of Stein's and Toklas's gendered roles among guests: "I knew the rules and regulations about wives at Gertrude's. They couldn't be kept from coming, but Alice had strict orders to keep them out of the way while Gertrude conversed with the husbands. . . . I couldn't see the necessity for the cruelty to wives that was practised in the rue de Fleurus. Still, I couldn't help being amused at Alice's wife-proof technique. Curiously, it was only applied to wives; non-wives were admitted to Gertrude's conversation" (31).

19. Gilbert and Gubar comment on this scene: "Although [Alice] is eventually 'terribly pleased with it,' her initial response is one of the first clues we have about the 'actual' author of *The Autobiography*. . . . The cooking and eating of Alice are interrupted by a telling that is a forced feeding which Stein's Alice can only feebly protest" (2:252).

20. Both Richard Bridgman (209 ff.) and Gilbert and Gubar (2:253 ff.) suggest that Toklas actually did author *The Autobiography*, either wholly or in part. I do not wish to weigh in on this controversy directly; however, I think that my obvious point—that Stein thematizes authorial partnership—is too often overlooked.

21. In "The Missing All" (1937), Bishop describes the real-life counterpart to this scene as follows: "We talked of books: those I had read, which were not many, those Fitzgerald had read, which were even less, those he said he had read, which were many, many more. It was the age at which we were discovering Meredith and the writers of the Yellow Book" (108).

22. "Whitman is the man that attracts me," Burne says elsewhere in the novel; "he's a definite ethical force" (118).

23. On the career-long influence of poet and critic Gourmont on Pound's thought and poetry, see Richard Sieburth, *Instigations* (1978).

24. Although the Spanish poet Luis de Góngora y Argote does not appear to have influenced Williams either positively or negatively, Williams's 1955 translation of Octavio Paz's "Hymn among the Ruins" includes an epigraph from Góngora's "Poliferro of Galatea."

25. I must disagree here with Ned Stuckey-French, who argues that "organic unity could only be viewed ironically, and so Williams encloses it in quotation marks. No longer could unity be characterized in terms of a human body or a flowering plant; now it must be seen in terms of a crystal and its angles or an engine and its parts, both tropes that Williams uses" (109–10). Williams is hardly consistent on this point; as I demonstrate below, he posits an organicist aesthetic—not yet realized but within the realm of possibility—as an alternative to consumer culture and mass production. Indeed, when writing about the intersection of his dual careers as doctor and as poet, Williams observes that the "physician enjoys a wonderful opportunity actually to witness the words being born. Their actual colors and shapes are laid before him carrying their tiny burdens which he is privileged to take into his care with their unspoiled newness. He may see the difficulty with which they have been born and

what they are destined to do. No one else is present but the speaker and ourselves, we have been the words' very parents" (*Autobiography* 361).

26. See esp. Jayne E. Marek, *Women Editing Modernism* (1995). Marek's focus on a handful of little magazines (e.g., Marianne Moore's *Dial,* Harriet Weaver's *Egoist,* Margaret Anderson's *Little Review,* and Harriet Monroe's *Poetry*) offers a tip-of-the-iceberg look at the increasingly prominent role played by women in the early-twentieth-century literary marketplace. Much work remains to be done in terms of reevaluating the role of women book and magazine publishers, editors, merchants, critics, consumers, and patrons.

27. Hettie Jones describes the impressive roster published in her journal: "From a quick first look at *Yugen 4* you'd say Beat, as the three Beat gurus—Kerouac, Corso, and Ginsberg—were represented. Except the 'new consciousness in arts and letters' was more inclusive. Like Basil King, Joel Oppenheimer, and Fielding Dawson, the poets Robert Creeley, John Wieners, and Charles Olson were out of Black Mountain College, where Olson was the last rector. Frank O'Hara, like the painters he knew, was a poet of the 'New York School.' Gilbert Sorrentino lived in Brooklyn, Gary Snyder in Japan, Ray Bremser in a Trenton, New Jersey, prison" (74).

28. See Donna Hollenberg, "Abortion, Identity Formation, and the Expatriate Woman Writer" (1997). Hollenberg writes: "Such *bildungsromans* as H.D.'s *Asphodel, Paint It Today,* and *Palimpsest* and Kay Boyle's *Plagued by the Nightingale, Year Before Last,* and *My Next Bride* embody a psychological drama of underlying, problem-ridden mother-daughter attachment that combines with a social drama of exile, with conflicting longings for freedom, and with yearnings for a maternal home. In addition, H.D. in her short story 'Two Americans,' written shortly after her abortion, uses geographical and racial metaphors to recast her anxiety about motherhood and authorship in cultural terms" (212). Susan Gubar demonstrates how modernist women writers transformed the view of the "so-called redundant woman" (i.e., the view that women are simply vessels for procreation) into the view that biological and literary creativity by women exist on equal footing: "From the Victorian anxiety of female authorship, which infects the woman artist with the fear that she is a monstrous contradiction in terms, we move toward a celebration of female artistry that blurs the distinction between life and art so as to privilege neither one, a political act that reevaluates the woman as the exemplary creator, the heroine as the artist" (25–26).

29. Williams celebrates his friendship with Miller in a 1944 poem, "To the Dean."

30. The cover and dust-jacket illustration for Williams's *Kora in Hell: Improvisations* (1920) literalizes his injunction that "there must be [an] implantation of the sperm" before poetic activity can take place. The illustration, designed by Williams, consists of a many-shaded ovum surrounded by twenty-eight spermatozoa of differing shapes and sizes. Williams explains the design's symbolism: "I myself improvised the idea, seeing, symbolically, a design using sperms of various breeds, various races let's say, and directed the artist to vary the shadings of the drawing from white to gray to black. The cell accepts one sperm—that is the beginning of life. I was feel-

ing fresh and I thought it was a beautiful thing and I wanted the world to see it" (*I Wanted* 28–29).

31. For a brief overview of myths (both Western and Eastern) explaining the genesis of language and writing, see Wayne M. Senner, "Theories and Myths on the Origins of Writing" (1987).

Chapter 4

1. Drug and alcohol use, sexual experimentation, and political radicalism are additional forms of bohemian outlawry that do not exhibit specifically nationalist tendencies, at least not in U.S. cultural history.

2. Beebe adds that the "retreat to Bohemia is a mild form of revolt. The potential artist, in rebellion against the standards of middle-class society, goes to the Latin Quarter or Greenwich Village not only to develop his art but also to find convivial companions, to join coteries, and to establish an environment congenial to his temperament. Thus the Bohemian, instead of alienating himself from society, substitutes one kind of society for another and usually stops short of the detachment of those who follow the ideal of the Ivory Tower" (*Ivory* 78).

3. Michael S. Reynolds pinpoints the historical moment when this type of criticism took firm hold within Hemingway studies: "The second wave of criticism [after 1960] spent unwarranted effort distinguishing between Hemingway's characters and their real-life prototypes. This game lasted until the prototypes all went under the earth; today readers have little interest in whether Duff Twysden really behaved as Brett Ashley did in Pamplona" (*Twenties* 14). I agree with Reynolds that this critical approach quickly leads to trivial results; more important, I think, is the extent to which the novel insists on its biographical foundations.

4. Loeb's memoir, for example, is designed with *The Sun Also Rises* very much in mind, even though he fails to mention the novel directly. It includes a chapter about his affair with Duff Twysden ("Spring in Paris") and a chapter about his exploits in Pamplona with Hemingway, Twysden, and several others who inspired the novel ("Fiesta," which was also the novel's title in England). Similarly, Baker's biography of Hemingway includes a section called "The Sun Also Rises," in which Baker details events of June and July 1925 that found their way into the novel. In his biography Baker writes, "Around Paris, much of the pleasure in reading the novel lay in identifying those who served as working models for the cast of characters" (*Life* 179).

5. Reynolds unfolds several insider jokes in the novel leveled against various Left Bank personalities. Ford, for instance, in the person of Braddocks, cannot recognize a prostitute (Georgette Hobin) when he meets one. Georgette Leblanc—the "fictional" name attributed to the prostitute by Jake when he introduces the woman as his fiancée (25–26)—was the name of the singer and lesbian lover of Margaret Anderson, for whom Anderson left Jane Heap. "Left Bank readers," Reynolds writes, "recognized the *bal musette* in rue de la Montagne Sainte Geneviève as a homosexual

bar. . . . [R]eaders in the Quarter would recognize [Brett's companions at the bar as] Arthur Lett-Haines, lover of Cedric Morris the painter, and Ernest's neighbors on Notre-Dame-des-Champs" (*Hemingway* 310–11).

6. Scott Donaldson demonstrates how Maxwell Perkins, Hemingway's editor at Scribner's, convinced Hemingway to make changes specifically to avoid the difficulties of a libel case or outright censorship (26–27). In a July 1926 letter to Hemingway, Perkins writes: "There are two points to consider that bear on this publication: the danger of trouble from referring to real people in a way to reflect upon them, and the danger of suppression." Perkins goes on in the letter to recommend specific name changes for four minor characters to avoid legal complications (Hemingway, *Only* 41–42).

7. According to Baker, "The book made Kitty Cannell so angry that she took to her bed for three days. Her deepest indignation was less for herself than for the virtual crucifixion of Harold Loeb. But she was also enraged by the portrait of Frances Cline, Cohn's jealous mistress in the novel. She saw at once that Ernest had listened carefully to her conversational style, which was highly individualized and unmistakable. . . . Loeb himself felt as if he had developed an ulcer. . . . Duff Twysden came only belatedly to a reading of the novel. Although furious at first, she afterwards relented. When Ernest happened to meet her one night at the Dingo, she said that she had not been at all disturbed. Her only quibble was that she had not in fact slept with the bloody bullfighter" (*Life* 179).

8. The statutory definition of libel varies from nation to nation, and in the United States from state to state; however, in most jurisdictions a jury measures malicious "intention" against the expected response of a "reasonable" or "typical" reader rather than the ideal response of an Iserian "implied" reader. Wittenberg explains why authors and publishers might include the title-page disclaimer: "The only possible use to which this sentence might be put is in the event of action by a person who was not known to the author and where the portrait, if applied to a living person, would be purely accidental. In that event the sentence might have some weight as indicating lack of intention and malice" (216).

9. However, one must also bear in mind that there is a long history of anti-Semitic rhetoric that identifies a Jewish cultural parasitism not unlike Cohn's. As Jean-Paul Sartre writes, "The anti-Semite reproaches the Jew with 'not being creative,' with having 'a destructive intelligence.' This absurd accusation (Spinoza, Proust, Kafka, Darius Milhaud, Chagall, Einstein, Bergson—are they not Jews?) has been given a semblance of truth by the fact that the Jewish intelligence willingly takes a critical turn" (113).

10. Hemingway himself made a similar accusation about the "lostness" of his fellow expatriates in "American Bohemians in Paris," a 1922 dispatch for the *Toronto Star Weekly*. "You can find anything you are looking for at the Rotonde—except serious artists," reports Hemingway. Visitors to the Latin Quarter, he continues, do not encounter "the real artists of Paris"; instead, they find "loafers expending the energy that an artist puts into his creative work in talking about what they are going to do

and condemning the work of all artists who have gained any degree of recognition. By talking about art they obtain the same satisfaction that the real artist does in his work" (*By-Line* 24–25). For a more detailed account of Hemingway's vexed attitude toward bohemianism, see my "Hemingway among the Bohemians" (2001).

11. That is, the *OED* lists a quotation from *The Sun Also Rises* (or *Fiesta*) as the first example for each of these entries. Three hundred quotation entries is not a surprisingly large or small number for a well-known writer like Hemingway. By comparison, the *OED* contains more than 550 quotations from T. S. Eliot, almost 12,500 from Milton, and well over 33,000 from Shakespeare.

12. Sarrason's collection of biographical material includes an interview with Bill Smith, Hemingway's companion on the "real" fishing trip. Smith recalls: "You can get pretty silly when you're tight. Yes, I actually remember using that word, utilize, and I remember it catching on somehow, even with the Englishman. We all have our moments, I guess" (183).

13. *The Random House Historical Dictionary of American Slang,* citing an article in *Jazz Talk,* dates a similar usage of "happening" ("goings-on of any nature in one's surroundings, esp. those of immediate interest; SCENE") as early as 1953. According to Kerouac biographer Ann Charters in her introduction to the Penguin edition of *On the Road,* Kerouac "intended at the end of his life to gather all his autobiographical novels together in a uniform binding published with all the names of the 'real life' people returned to them" (xxviii).

14. Holmes puns on the social and religious dimensions of "visitation." He took the section title from a passage in Hosea (9:7), reproduced as an epigraph. The other two sections are titled "Children in the Markets" (after a passage in Matthew [11:16, 17]) and "Hell" (after a quotation by Father Zossima in Dostoyevsky's *The Brothers Karamazov*).

15. According to Ginsberg, this 1948 revelation actually took place on 121st Street, in Russell Durgin's Spanish Harlem apartment (*Howl* 126 n. 19).

16. The lines quoted here are from "The look of love alarms," "A Little Boy Lost," and "My Pretty Rose Tree."

17. While Eberhart covers a wide range of poets and locales in the article, he argues that the "most remarkable poem of the young group, written during the past year, is 'Howl,' by Allen Ginsberg, a 29-year-old poet who is the son of Louis Ginsberg, a poet known to newspaper readers in the East. . . . This poem has created a furor of praise or abuse whenever read or heard" (7, 18).

18. Of course, communities that imagine themselves as generations (Beat or otherwise) cannot meet all the criteria outlined by Anderson in his definition of the modern nation-state ("an imagined political community") because generations are neither "inherently limited" in scope nor "sovereign" (6) political entities.

19. Even today the source of "ragtime"—both the music and the word—remains a mystery. The best available evidence suggests that ragtime has been played since at least the 1870s, if not earlier, although the word appeared in print for the first time in 1896. In August of that year Ben Harvey's "You've Been a Good Old Wagon

but You've Done Broke Down" was entered into copyright with a cover proclaiming Harvey the "Original Introducer to the Stage of the Now Popular 'Rag Time' in Ethiopian Song" (Hasse 7). These lines from Johnson are used as one of the epigraphs to Reed's *Mumbo Jumbo.*

20. My investigations into the etymology of "jazz" are particularly indebted to Alan P. Merriam and Fradley H. Garner, "Jazz—the Word" (1968). I have also benefited from Dick Holbrook, "Our Word Jazz" (1974), as well as the *OED* and the *Random House Historical Dictionary of American Slang.*

21. In 1926, Irving Schwerke wrote, "Le mot jazz est d'origine française et son application a la musique est la fidèle image de son sens literal. Il y a 250 ans, la civilisation française trouva un solide point d'appui dans les provinces (plus tard devenues États) de la Louisiane et de la Caroline du Sud. Dans les villes cultivées du Sud (la Nouvelle-Orléans et Charleston), le Français fut pour un certain temps la langue dominante, et, dans les plantations possédées par les Français, c'était la seule langue dont on usât. Les esclaves au service de Français furent obligés d'apprendre la langue de leurs maitres, ce qu'ils apprennent, des inflexions et des modifications propres à leur race. S'il faut en croire Larousse, le verbe français *jaser* signfie *causer, bavarder, parler beaucoup*" (qtd. in Merriam and Garner 383). The *Random House Historical Dictionary of American Slang* records English appropriations of the term as early as 1831, in which the sexual overtones of *jaser* are Anglicized as "jazz."

22. Henry Louis Gates Jr. argues that "after Descartes, reason was privileged, or valorized, over all human characteristics. Writing, especially after the printing press became so wide-spread, was taken to be the visible sign of reason. Blacks were reasonable, and hence 'men,' if—and only if—they demonstrated mastery of 'the arts and sciences,' the eighteenth century's formula for writing" (129).

23. This statement is an almost verbatim repetition of the words of the unnamed narrator in Johnson's novel, *The Autobiography of an Ex-Colored Man* (1912), who observes that "no one who has traveled can question the world-conquering influence of ragtime, and I do not think that it would be an exaggeration to say that in Europe the United States is popularly known better by ragtime than by anything else it has produced in a generation. In Paris they call it American music" (63).

24. The best of these are Kathy J. Ogren, *The Jazz Revolution* (1989), and Burton W. Peretti, *Jazz in American Culture* (1997). Among the many fine studies available on the early history of jazz music, I have benefited most from Marshall W. Stearns, *The Story of Jazz* (1956), and Gunther Schuller, *Early Jazz* (1968).

25. In his autobiography, *A Long Way from Home* (1937), McKay comments on the "modernism" of Lawrence, arguing that "D. H. Lawrence was more modern than James Joyce. In D. H. Lawrence I found confusion—all of the ferment and torment and turmoil, the hesitation and hate and alarm, the sexual inquietude and the incredulity of this age, and the psychic and romantic groping for a way out" (247).

26. Similarly, James Weldon Johnson calls the "power of the Negro to suck up the national spirit from the soil and create something artistic and original" a "transfusive quality." Indeed, he argues that "the Negro has exercised this transfusive quality not

only here in America, where the race lives in large numbers, but in European countries, where the number has been almost infinitesimal" (*Negro Poetry* xix).

27. McKay responds in his autobiography to accusations that his depiction of Jake's doings were a transcript of his own life: "I haven't arrived at that high degree of civilized culture where I can make a success of producing writing carefully divorced from reality. Yet I couldn't indulge in such self-flattering as to claim Jake in *Home to Harlem* as a portrait of myself. My damned white education has robbed me of much of the primitive vitality, the pure stamina, the simple unswaggering strength of the Jakes of the Negro race" (*Long Way* 229). As Tracy McCabe smartly points out, "Ray seems to be struggling with what Maurice Beebe describes in *Ivory Towers and Sacred Founts* as the two major modes pursued by fictional artist figures" (481).

28. At a late point in *Go,* for instance, Hobbes "had been half-heartedly trying to explain to [his lover] what was suggested by the term 'cool,' as hipsters use it. 'When the music is cool, it's pleasant, somewhat meditative and without tension. Everything before, you see, just last year, was "crazy," "frantic," "gone." Now everybody is acting cool, unemotional, withdrawn'" (209). William S. Burroughs, in *Junky* (1953), describes how he "learned the new hipster vocabulary: 'pot' for weed, 'twisted' for busted, 'cool,' an all-purpose word indicating anything you like or any situation that is not hot with the law. Conversely, anything you don't like is 'uncool'" (143). In *Fear and Loathing in Las Vegas* (1971), Hunter S. Thompson mocks the efforts of "drug expert" Dr. E. R. Bloomquist, M.D., to explain to his law enforcement readership the vagaries of drug culture: "Dr. Bloomquist's book is a compendium of state bullshit. On page 49 he explains, the 'four states of being' in the cannabis society: 'Cool, Groovy, Hip & Square'—in that descending order. 'The square is seldom if ever cool,' says Bloomquist. 'He is "not with it," that is, he doesn't know "what's happening." But if he manages to figure it out, he moves up a notch to "hip." And if he can bring himself to approve of what's happening, he becomes "groovy." And after that, with much luck and perseverance, he can rise to the rank of "cool"'" (139).

Works Cited

Aberdeen and Tamir, Ishbel Gordon, Marchioness of. "The Present Irish Literary Revival." *Catholic World* 61 (1895): 574–76.

Abrams, M. H. *The Mirror and the Lamp: Romantic Theory and the Critical Tradition.* New York: Oxford UP, 1953.

Acosta, Oscar Zeta. *The Autobiography of a Brown Buffalo.* 1972. New York: Vintage, 1989.

———. *The Revolt of the Cockroach People.* 1973. New York: Vintage, 1989.

Adams, Robert Martin. "What Was Modernism?" *Hudson Review* 31 (1978): 19–33.

Adorno, Theodor W. *Aesthetic Theory.* 1970. Trans. Robert Hullot-Kentor. Minneapolis: U of Minnesota P, 1997.

———. "On Popular Music." *Studies in Philosophy and Social Science* 9 (1941): 17–48.

Aldridge, John. *After the Lost Generation: A Critical Study of the Writers of Two Wars.* New York: McGraw, 1951.

Allen, Frederick Lewis. *Only Yesterday.* 1931. New York: Harper, 1964.

"American Negro Art." *Opportunity* 4 (1926): 238–39.

"America's Golden Age in Poetry." *Century* 69 (1916): 793–94.

Anderson, Benedict. *Imagined Communities: Reflections on the Origin and Spread of Nationalism.* Rev. ed. London: Verso, 1991.

Appadurai, Arjun. *Modernity at Large: Cultural Dimensions of Globalization.* Minneapolis: U of Minnesota P, 1996.

Arlen, Michael. *Babes in the Wood.* London: Hutchinson, 1929.

———. *The Green Hat.* New York: G. H. Doran, 1924.

Arnold, Matthew. *Discourses in America.* London: Macmillan, 1885.

———. *On the Study of Celtic Literature.* London: Smith, Elder, 1867.

Avallone, Charlene. "What American Renaissance? The Gendered Genealogy of a Critical Discourse." *PMLA* 112 (1997): 1102–20.

Baker, Carlos. *Ernest Hemingway: A Life Story.* New York: Scribner, 1969.

———. *Hemingway: The Writer as Artist.* Princeton: Princeton UP, 1952.

Baker, Houston. *Modernism and the Harlem Renaissance.* Chicago: U of Chicago P, 1987.

Baldwin, James. "Sonny's Blues." *Partisan Review* 24 (1957): 327–58.

Baraka, Amiri. "Social Change and Poetic Tradition." *Chicago Review* 43 (1997): 109–13.

Barber, J. Max. "The Morning Cometh." *Voice of the Negro* 1 (1904): 37–38.

Barnes, Albert C. "Negro Art and America." *Survey Graphic* 6 (1925): 668–69.

Barnouw, Erik. *A History of Broadcasting in the United States.* 3 vols. New York: Oxford UP, 1966–70.

Barthes, Roland. *The Pleasure of the Text.* Trans. Richard Miller. New York: Hill and Wang, 1975.

Beach, Sylvia. *Shakespeare and Company.* New York: Harcourt, 1959.

Bechhofer, C. E. *The Literary Renaissance in America.* London: Heinemann, 1923.

Beebe, Maurice. *Ivory Towers and Sacred Founts.* New York: New York UP, 1964.

———. "What Modernism Was." *Journal of Modern Literature* 3 (1974): 1065–84.

Bell, Clive. "Plus De Jazz." *New Republic* 28 (1921): 92–96.

Bellow, Saul. *The Adventures of Augie March.* New York: Viking, 1953.

Bercovitch, Sacvan, ed. *The Cambridge History of American Literature.* 9 vols. Cambridge: Cambridge UP, 1994–.

Berlant, Lauren. *The Anatomy of National Fantasy: Hawthorne, Utopia, and Everyday Life.* Chicago: U of Chicago P, 1991.

Bhabha, Homi K., ed. *Nation and Narration.* London: Routledge, 1990.

Bishop, John Peale. "The Missing All." *Virginia Quarterly Review* 13 (1937): 106–21.

Blankenship, Russell. *American Literature as an Expression of the National Mind.* Rev. ed. New York: Cooper Square, 1949.

Blenner-Hassett, Roland. "A Brief History of Celtic Studies in North America." *PMLA* 64.4 (1954): 3–21.

Bourdieu, Pierre. *Distinction: A Social Critique of the Judgement of Taste.* Trans. Richard Nice. Cambridge: Harvard UP, 1984.

———. "The Historical Genesis of a Pure Aesthetic." *Analytic Aesthetics.* Ed. Richard Schusterman. Oxford: Basil Blackwell, 1989. 147–60.

———. *Language and Symbolic Power.* Ed. John B. Thompson. Trans. Gino Raymond and Matthew Adamson. Cambridge: Harvard UP, 1991.

———. *Outline of a Theory of Practice.* Trans. Richard Nice. Cambridge: Cambridge UP, 1977.

Bourne, Randolph. *History of a Literary Radical and Other Essays.* Ed. Van Wyck Brooks. New York: Huebsch, 1920.

———. *Youth and Life.* Boston: Houghton, 1913.

Boyd, Ernest. "The Irish Renaissance—Renascent." *Dial* 67 (1919): 53–55.

Boynton, Percy. *Some Contemporary Americans: The Personal Equation in Literature.* Chicago: U of Chicago P, 1924.

Bradbury, Malcolm. *The Modern American Novel.* Rev. ed. New York: Viking, 1992.

Bradbury, Malcolm, and James McFarlane. "The Name and Nature of Modernism."

Modernism: A Guide to European Literature, 1890–1930. Ed. Malcolm Bradbury and James McFarlane. New York: Penguin, 1991. 19–55.
Braithwaite, William Stanley. "Book Reviews." *Colored American Magazine* 4 (1901): 72–75.
Brawley, Benjamin. "The Negro in American Fiction." *Dial* 60 (1916): 445–50.
———. "The Negro Literary Renaissance." *Southern Workman* 56 (1927): 177–84.
Brennan, Timothy. "The National Longing for Form." Bhabha 44–70.
Brickell, Herschel. "The Literary Awakening in the South." *Bookman* 66 (1927): 138–43.
Bridgman, Richard. *Gertrude Stein in Pieces*. New York: Oxford UP, 1970.
Bristed, Charles Astor. "The Gypsies of Art. Translated for the Knickerbocker from Henry Murger's 'Scenes de la Bohème.'" *Knickerbocker* 41 (1853): 12–23, 218–25, 336–40, 419–24; *Knickerbocker* 42 (1853): 19–24, 227–33, 362–66, 596–601; *Knickerbocker* 43 (1854): 20–30, 165–69, 378–83, 485–91.
———. "A New Theory of Bohemians." *Knickerbocker* 57 (1861): 311–17.
Brooks, Van Wyck. *An Autobiography*. New York: Dutton, 1965.
———. "Literary Generations." 1921. *Sketches in Criticism*. New York: Dutton, 1932. 58–69.
———. *New England: Indian Summer, 1865–1915*. New York: Dutton, 1940.
Brubacher, John S., and Willis Rudy. *Higher Education in Transition: An American History, 1636–1956*. New York: Harper, 1958.
Buell, Frederick. *National Culture and the New Global System*. Baltimore: Johns Hopkins UP, 1994.
Buell, Lawrence. "American Literary Emergence as Postcolonial Phenomenon." *American Literary History* 4 (1992): 411–42.
Burckhardt, Jacob. *The Civilization of the Renaissance in Italy*. 1860. 15th ed. Trans. S. G. C. Middlemore. London: George G. Harrap, 1929.
Bürger, Peter. "Literary Institution and Modernization." *Poetics* 12 (1983): 419–33.
———. *Theory of the Avant-Garde*. Trans. Michael Shaw. Minneapolis: U of Minnesota P, 1984.
Burroughs, William S. *Junky*. 1953. New York: Penguin, 1977.
Byerman, Keith E. "Words and Music: Narrative Ambiguity in 'Sonny's Blues.'" *Critical Essays on James Baldwin*. Ed. Fred L. Standley and Nancy V. Burt. Boston: G. K. Hall, 1988. 198–204.
Cabell, James Branch. *Jurgen: A Comedy of Justice*. New York: Robert M. McBride, 1919.
Calderón, Héctor. "To Read Chicano Narrative: Commentary and Metacommentary." *Mester* 11 (1982): 3–14.
Calinescu, Matei. *Five Faces of Modernity*. Durham: Duke UP, 1987.
Calverton, V. F. "The Advance of the Negro." *Opportunity* 4 (1926): 54–55.
Calza, A. "La rivincita dei 'negri.'" *Nuova Antologia* 64 (1929): 531–33.
Campbell, Frazelia. "The Sixteenth Century in the Education of Modern Thought." *AME Church Review* 20 (1903): 31–40.
Canby, Henry Seidel. *Definitions: Essays in Contemporary Criticism*. New York: Harcourt, 1922.

Cather, Willa. *My Antonia.* 1918. Boston: Houghton, 1954.

Chase, Richard. *The American Novel and Its Tradition.* Baltimore: Johns Hopkins UP, 1957.

———. "The Fate of the Avant-Garde." *Partisan Review* 24 (1957): 363–75.

Chatterjee, Partha. *Nationalist Thought and the Colonial World: A Derivative Discourse?* London: Zed, 1986.

Chessman, Harriet Scott. *The Public Is Invited to Dance: Representation, the Body, and Dialogue in Gertrude Stein.* Stanford: Stanford UP, 1989.

Chopin, Kate. *The Awakening.* 1899. Ed. Margo Culley. New York: Norton, 1994.

Conrad, Bryce. *Refiguring America: A Study of William Carlos Williams'* In the American Grain. Urbana: U of Illinois P, 1990.

Conway, Moncure D. "The Negro as Artist." *Radical* 2 (1866): 39–42.

Corbie, Eugene. "The German Youth Movement." *Crisis* 27 (1924): 157–60.

Coupland, Douglas. *Generation X: Tales for an Accelerated Culture.* New York: St. Martin's, 1991.

Cowley, Malcolm. *The Dream of the Golden Mountains: Remembering the 1930s.* New York: Viking, 1980.

———. *Exile's Return: A Literary Odyssey of the 1920s.* 1934. 2nd ed. New York: Viking, 1951.

———. *A Second Flowering: Works and Days of the Lost Generation.* London: André Deutsch, 1956.

Crunden, Robert. *American Salons: Encounters with European Modernism, 1885–1917.* New York: Oxford UP, 1993.

Cullen, Countee. "The League of Youth." *Crisis* 26 (1923): 167–68.

Davidson, Donald. "A Mirror for Artists." *I'll Take My Stand: The South and the Agrarian Tradition.* Twelve Southerners. 1930. Baton Rouge: Louisiana State UP, 1977. 28–60.

Davidson, Michael. *The San Francisco Renaissance: Poetics and Community at Mid-Century.* New York: Cambridge UP, 1989.

Davis, Allison. "Our Negro 'Intellectuals.'" *Crisis* 35 (1928): 268–69, 284–86.

Davis, Maxine. *The Lost Generation: A Portrait of American Youth Today.* New York: Macmillan, 1936.

"The Debut of the Younger School of Negro Writers." *Opportunity* 2 (1924): 143–44.

Devereux, George. "Ethnic Identity: Its Logical Foundations and Its Dysfunctions." *Theories of Ethnicity: A Classical Reader.* Ed. Werner Sollors. New York: New York UP. 385–414.

DeVoto, Bernard. "A Generation Beside the Limpopo." *Saturday Review* 26 September 1936: 3–4, 14, 16, 18.

Diggins, John P. *The American Left in the Twentieth Century.* New York: Harcourt, 1973.

Di Prima, Diane. *Memoirs of a Beatnik.* 1969. San Francisco: Last Gasp, 1988.

Dolan, Marc. *Modern Lives: A Cultural Re-reading of "The Lost Generation."* West Lafayette: Purdue UP, 1996.

Donaldson, Scott. "Fitzgerald's Blue Pencil." *French Connections: Hemingway and Fitzgerald Abroad.* Ed. J. Gerald Kennedy and Jackson R. Bryer. New York: St. Martin's, 1998. 15–29.

Dos Passos, John. *John Dos Passos: The Major Nonfictional Prose.* Ed. Donald Pizer. Detroit: Wayne State UP, 1988.

Douglas, Ann. *Terrible Honesty: Mongrel Manhattan in the 1920s.* New York: Farrar, 1995.

Douglas, Susan J. *Listening In: Radio and the American Imagination from Amos 'n' Andy and Edward R. Murrow to Wolfman Jack and Howard Stern.* New York: Random, 1999.

Dowling, Linda C. *Language and Decadence in the Victorian Fin de Siècle.* Princeton: Princeton UP, 1986.

Du Bois, W. E. B. *The Gift of Black Folk: The Negroes in the Making of America.* Boston: Stratford, 1924.

———. "Negro Art Renaissance." *Los Angeles Times* 14 June 1925, sec. 3: 26–27.

———. "The Negro College." *Crisis* 40 (1933): 175–77.

———. "The Negro in Literature and Art." *Annals of the American Academy of Political and Social Science* 49 (1913): 233–37.

———. "Negro Writers." *Crisis* 19 (1920): 298–99.

———. "The New Crisis." *Crisis* 30 (1925): 7–9.

———. "Our Book Shelf." *Crisis* 31 (1926): 140–41.

———. *The Souls of Black Folk.* 1903. Ed. Henry Louis Gates Jr. and Terri Hume Oliver. New York: Norton, 1998.

———. "Two Novels." *Crisis* 35 (1928): 202, 211.

Du Bois, W. E. B., and Alain Locke. "The Younger Literary Movement." *Crisis* 27 (1924): 161–63.

Duffey, Bernard I. *The Chicago Renaissance in American Letters: A Critical History.* East Lansing: Michigan State College P, 1954.

Du Maurier, George. *Trilby.* London: Osgood, McIlvaine, 1894.

Dumenil, Lynn. *The Modern Temper: American Culture and Society in the 1920s.* New York: Farrar, 1995.

Dupuis, Margaret Helen. "Birthing the Text: Authorship and Childbirth in Early Modern England." Diss. U of Oregon, 1998.

Eberhart, Richard. "West Coast Rhythms." *New York Times Book Review* 2 September 1956: 7, 18.

Elliott, Emory, ed. *Columbia Literary History of the United States.* New York: Columbia UP, 1988.

Emerson, Ralph Waldo. *The Collected Works of Ralph Waldo Emerson.* Ed. Robert Spiller et al. 5 vols. Cambridge: Harvard UP, 1971–.

———. *Journals and Miscellaneous Notebooks of Ralph Waldo Emerson.* Ed. William Gillman et al. 16 vols. Cambridge: Harvard UP, 1960–.

———. "Thoughts on Modern Literature." *Dial* 1 (1840): 137–58.

Enzensberger, Hans Magnus. "The Aporias of the Avant Garde." 1962. *The Conscious-*

ness Industry: On Literature, Politics, and the Media. Ed. Michael Roloff. New York: Seabury Press, 1974. 16–41.

Eysteinsson, Astradur. *The Concept of Modernism.* Ithaca: Cornell UP, 1990.

Fisher, Rudolph. "Harlem Manor." *New York Herald Tribune Books,* 21 February 1932: 16.

Fitzgerald, F. Scott. *The Beautiful and Damned.* New York: Scribner, 1922.

———. *The Crack-Up.* Ed. Edmund Wilson. New York: New Directions, 1954.

———. *The Great Gatsby.* 1925. New York: Collier, 1992.

———. *A Life in Letters.* Ed. Matthew J. Bruccoli. New York: Simon, 1994.

———. *Tales of the Jazz Age.* New York: Scribner, 1922.

———. *This Side of Paradise.* 1920. Ed. James L. W. West III. New York: Cambridge UP, 1995.

Fleming, Robert E. *The Face in the Mirror: Hemingway's Writers.* Tuscaloosa: U of Alabama P, 1994.

Ford, Mary K. "Is the Celtic Revival Really Irish?" *North American Review* 183 (1906): 771–75.

Fordham, Mary Weston. *Magnolia Leaves.* 1897. New York: AMS, 1973.

Foucault, Michel. *The History of Sexuality.* Vol. 1. Trans. Robert Hurley. New York: Vintage, 1978.

———. "What Is an Author?" *The Foucault Reader.* Ed. Paul Rabinow. New York: Pantheon, 1984. 101–20.

Fox, R. M. "The Negro Renaissance." *Labour Magazine* 7 (1928): 306–8.

Frank, Waldo. *Our America.* New York: Boni and Liveright, 1919.

Freud, Sigmund. *Civilization and Its Discontents.* 1930. Trans. James Strachey. New York: Norton, 1961.

Frothingham, Octavius Brooks. *Transcendentalism in New England: A History.* New York: Putnam's, 1876.

"The Gaelic Revival in Literature." *Quarterly Review* 195 (1902): 423–49.

Gates, Henry Louis, Jr. *The Signifying Monkey: A Theory of African-American Literary Criticism.* New York: Oxford UP, 1988.

Gates, Henry Louis, Jr., and Nellie Y. McKay, eds. *The Norton Anthology of African American Literature.* New York: Norton, 1997.

Gerig, John L. "Celtic Studies in the United States." *Columbia University Quarterly* 19.1 (1916): 30–43.

Gide, André. *The Counterfeiters with Journal of "The Counterfeiters."* 1926. Trans. Dorothy Bussy and Justin O'Brien. New York: Vintage, 1955.

Gilbert, Sandra M., and Susan Gubar. *No Man's Land.* 2 vols. New Haven: Yale UP, 1988.

Ginsberg, Allen. *Howl: Original Draft Facsimile, Transcript and Variant Versions, Fully Annotated by Author With Contemporaneous Correspondence, Account of First Public Reading, Legal Skirmishes, Precursor Texts and Bibliography.* Ed. Barry Miles. New York: Harper, 1986.

Goldman, Suzy Bernstein. "James Baldwin's 'Sonny's Blues': A Message in Music." *Negro American Literature Forum* 8 (1974): 231–33.

Gorki, Maxim. "The Music of the Degenerate." Trans. Marie Budberg. *Dial* 85 (1928): 480–84.

Gottesman, Ronald, ed. *Critical Essays on Henry Miller.* New York: G. K. Hall, 1992.

Gourmont, Remy de. *The Natural Philosophy of Love.* 1922. Trans. Ezra Pound. New York: Collier, 1972.

Gruening, Martha. "The Negro Renaissance." *Hound and Horn* 5 (1932): 504–14.

Gubar, Susan. "The Birth of the Artist as Heroine: (Re)production, the *Kunstlerroman* Tradition, and the Fiction of Katherine Mansfield." *The Representation of Women in Fiction.* Ed. Margaret R. Higonnet. Baltimore: Johns Hopkins UP, 1983. 19–59.

Gwynn, Stephen L. "The Gaelic Revival in Literature." *Quarterly Review* 195 (1902): 423–49.

———. "The Revival of a Language." *Living Age* 232 (1902): 550–59.

Hahn, Emily. *Romantic Rebels: An Informal History of Bohemianism in America.* Boston: Houghton, 1967.

Hansen, Marcus Lee. "The Third Generation in America: A Classic Essay in Immigrant History." 1938. *Commentary* 14 (1952): 492–500.

Hasse, John Edward. "Ragtime: From the Top." *Ragtime: Its History, Composers, and Music.* Ed. John Edward Hasse. New York: Schirmer, 1985. 1–39.

Hawley, John G. *An Appendix to* Trilby: *Translation and Notes.* Rev. ed. Detroit: Richmond and Backus, 1895.

Hearn, Lafcadio. *Two Years in the French West Indies.* New York: Harper, 1890.

Hemenway, Robert E. *Zora Neale Hurston: A Literary Biography.* Urbana: U of Illinois P, 1977.

Hemingway, Ernest. *By-Line: Earnest Hemingway; Selected Articles and Dispatches of Four Decades.* Ed. William White. New York: Scribner, 1967.

———. *Death in the Afternoon.* 1932. New York: Touchstone, 1996.

———. *Ernest Hemingway: Selected Letters, 1917–1961.* Ed. Carlos Baker. New York: Scribner, 1981.

———. *Fiesta.* London: Jonathan Cape, 1927.

———. *A Moveable Feast.* New York: Simon, 1964.

———. *Only Thing That Counts: The Ernest Hemingway–Maxwell Perkins Correspondence, 1925–1947.* Ed. Matthew J. Bruccoli. New York: Scribner, 1996.

———. *The Sun Also Rises.* 1926. New York: Scribner, 1954.

———. *The Sun Also Rises.* Facsimile ed. Ed. Matthew J. Bruccoli. Detroit: Omnigraphics, 1990.

———. *Three Stories and Ten Poems.* Paris: Contact, 1923.

Higham, John. *Strangers in the Land: Patterns of American Nativism, 1860–1925.* New Brunswick: Rutgers UP, 1955.

Hinkson, Katherine Tynan. "The Literary Revival in Ireland." *Outlook* 49 (1894): 1189–91.

Holbrook, Dick. "Our Word Jazz." *Storyville* 50 (1974): 46–58.

Hollenberg, Donna. "Abortion, Identity Formation, and the Expatriate Woman

Writer: H.D. and Kay Boyle in the Twenties." *Critical Essays on Kay Boyle*. Ed. Marylin Elkins. New York: G. K. Hall, 1997. 211–27.

Holmes, John Clellon. *Go*. 1952. New York: Thunder's Mouth, 1988.

———. "This Is the Beat Generation." 1952. *Passionate Opinions: The Cultural Essays*. Fayetteville: U of Arkansas P, 1988. 57–64.

Holton, Robert. "Kerouac among the Fellahin: *On the Road* to the Postmodern." *MFS* 41 (1995): 265–83.

Hourwich, Rebecca. "Where the Jazz Begins." *Collier's* 23 January 1926: 14.

Howard, Lillie P. *Zora Neale Hurston*. Boston: Twayne, 1980.

Howells, William Dean. *Literary Friends and Acquaintance: A Personal Retrospect of American Authorship*. New York: Harper, 1900.

Huggins, Nathan Irvin. *Harlem Renaissance*. London: Oxford UP, 1971.

Hughes, Langston. *The Big Sea*. 1940. New York: Farrar, 1993.

———. "The Negro Artist and the Racial Mountain." *Nation* 122 (1926): 692–94.

———. *The Ways of White Folks*. 1934. New York: Vintage, 1990.

Hurston, Zora Neale. *Dust Tracks on a Road*. 1942. New York: Harper, 1991.

———. *Their Eyes Were Watching God*. 1937. New York: Harper, 1990.

Hutchinson, Earl R. Tropic of Cancer *on Trial: A Case History of Censorship*. New York: Grove, 1968.

Hutchinson, George. *The Harlem Renaissance in Black and White*. Cambridge: Harvard UP, 1995.

Ignatiev, Noel. *How the Irish Became White*. New York: Routledge, 1995.

"The Irish Literary Revival." *Harper's* 47 (1903): 958.

Jacobs, George W. "Negro Authors Must Eat." *Nation* 128 (1929): 710–11.

James, Henry. *The Bostonians*. 1886. London: Penguin, 1984.

Jenkins, Emily. "*Trilby:* Fads, Photographers, and 'Over-Perfect Feet'." *Book History* 1 (1998): 221–67.

Johnson, Abby Arthur, and Ronald Maberry Johnson. *Propaganda and Aesthetics: The Literary Politics of African-American Magazines in the Twentieth Century*. Rev. ed. Amherst: U of Massachusetts P, 1991.

Johnson, Charles S. "The Negro Enters Literature." *Carolina Magazine* 57 (1927): 44–48.

———. "The Rise of the Negro Magazine." *Journal of Negro History* 13 (1928): 7–21.

Johnson, James Weldon. *The Autobiography of an Ex-Colored Man*. 1912. New York: Penguin, 1990.

———, ed. *The Book of American Negro Poetry*. New York: Harcourt, 1922.

Johnson, Joyce. *Minor Characters*. Boston: Houghton, 1983.

Jones, Hettie. *How I Became Hettie Jones*. New York: Dutton, 1990.

Jones, Howard Mumford. "Is There a Southern Renaissance?" *Virginia Quarterly Review* 6 (1930): 184–97.

Kaestle, Carl F. "Literacy in Mainstream Culture in American History." *Language Arts* 58 (1981): 207–18.

Kaestle, Carl F., et al. *Literacy in the United States: Readers and Reading since 1880*. New Haven: Yale UP, 1991.

Kazin, Alfred. *On Native Grounds: An Interpretation of Modern American Prose Literature.* 1942. San Diego: Harcourt, 1995.

Kenner, Hugh. *A Homemade World: The American Modernist Writers.* New York: Knopf, 1975.

Kerouac, Jack. *Book of Dreams.* San Francisco: City Lights, 1961.

———. *Desolation Angels.* New York: Perigree, 1965.

———. *The Dharma Bums.* New York: Viking, 1958.

———. *On the Road.* 1957. New York: Penguin, 1991.

———. *The Subterraneans.* 1958. New York: Grove, 1981.

———. *The Town and the City.* New York: Harcourt, 1950.

———. *Visions of Cody.* New York: McGraw-Hill, 1972.

Keyishian, Harry. *Michael Arlen.* Boston: Twayne, 1975.

Keys, Florence Valentine. "A Generation Lost?" *North American Review* 212 (1920): 678–85.

———. *Return.* Toronto: T. Nelson, 1954.

King, Richard H. *A Southern Renaissance: The Cultural Awakening of the American South, 1930–1955.* Oxford: Oxford UP, 1980.

Kingsley, Walter. "Whence Comes Jass?" *New York Sun* 5 August 1917, sec. 3: 6–8.

Kingston, Maxine Hong. *Tripmaster Monkey: His Fake Book.* 1989. New York: Vintage, 1990.

Kowalczyk, Kimberly A. "Oscar Zeta Acosta: The Brown Buffalo and His Search for Identity." *Americas Review* 16 (1988): 198–209.

Kramer, Dale. *Chicago Renaissance: The Literary Life in the Midwest, 1900–1930.* New York: Appleton, 1966.

Kreuzer, Helmut. "Bohemia(nism)." Trans. Glen Burns. *Idee, Gestalt, Geschichte: Festschrift fur Klaus von See.* Ed. Gerd Wolfgang Weber. Odense, Denmark: Odense UP, 1988. 533–46.

Lang, A. "The Celtic Renaissance." *Blackwood's* 161 (1897): 181–91.

Larbaud, Valéry. "The Rebirth of American Poetry." *Living Age* 311 (1921): 589–94.

Lawrence, D. H. "America, Listen to Your Own." *New Republic* 25 (1920): 68–70.

Lecky, Walter. "The American Celt and His Critics." *Catholic World* 63 (1896): 355–69.

Levin, Harry. "What Was Modernism?" 1960. *Varieties of Literary Experience: Eighteen Essays in World Literature.* Ed. Stanley Burnshaw. New York: New York UP, 1962. 307–29.

Levine, Lawrence W. *Highbrow/Lowbrow: The Emergence of Cultural Hierarchy in America.* Cambridge: Harvard UP, 1988.

———. "Jazz and American Culture." *Journal of American Folklore* 102 (1989): 6–22.

Lewis, David Levering. *When Harlem Was in Vogue.* New York: Knopf, 1981.

Lincoln, Kenneth. *Native American Renaissance.* Berkeley: U of California P, 1983.

Lindsay, Vachel. *The Poetry of Vachel Lindsay: Complete and with Lindsay's Drawings.* Ed. Dennis Camp. Peoria: Spoon River, 1984–85.

Lionnet, Françoise. *Autobiographical Voices: Race, Gender, Self-Portraiture.* Ithaca: Cornell UP, 1987.

Locke, Alain. "American Literary Tradition and the Negro." *Modern Quarterly* 3 (1926): 215–22.

———. "Art or Propaganda?" *Harlem* 1 (1928): 12.

———, ed. *Four Negro Poets.* New York: Simon, 1927.

———. *The Negro and His Music.* Washington, DC: Associates in Negro Folk Education, 1936.

———. "Negro Contributions to America." *World Tomorrow* 12 (1929): 255–57.

———. "The Negro's Contribution to American Art and Literature." *Annals of the American Academy of Political and Social Science* 140 (1928): 234–47.

———, ed. *The New Negro: Voices of the Harlem Renaissance.* New York: Atheneum, 1992. Orig. *The New Negro: An Interpretation.* New York: Albert and Charles Boni, 1925.

———. "Our Little Renaissance." *Ebony and Topaz: A Collectanea.* Ed. Charles S. Johnson. New York: National Urban League, 1927. 117–18.

———. "Spiritual Truancy." *New Challenge* 2 (1937): 81–85.

Loeb, Harold. *The Way It Was.* New York: Criterion, 1959.

Longenbach, James. *Stone Cottage: Pound, Yeats, and Modernism.* New York: Oxford UP, 1988.

Loos, Anita. *Gentlemen Prefer Blondes.* New York: Boni and Liveright, 1925.

Lowell, Amy. *Tendencies in Modern American Poetry.* New York: Macmillan, 1917.

———. "Two Generations in American Poetry." *New Republic* 37 (1923–24): supp. 1–3.

Lowney, John. *The American Avant-Garde Tradition: William Carlos Williams, Postmodern Poetry, and the Politics of Cultural Memory.* Lewisburg, PA: Bucknell UP, 1997.

Loy, Mina. "Modern Poetry." 1925. *The Lost Lunar Baedeker.* Ed. Roger L. Conover. New York: Farrar, 1996. 157–61.

Lyons, F. S. L. *Culture and Anarchy in Ireland, 1890–1939.* Oxford: Oxford UP, 1979.

Mahaffy, J. P. "The Recent Fuss about the Irish Language." *Living Age* 223 (1899): 110–17.

Mailer, Norman. "The White Negro: Superficial Reflections on the Hipster." 1957. *Advertisements for Myself.* Cambridge: Harvard UP, 1992. 340–58.

Malraux, André. *Museum without Walls.* 1947. Trans. Stuart Gilbert and Francis Price. Garden City: Doubleday, 1967.

Mannheim, Karl. "The Problem of Generations." 1927. *From Karl Mannheim.* Ed. Kurt H. Wolf. 2nd ed. New Brunswick: Transaction, 1993. 351–98.

Marek, Jayne E. *Women Editing Modernism: "Little" Magazines and Literary History.* Lexington: UP of Kentucky, 1995.

Martinez, Manuel Luis. "'With Imperious Eye': Kerouac, Burroughs, and Ginsberg on the Road in South America." *Aztlán* 23 (1998): 33–53.

Matthiessen, F. O. *American Renaissance: Art and Expression in the Age of Emerson and Whitman.* London: Oxford UP, 1941.

McAlmon, Robert. *McAlmon and the Lost Generation: A Self-Portrait.* Ed. Robert E. Knoll. Lincoln: U of Nebraska P, 1962.

McCabe, Tracy. "The Multifaceted Politics of Primitivism in Harlem Renaissance Writing." *Soundings* 80 (1997): 475–97.

McCarthy, Justin. "Revival of Irish Language and Literature." *Living Age* 230 (1901): 190–93.

McKay, Claude. *Home to Harlem.* 1928. Boston: Northeastern UP, 1987.

———. *A Long Way from Home.* New York: Lee Furman, 1937.

McManus, L. "The Irish Literary Revival." *Living Age* 241 (1904): 189–90.

McRuer, Robert. *The Queer Renaissance: Contemporary American Literature and the Reinvention of Lesbian and Gay Identities.* New York: New York UP, 1997.

Mencken, H. L. *The American Language: An Inquiry into the Development of English in the United States.* 4th ed., abridged. New York: Knopf, 1963.

Merriam, Allan P., and Fradley H. Garner. "Jazz—the Word." *Ethnomusicology* 12 (1968): 373–96.

Merton, Robert K. "Insiders and Outsiders: A Chapter in the Sociology of Knowledge." 1972. *Theories of Ethnicity: A Classical Reader.* Ed. Werner Sollors. New York: New York UP, 1996. 325–69.

Michaels, Walter Benn. *Our America: Nativism, Modernism, and Pluralism.* Duke UP, 1995.

Miller, Henry. *The Air-Conditioned Nightmare.* New York: New Directions, 1941.

———. *Tropic of Cancer.* 1934. New York: Modern Library, 1961.

Miller, J. D. "Celtic Renaissance." *Era* 12 (1903): 415–19.

Mishkin, Tracy, and George Bornstein. *The Harlem and Irish Renaissances: Language, Identity, and Representation.* Gainesville: UP of Florida, 1998.

Mizener, Arthur. "The Lost Generation." *Voice of America Forum Lectures: Literature Series* 8 (1961): 1–8.

Montgomery, K. L. "Some Writers of the Celtic Renaissance." *Fortnightly Review* 96 (1911): 545–61.

Moore, Charles Leonard. "The Celtic Revival." *Dial* 40 (1906): 185–87.

Moore, Virginia. "The Youngest Generation." *Saturday Review of Literature* 25 January 1930: 672–73.

Moore, W. H. A. "The New Negro Literary Movement." *AME Church Review* 21 (1904): 49–54.

More, Paul Elmer. *Shelburne Essays.* 1st ser. Boston: Houghton, 1904.

Morris, Lloyd. "The Negro 'Renaissance.'" *Southern Workman* 59 (1930): 82–86.

Mumford, Lewis. *The Brown Decades: A Study of the Arts in America.* New York: Harcourt, 1931.

Murger, Henri. *Bohemians of the Latin Quarter.* 1851. Paris: Société des Beaux-Arts, 1910.

Murray, Donald C. "James Baldwin's 'Sonny's Blues': Complicated and Simple." *Studies in Short Fiction* 14 (1977): 353–57.

Nash, Gerald D. *Creating the West: Historical Interpretations, 1890–1990.* Albuquerque: U of New Mexico P, 1991.

Nash, Laura L. "Concepts of Existence: Greek Origins of Generational Thought." *Daedalus* 107 (1978): 1–21.

"A Negro Renaissance." *Opportunity* 3 (1925): 187.

The New Quotable Woman. Ed. Elaine Partnow. Rev. ed. New York: Facts on File, 1992.

Norris, Margot. "The 'Wife' and the 'Genius': Domesticating Modern Art in Stein's *Autobiography of Alice B. Toklas.*" *Modernism, Gender, and Culture: A Cultural Studies Approach.* Ed. Lisa Rado. New York: Garland, 1997. 79–99.

North, Michael. *The Dialect of Modernism: Race, Language, and Twentieth-Century Literature.* New York: Oxford UP, 1994.

O'Brien, Fitz-James. "The Bohemian." *Harper's* 11 (1855): 233–42.

O'Byrne, M. A. "How the Celtic Revival Arose." *Catholic World* 62 (1896): 764–74.

O'Donnell, T. "The Gaelic Revival in Ireland." *Review of Reviews* 24 (1901): 188–91.

Ogren, Kathy J. *The Jazz Revolution: Twenties America and the Meaning of Jazz.* New York: Oxford UP, 1989.

Olds, Sharon. *Satan Says.* Pittsburgh: U of Pittsburgh P, 1980.

Ortega y Gasset, José. *The Modern Theme.* Trans. James Cleugh. New York: Norton, 1931.

Ortego, Philip D. "The Chicano Renaissance." *Social Casework* 52 (1971): 294–307.

Osgood, Samuel. "Transcendentalism in New England." *International Review* (1876): 742–63.

O'Shea, J. J. "Gaelic Revival Pioneers." *American Catholic Quarterly* 35 (1910): 173–85.

"Our Literary 'Rebirth' Doubted." *Literary Digest* 23 April 1921: 23–24.

Padilla, Genaro M. "The Self as Cultural Metaphor in Acosta's *Autobiography of a Brown Buffalo.*" *Journal of General Education* 35 (1984): 242–58.

Panish, Jon. *The Color of Jazz: Race and Representation in Postwar American Culture.* Jackson: UP of Mississippi, 1997.

Parker, Dorothy. "The Artist's Reward." 1929. *The Portable Dorothy Parker.* Rev. ed. New York: Penguin, 1973. 582–88.

Parrington, Vernon Louis. *Main Currents in American Thought: An Interpretation from the Beginnings to 1920.* 3 vols. New York: Harcourt, 1930.

Parry, Albert. *Garrets and Pretenders: A History of Bohemianism in America.* Rev. ed. New York: Dover, 1960.

Pattee, Fred Lewis. *A History of American Literature: With a View to the Fundamental Principles Underlying Its Development: A Text Book for Schools and Colleges.* Boston: Silver, Burdett, 1896.

Paz, Octavio. "Antevíspera: *Taller* (1938–1941)." *Sombras de Obras: Arte y Literatura.* Barcelona: Seix Barral, 1983. 94–113.

Peretti, Burton W. *Jazz in American Culture.* Chicago: Ivan R. Dee, 1997.

Pfemfert, Franz. "Die Jugend Spricht!" *Die Aktion* 11 October 1913: 1.

———. "Unsere Hoffnung." *Die Aktion* 11 December 1912: 1.

Pinder, Wilhelm. *Das Problem der Generationen in der Kunstgeschichte Europas.* Berlin: Frankfurter Verlags-Anstalt, 1926.

Pitkin, Walter B. *The Chance of a Lifetime: Marching Orders for the Lost Generation.* New York: Simon, 1934.

Pizer, Donald. "The Sexual Geography of Expatriate Paris." *Twentieth-Century Literature* 36 (1990): 173–85.

Poggioli, Renato. *The Theory of the Avant-Garde.* Trans. Gerald Fitzgerald. Cambridge: Harvard UP, 1968.

Porter, Horace A. *Stealing the Fire: The Art and Protest of James Baldwin.* Middletown, CN: Wesleyan UP, 1989.

Pound, Ezra. *Literary Essays of Ezra Pound.* Ed. T. S. Eliot. New York: New Directions, 1968.

———. "The Renaissance." *Poetry* 5 (1915): 227–33, 283–87; 6 (1915): 84–91.

Pulliam, John D. *History of Eduction in America.* 5th ed. New York: Merrill, 1991.

Purcell, L. Edward. "Trilby and Trilby-Mania: The Beginning of the Bestseller System." *Journal of Popular Culture* 11 (1977): 62–76.

Quinn, Arthur Hobson, ed. *The Literature of the American People: An Historical and Critical Survey.* New York: Appleton, 1951.

Ray, Moira L. "The Irish Literary Revival and Its Gaelic Writers." *Sewanee Review* 14 (1906): 20–27.

Reed, Ishmael. *Mumbo Jumbo.* Garden City: Doubleday, 1972.

Rembar, Charles. *The End of Obscenity: The Trials of* Lady Chatterly, Tropic of Cancer, *and* Fanny Hill. New York: Random, 1968.

Renan, Ernest. "The Poetry of the Celtic Races." 1851. *The Poetry of the Celtic Races, and Other Studies by Ernest Renan.* Trans. William G. Hutchison. Port Washington, NY: Kennikat, 1976. 1–60.

———. "What Is a Nation?" 1882. Trans. Martin Thom. Bhabha 8–22.

Reynolds, Michael S. *Hemingway: The Paris Years.* Oxford: Basil Blackwell, 1989.

———. The Sun Also Rises: *A Novel of the Twenties.* Boston: Twayne, 1988.

Richardson, Charles Francis. *American Literature, 1607–1885.* 2 vols. New York: Putnam, 1886–88.

Ricoeur, Paul. "The Metaphorical Process as Cognition, Imagination, and Feeling." *On Metaphor.* Ed. Sheldon Sacks. Chicago: U of Chicago P, 1978. 141–57.

Robertson, Roland. *Globalization: Social Theory and Global Culture.* London: Sage, 1992.

Rodriguez-Hunter, Suzanne. *Found Meals of the Lost Generation: Recipes and Anecdotes from 1920s Paris.* Boston: Faber, 1994.

Rosenfeld, Paul. "The Younger Generation and Its Critics." *Vanity Fair* September 1922: 53, 84, 106.

Roz, Firmin. "L'esprit nouveau du roman Américain." *Revue des Deux Mondes* 95 (1925): 878–900.

Saldívar, Ramón. *Chicano Narrative: The Dialectics of Difference.* Madison: U of Wisconsin P, 1990.

Sanders, Ed. *Tales of Beatnik Glory.* 2 vols. 1975. New York: Citadel, 1990.

Sarason, Bertram D., comp. *Hemingway and* The Sun *Set.* Washington, DC: NCR, 1972.

Sartre, Jean-Paul. *Anti-Semite and Jew.* 1948. Trans. George J. Becker. New York: Schocken, 1995.

Schauffler, Robert Haven. "Who Invented Jazz?" *Collier's* 3 January 1925: 38.

Schermerhorn, R. A. *Comparative Ethnic Relations: A Framework for Theory and Research.* New York: Random, 1970.

Schoell, Franck L. "La 'renaissance nègre' aux États-Unis." *Revue de Paris* 36 (January–February 1929): 124–65.

Schönberg, James. *The Comparative "Trilby" Glossary.* New York: J. Hovendon, 1895.

Schuller, Gunther. *Early Jazz: Its Roots and Musical Development.* New York: Oxford UP, 1968.

Schuyler, George S. "The Negro-Art Hokum." *Nation* 122 (1926): 662–63.

———. "Negroes and Artists." *Nation* 123 (1926): 50.

Seldes, Gilbert. *The Seven Lively Arts.* New York: Harper, 1924.

Self, Robert T. *Barrett Wendell.* Boston: Twayne, 1975.

Senner, Wayne M. "Theories and Myths on the Origins of Writing: A Historical Overview." *The Origins of Writing.* Ed. Wayne M. Senner. Lincoln: U of Nebraska P, 1987. 1–26.

Sieburth, Richard. *Instigations: Ezra Pound and Remy de Gourmont.* Cambridge: Harvard UP, 1978.

Simpson, Catherine R. "Gertrude Stein and the Lesbian Lie." *American Women's Autobiography: Fea(s)ts of Memory.* Ed. Margo Culley. Madison: U of Wisconsin P, 1992. 152–66.

Singal, Daniel Joseph. "Modernist Culture in America: Introduction." *American Quarterly* 39 (1987): 5–6.

Sollors, Werner. *Beyond Ethnicity: Consent and Descent in American Culture.* New York: Oxford UP, 1986.

———. *Neither Black Nor White Yet Both: Thematic Explorations of Interracial Literature.* New York: Oxford UP, 1997.

Soltow, Lee, and Edward Stevens. *The Rise of Literacy and the Common School in the United States: A Socioeconomic Analysis to 1870.* Chicago: U of Chicago P, 1981.

Soto, Michael. "Hemingway among the Bohemians: A Generational Reading of *The Sun Also Rises.*" *Hemingway Review* 21 (2001): 5–21.

Spengemann, William C. *The Forms of Autobiography: Episodes in the History of a Literary Genre.* New Haven: Yale UP, 1980.

Spiller, Robert E., et al., eds. *Literary History of the United States.* 3 vols. New York: Macmillan, 1948.

———. *Literary History of the United States.* Rev. ed. 2 vols. New York: Macmillan, 1953.

Spring, Joel. *The American School, 1642–1996.* 4th ed. New York: McGraw-Hill, 1997.

Stearns, Harold, ed. *Civilization in the United States: An Inquiry by Thirty Americans.* New York: Harcourt, 1922.

Stearns, Marshall W. *The Story of Jazz.* New York: Oxford UP, 1956.

Stein, Gertrude. *The Autobiography of Alice B. Toklas.* 1933. New York: Vintage, 1990.

———. *Everybody's Autobiography.* 1937. Cambridge: Exact Change, 1993.

———. *Selected Writings of Gertrude Stein.* Ed. Carl Van Vechten. New York: Vintage, 1962.

Stephens, Robert O., ed. *Ernest Hemingway: The Critical Reception.* New York: B. Franklin, 1977.

Stoddard, Lothrop. *The Rising Tide of Color against White World-Supremacy.* New York: Scribner, 1920.

Stuckey-French, Ned. "'An Essay on Virginia': William Carlos Williams and the Modern(ist) Essay." *American Literature* 70 (1998): 97–130.

Sundquist, Eric J. *To Wake the Nations: Race in the Making of American Literature.* Cambridge: Harvard UP, 1993.

Survey Graphic (Harlem, Mecca of the New Negro) 6 (1925): 621–724.

Swinnerton, Frank. "The Younger Generation." *Saturday Review* 10 December 1927: 421–22.

Taeuber, Conrad, and Irene B. Taeuber. *The Changing Population of the United States.* New York: Russell and Russell, 1975.

Tate, Allen. "American Poetry since 1920." *Bookman* 68 (1929): 503–8.

———. "The New Provincialism." 1945. *Collected Essays.* Denver: Alan Swallow, 1959. 282–93.

Tavernier-Courbin, Jacqueline. *Ernest Hemingway's* A Moveable Feast: *The Making of a Myth.* Boston: Northeastern UP, 1991.

Taylor, Bayard. *Diversions of the Echo Club, a Companion to "Autocrat of the Breakfast Table."* London: J. C. Hotten, 1876.

Thomas, William Hannibal. *The American Negro: What He Is, and What He May Become.* New York: Macmillan, 1901.

Thompson, Hunter S. *Fear and Loathing in Las Vegas: A Savage Journey into the Heart of the American Dream.* 1971. New York: Vintage, 1989.

Thurman, Wallace. *The Blacker the Berry.* 1929. New York: Arno, 1969.

———. *Infants of the Spring.* New York: Macaulay, 1932.

———. "Negro Poets and Their Poetry." *Bookman* 67 (1928): 555–61.

———. "Nephews of Uncle Remus." *Independent* 119 (1927): 296–98.

Toklas, Alice B. *What Is Remembered.* New York: Holt, 1963.

Toomer, Jean. *Cane.* 1923. Ed. Darwin T. Turner. New York: Norton, 1988.

Trent, W. P., et al., eds. *The Cambridge History of American Literature.* 4 vols. New York: Putnam, 1917–21.

Trilling, Lionel. *Beyond Culture: Essays on Literature and Learning.* New York: Viking, 1965.

Untermeyer, Louis. *Modern American Poetry: An Introduction.* New York: Harcourt, 1919.

Urban, Wayne T., and Jennings L. Wagoner Jr. *American Education: A History.* New York: McGraw-Hill, 1996.

Van Doren, Carl. "The Negro Renaissance." *Century* 11 (1925–26): 635–37.

———. "The Younger Generation of Negro Writers." *Opportunity* 2 (1924): 144–45.

Van Vechten, Carl. *Nigger Heaven.* New York: Knopf, 1926.

Wagner-Martin, Linda. *"Favored Strangers": Gertrude Stein and Her Family.* New Brunswick: Rutgers UP, 1995.

Weigley, Russell F. *History of the United States Army.* Enl. ed. Bloomington: Indiana UP, 1984.

Weitenkampf, Frank. "The Irish Literary Revival." *Lamp* 29 (1904): 238–40.

Wellek, René, and Austin Warren. *Theory of Literature.* 3rd ed. New York: Harcourt, 1956.

Wendell, Barrett. *A Literary History of America.* New York: Scribner, 1900.

Wertheim, Arthur Frank. *The New York Little Renaissance: Iconoclasm, Modernism, and Nationalism in American Culture, 1908–1917.* New York: New York UP, 1976.

West, Nathanael. *The Day of the Locust.* New York: New Directions, 1950.

Weygandt, Cornelius. "The Irish Literary Revival." *Sewanee Review* 12 (1904): 420–31.

———. *Irish Plays and Playwrights.* Boston: Houghton, 1913.

Wharton, Edith. *The House of Mirth.* 1905. Ed. Elizabeth Ammons. New York: Norton, 1990.

White, Walter. "The Negro Renaissance." *Palms* 4 (1926): 3–7.

Whitman, Walt. *Leaves of Grass.* 1855–92. New York: Vintage, 1992.

Wickes, George, ed. *Henry Miller and the Critics.* Carbondale: Southern Illinois UP, 1963.

Widmer, Edward L. *Young America: The Flowering of Democracy in New York City.* New York: Oxford UP, 1999.

Wiegand, Wayne A., and Donald G. Davis Jr., eds. *Encyclopedia of Library History.* New York: Garland, 1994.

Williams, Raymond. *The Politics of Modernism: Against the New Conformists.* Ed. Tony Pinkney. London: Verso, 1989.

Williams, William Carlos. *The Autobiography of William Carlos Williams.* New York: New Directions, 1951.

———. *The Collected Poems of William Carlos Williams.* 2 vols. New York: New Directions, 1986.

———. "Comment." *Contact* 4 (1921): 18–19.

———. "Glorious Weather." *Contact* 5 (1923): n.p.

———. *In the American Grain.* 1925. New York: New Directions, 1933.

———. *I Wanted to Write a Poem: The Autobiography of the Works of a Poet.* Ed. Edith Heal. New York: New Directions, 1958.

———. *Kora in Hell: Improvisations.* Boston: Four Seas, 1920.

———. "Yours, O Youth." *Contact* 3 (1921): 14–16.

Wilson, Edmund. *Axel's Castle: A Study in the Imaginative Literature of 1870–1930.* New York: Scribner, 1931.

Wittenberg, Philip. *The Law of Literary Property.* Cleveland: World, 1957.

Wohl, Robert. *The Generation of 1914.* Cambridge: Harvard UP, 1979.

Wolfe, Thomas. *Look Homeward, Angel: A Story of the Buried Life.* New York: Modern Library, 1929.

Woods, Tom. "Origin of the Term Lost Generation." *Lost Generation Journal* 1 (1973): 3–5.

Wright, Edward. "A Celtic Renaissance of the Past." *Fortnightly Review* 87 (1907): 128–36.

Wright, Richard. "Blueprint for Negro Writing." *New Challenge* 2 (1937): 53–65.

Yeats, W. B. *Essays and Introductions.* New York: Macmillan, 1961.

———. *Letters to the New Island.* Ed. Horace Reynolds. Cambridge: Harvard UP, 1934.

———. *Uncollected Prose.* 2 vols. Ed. John P. Frayne and Colton Johnson. New York: Columbia UP, 1970–75.

Ziff, Larzer. *American 1890s: Life and Times of a Lost Generation.* New York: Viking, 1966.

Index